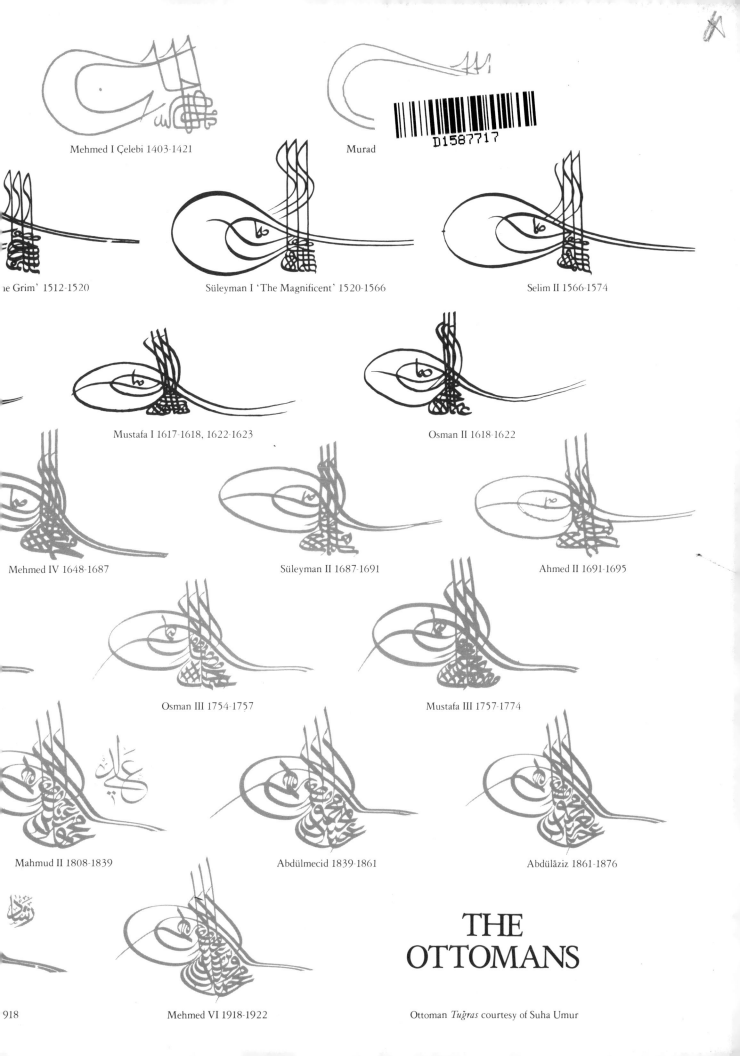

Mehmed I Çelebi 1403-1421

Murad

ne Grim' 1512-1520

Süleyman I 'The Magnificent' 1520-1566

Selim II 1566-1574

Mustafa I 1617-1618, 1622-1623

Osman II 1618-1622

Mehmed IV 1648-1687

Süleyman II 1687-1691

Ahmed II 1691-1695

Osman III 1754-1757

Mustafa III 1757-1774

Mahmud II 1808-1839

Abdülmecid 1839-1861

Abdülāziz 1861-1876

918

Mehmed VI 1918-1922

THE
OTTOMANS

Ottoman *Tuğras* courtesy of Suha Umur

To Constantinople/İstanbul—The City

Tulips, Arabesques & Turbans

Decorative Arts from the Ottoman Empire

Edited by
Yanni Petsopoulos

Alexandria Press, London
Distributed by
SOTHEBY PUBLICATIONS

Acknowledgements

This book is the result of advice, help, encouragement and contributions by a great number of people and institutions. The editor would like to thank the authors in particular for their efforts over and above the call of duty and Dr. Nurhan Atasoy for opening the magical gates of Turkey.

The museums, institutions and collectors who graciously permitted their objects or photographs to be used are listed alphabetically below.

The Art Institute of Chicago; The Ashmolean Museum and Dr James Allan; Dr Herwig Bartels; The Benaki Museum and Mrs Helen Philon; Mr Edwin Binney 3rd; Biblioteca Marciana, Venice; Mr Wilfrid Blunt; The British Museum and Dr Michael Rogers; Mr Alessandro Bruschettini; The Chester Beatty Library and Mr David James; The Cleveland Museum of Art; Dr Marino and Mrs Clara Dall'Oglio; Dumbarton Oaks; Mr Alistair Duncan; The Freer Gallery of Art and Dr Esin Atil; The State Hermitage Museum and Dr Yuri Miller; Mr Jasim El Homaizi; Mr Hans König; The Kunstgewerbe Museum, Cologne; Dr Maan Madina; Mr Gawain McKinley; The Metropolitan Museum of Art; Musée de la Céramique, Sèvres; Musée du Louvre and Mrs Marthe Bernus; Musée des Tissus, Lyons; Museum für Islamische Kunst in West Berlin and Dr Klaus Brisch and Dr Friedrich Spuhler; Oesterreichische Nationalbibliothek and Dr Irblich; The Hon. Anthony Ramsay; Mr Peter Scarisbrick; Miss Philippa Scott; Mr Zia Sofu; The Textile Museum and Mrs Patricia Fiske; The Topkapı Sarayı Müzesi and Dr Filiz Çağman, Dr Zeren Tanindi and Mrs Selma Delibaş; The Türk ve İslam Eserleri Müzesi and Dr Nazan Tapan; The University Library, İstanbul; The Victoria and Albert Museum and Dr Oliver Watson and Mr Anthony North; The Walters Art Gallery, Baltimore, and Dr Ellen Smart.

Finally my sincere thanks go to Gordon Roberton and his team at A.C. Cooper and Dr Reha Günay for their excellent photography.

Editorial
Venetia Porter
Tim Stanley
Manijeh Bayani
Caroline Ogilvie

Design
Richard Foenander

Key to Abbreviations

Measurements
H: Height
Diam: Diameter
L: Length
W: Width
w: Weight

Institutions
TKS Topkapı Sarayı
TVIEM Türk ve İslam Eserleri Müzesi
BM British Museum
V&A Victoria and Albert Museum
MMA Metropolitan Museum of Art
Cleveland The Cleveland Museum of Art
Freer The Freer Gallery of Art, Washington DC
Textile Museum The Textile Museum, Washington DC
Berlin-Dahlem Museum für Islamische Kunst, Berlin-Dahlem

AH Muslim year
AD Christian year

Transliteration

Place names and personal names are given in their modern Turkish forms, while the transliteration of other Turkish words follows the IJMES system, as does that of Arabic terms.

Cover illustration
Rectangular border tile with 'sealing wax' red in high relief, cobalt blue, white and black, c. 1575. H. 14.1 cm; W. 24.3 cm. Ex coll. Princess Kamal el-Din.

This book was designed and produced by Alexandria Press in collaboration with AXIA and John Calmann and Cooper Ltd., London

First published in 1982 by Alexandria Press, London

Distributed by
SOTHEBY PUBLICATIONS
Philip Wilson Publishers Ltd
Russell Chambers
Covent Garden
London WC2E 8AA

© 1982 Alexandria Press

ISBN 0 85667 151 7

Filmset by Southern Positives and Negatives (SPAN), Lingfield, Surrey
Printed and bound by Toppan Printing, Singapore

Contents

Introduction—the Ottoman Style
Yanni Petsopoulos

The general view of the Ottoman Empire is that of a Muslim, Oriental, Turkish state. The most superficial examination, however, shows that the house of Osman built for itself an empire from both east and west. From their modest beginning in the fourteenth century and long before they gained total control of Anatolia, the Ottomans had established a European presence. Eventually, with the capture of Constantinople, they inherited the throne and civilization of Byzantium to which they added their Central Asian traditions and vitality coupled with the sophisticated culture of Islam. The subsequent phases of Ottoman art constantly reflect this east-west duality; not, however, in terms of coexisting opposites, but rather as a synthesis of heterogeneous elements into an articulate decorative vocabulary with an unmistakable identity of its own.

Ottoman art, whose highest achievements span the sixteenth century, is approximately half a century out of phase with the peak period of Ottoman political and military power as defined by the conquest of Constantinople in 1453 by Mehmed the Conqueror and the death of Süleyman the Magnificent in 1566. During this time the cultural, intellectual and artistic production of the Empire develops from tentative and conservative beginnings to assert its individuality and freedom as befits the arts of a confident and outward-looking Empire.

The purpose of this book has been to outline the formation, gradual development and full flowering of this art. With the exception of calligraphy and, to a lesser extent, textiles, which show a remarkable conservatism, this process comes to an end in the seventeenth century. The subsequent period sees a surrender to western Baroque and Rococo, and charming as this later phase of Ottoman art can be, it is clearly the subject of a separate study.

The central theme which the authors develop succinctly in their respective sections is the cohesive unity and interdependence of the main Ottoman decorative arts and their stylistic origins on the designs provided by the Imperial design ateliers, *nakkāṣhāne*.

In contrast with many other aspects of Islamic art we are fortunate that enough material has survived from the classical Ottoman period to allow us to paint a comprehensive picture of it. Such, in fact, is the available quantity and quality of the material that in order to emphasize the main trends and stylistic developments, many facets of Ottoman art have, by necessity, been left out—bookbinding, mural painting, arms and armour, glass-making;

carving and inlaying in wood, stone, ivory and jade, not to mention the most popular Turkish art form: carpets.

In artistic terms, the sixteenth century witnesses the gradual growth of realism and legibility. Leaving aside intermediary styles and direct foreign implantations, five basic stylistic categories emerge during that period in the main decorative arts: 'The plain tradition', 'Abraham of Kütahya', arabesque, 'saz leaf and rosette' and 'quatre fleurs'. The last four originated in the Imperial nakkāşhāne and while their introduction was consecutive they were by no means mutually exclusive, so that by the end of the sixteenth century all four coexisted although their popularity differed markedly from medium to medium. The relative popularity of each style, however, was not so much arbitrary or subject to fashion, but depended largely on the decorative values and possibilities it afforded each branch of the decorative arts. The 'plain tradition', the first stylistic category mentioned, has an existence and lifespan independent of the other four, almost in the nature of a counterpoint to them, and therefore shall be examined last.

The 'Abraham of Kütahya' style was named after the Armenian artist who signed a ceramic ewer of the early sixteenth century painted in this style (plate 63a).[1] Rooted in the international Timurid style of the fifteenth century, it is, together with the 'arabesque' style, the most formal and least naturalistic of the four (plates 70 and 72). Directly related to manuscript illumination, it is dense, delicate, compact and intricate, and is best viewed from close-up. It creates an overall impression and does not emphasize individual elements. Its flexible nature makes it suitable for application on any surface whether flat or curved and it is, therefore, ideal for the decoration of metal and ceramic objects. Its qualities being rather ill-suited for transposition on a large scale, it was never applied to the decoration of textiles, or the coverage of extensive wall areas.

A variant and development of 'Abraham of Kütahya' is the so-called 'Golden Horn' style.[2] Here the calligraphic, scrolling tendrils have shed most of their foliage and flowers, save for some tiny cusp-like leaves, and the spiralling has been tightened to the point of creating an illusion of concentric circles. The effect is strongly reminiscent of background designs on Syrian Mamluk metalwork or tiles and appears to be closely associated with manuscript illumination during the reign of Süleyman the Magnificent (plate 185).

The 'Abraham of Kütahya' style is occasionally also referred to as hatāyī or Chinese.[3] This term has been avoided as being too general and incapable of drawing the distinction between direct copies of Chinese prototypes (plate 77) on the one hand, and the orientalism of the international Timurid style (plate 72) or the subsequent 'saz leaf and rosette' style (plate 81) on the other. It is worth noting in this context that the spiralling leafy motifs that Ottoman art historians often attribute to Chinese inspiration are called by the Chinese themselves 'Mohammedan scrolls'.[4]

A similar lack of clarity concerns the term rūmī when used to identify the arabesque style of decoration.[5] Literally 'Romaic', this term was used to describe Greek lands under Muslim control, hence, first, the Seljuk Sultanate in Central Anatolia, and then extended to the Balkans (Rumelia). As an identification of an artistic style its use is too vague; a vagueness, however, which is totally alien to the decorative style itself. Consisting primarily of split-leaf palmettes and other forms of stylized foliage connected by spiralling or undulating stems, it is a very vigorous and flexible style. This flexibility can be seen in terms of scale on the one hand, since it is equally suited to miniaturized metalwork decoration (plate 21) and to large-scale patterns on kaftans and tiles (plate 94), and on the other in terms of the surfaces on which it can be applied, since it can be extended in any direction and can, therefore, cover both flat and curved surfaces. As a result it found multiple uses (plates 25, 104, 137, and 171) and its popularity was long-lasting. It can be said to be the most formal and 'intellectual' of the four Ottoman decorative styles.

The '*saz*' style, or as we have chosen to call it here, the '*saz* leaf and rosette style', derives its name from the reed pen (*saz*) used to execute the exquisite drawings on which this style is based.[6] Its joyful exuberance stems from its illusory naturalism, while its organic structure renders it immediately readable. The patterns are full of sweeping, rotational movement with the long and directional serrated leaves contrasting boldly with the rather static rounded blossoms and fleshy palmettes.

Unlike the 'Abraham of Kütahya' style it can be successfully adapted for use in both large- and small-scale decoration. Thus we see it in its full glory in the pages of the Vienna Album (plates 186 and 202), the tiles in the entrance of the Sünnet Odası (plate 2d) or those in plate 86, and in the Royal silk kaftans erroneously associated with Bayezid II (plate 123) while miniaturized versions are common to bookbinding and metalwork (plates 5 and 51). No constraint is placed on the large-scale variants, whereas their miniaturized counterparts are invariably confined within medallions and lack the fine, detailed drawing as well as the polychromy of their larger brothers.

The Ottoman style par excellence, however, is the so-called '*quatre fleurs*'. Again a misnomer, with which Ottoman art seems to be riddled, since the flowers appearing in it exceed by far the four—tulips, carnations, hyacinths and roses—from which it was named,[7] it is, nevertheless, more accurate than the term 'Rhodian' by which it had in the past been known.[8] Undeniably the most loved of these decorative styles, it is the most readily recognizable as Ottoman, and reaches its apogee in the splendid ceramic vessels and wall revetments of the second half of the sixteenth century (plate 96). Consisting primarily of flowers from the real world, it goes far beyond the illusory naturalism of the '*saz* leaf and rosette' style to reach a super-realism that finds no parallel in the Islamic world. The flowers, directional as in nature and growing from leafy shrubs, are instantly recognizable both in terms of form and colour. It is, therefore, the most legible of the classical Ottoman decorative styles. However, since it is directional by nature it is rather ill-suited for use in endless repeat lattice patterns, a characteristic which defines the limits

2a. The 'Abraham of Kütahya' style

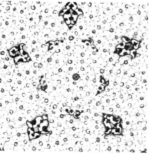
2b. The 'Golden Horn' style

2c. The 'Arabesque' style

of its use in the decorative arts. Strangely in this context, it does not appear in book-bindings for which its directionality might have been well suited, nor in objects of precious metal. Its only use in metalwork is in gilt copper objects such as the jug in plate 34 and the horse chamfron in plate 16d. It is interesting to note that the '*saz* leaf and rosette' style appears as an overall pattern on textiles and ceramics, whereas in metalwork it is always confined within cartouches; conversely, the '*quatre fleurs*' style appears as overall decoration on ceramic vessels and tiles, and more usually within ogival cartouches on textiles.

In parallel with these four styles, however, runs a totally different current in Ottoman art. The 'plain tradition' is a stylistic phenomenon seldom encountered elsewhere in the Islamic world and one which has to date received scant recognition. In terms of form, texture and decoration it can best be described as the triumph of simplicity over elaboration. In this it parallels the austerity and geometric purity so characteristic of the exteriors of Ottoman buildings in contrast with their lavishly decorated interiors.

The roots of the plain tradition can be traced to the fifteenth century, witness the plain hexagonal blue and turquoise tiles in the Green Tomb in Bursa. It reaches its apogee in the sixteenth century, but continues unabated until the nineteenth, as in the silver bowl on plate 31. It is manifest in most aspects of the decorative arts including ceramics and textiles, examples being the red bottle on plate 88, the glorious *saf* carpet on plate 157 and the black silk kaftan of Süleyman the Magnificent on plate 126; but nowhere is this tradition more evident than in metalwork, where it is exemplified by the splendid silver bottle on plate 30. Unlike Mamluk art, where shapes and forms are conservative and subservient to intricate surface decoration, here the roles are reversed. Even in the case of lavishly decorated objects, there is a tectonic quality, a volumetric purity, a search for the bold and powerful statement, where decoration is dominated—even dictated—by shape, such as the large ceramic deep bowls on high feet (plate 2a) or the bottles with tall necks (plate 73).

It may well be through this aspect of Ottoman art that one gains the best insight into the Ottoman character. It demonstrates a paradoxical quest of simple austerity in life coupled with an insatiable appetite and love for the good and beautiful things of this world. Simplicity they may have sought; simplistic they never were.

2d. The '*Saz* leaf and rosette' style

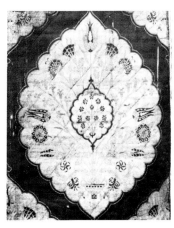

2e. The 'Quatre fleurs' style

2f. The 'Plain Tradition'

The Ottoman Milieu
Godfrey Goodwin

There is a distinct character alive in Ottoman artifacts, just as slender minarets and hemispherical domes set on severe cubes distinguish their architecture. While Ottoman art achieved great splendour, vivid colours and virile arabesque designs it could also be severely disciplined, using puritanical forms for their own sakes, devoid of any but structural decoration. It could be argued that it was at just such moments that the Ottomans achieved their perfect style, if we take perfection in art to lie in the ultimate expression of the possibilities of a particular approach to form: the mosque of Selim II at Edirne, built in the 1570s, or certain İznik tile panels of the same epoch. This creative conflict between the austere and the sumptuous, found elsewhere in Islam, reflects tension within religion and society, but there is a quality in Ottoman art which can be distinguished from that of other Islamic states. Moreover, this distinction was never drowned in the torrent of influences flowing in from every side—loot or gifts or imports—to be absorbed into Ottoman society.

The hereditary élan of the Ottoman style was sustained by the patronage of Sultans, the first dozen of whom were remarkable men with the ability to adapt to constantly changing circumstances. An awareness that fortune owes allegiance to no one was a force in Ottoman thinking which is not to be dismissed as mere fatalism, for Turks are not suicidal by nature. The earlier members of the dynasty were quasi-mythical figures like Osman—who gave his name to the house—or his sire, Ertuğrul, who pitched his tent in the pleasant valley of Söğüt. These frontiersmen were armed shepherds, who migrated from pasture to pasture, an activity which many of these settlers in former Byzantine lands continued for at least part of each year long after the centre of government had been established at Bursa and, later, Edirne (Adrianople).

The roots of such a family were as artless as those of any nomadic clan's, whatever their womenfolk achieved in weaving while passing the time between striking camp and re-erecting tents, trimming the mutton and stirring the pot. Tents continued to be the favourite dwellings of the sophisticated monarchs of later centuries—as many miniature paintings attest—just as hunting remained their favourite sport in common with their western brother kings. Kings who were doomed to perpetual motion within their dominions used nature not for itself like Pius II, but for its open-air pleasures from falconry to feasting.

The Sultans had far more in common with the princes of Italy and the West than many suppose. Their economic problems were akin and their patronage of music, poetry, books and the company of learned men mirrored each other's; indeed, even a love of gorgeous tents and awnings for the Sultan's camp was like a perpetual Field of the Cloth of Gold. For the Ottoman camp was not only the seat of war. In the precision with which it was laid out in streets and bazaars and cookhouses and privies, it showed an orderly array that underlies Ottoman art.

This ability to organize in detail is reflected in the various art forms. Their formalism was only to break down when the central authority itself lost strength. Although efficiency could not mask inevitable stress and strain it is, nevertheless, worth considering what foresight was needed to build a great complex, such as the Süleymaniye in İstanbul, in seven years, with its mosques and colleges, hospital, *hammām* or bath, hospice and kitchens, drains and terraces.

At the time when Orhan ruled (1324-60) the arts were not yet tainted with decadent luxury. Woodcarving and stone-masonry combined with some plasterwork to form most of what has survived from those times. Before the capture of Bursa the buildings were small and the ruined farms and churches of the former Byzantine lands could have had little influence. But with the occupation of a great trading centre on the Silk Road the Ottomans had to adapt themselves to trading abroad. They met with and had to grow accustomed to luxury products and the astute merchants from East and West who purveyed them. There began that extraordinary love-hate relationship with Venice that continued into the nineteenth century. If there was a sudden transition from sheepskins to silks and the service of craftsmen supplanted that of village carpenters, more important was that new wealth in coin made it possible to pay for a standing army which was capable of invading the Balkans. The Sultans were capable students who learnt quickly and developed shrewd judgement in the running of their new state. They were also aware of the proximity of Constantinople, unique even in decay, as they were of the temporary nature of their boundary onto the Sea of Marmara. The call of Europe was irresistible, particularly to those freebooting horsemen who responded to Orhan's drum. For the earliest Ottomans were modest Beys, not Sultans, and laid no claim to crowns. Yet at Bursa they met with aloes and porcelain—for which the dynasty was to develop a love— and such glamorous materials as taffeta from Samarkand and gold brocade from China. Their *nārgiles* or pipes now had crystal bowls and mouthpieces of amber. Such luxuries, together with the pride taken in striking a coinage, change the status of a commander however modest he may be.

Orhan married the daughter of a Christian lord. She took the name of Nilüfer and was the first known member of a formidable line of women of strong character for whom the Sultans showed a preference. They were not then forced to conform to orthodox laws and women still went unveiled in the old Turkish manner. The Sunni *müftīs* had not yet usurped the religious authority of the Sufi mystics like Erdebil and Emir Sultan who were the religious advisers of the government in Bursa. Bursa was thronged with dervishes of many orders and among these mountebanks and genuine mystics were those who retained Shamanist and other pagan beliefs that had been nourished by the superstitions of Anatolia and those central Asian provinces from which they had been driven. At the same time, a new if small class of Sunni or orthodox Muslim jurists was growing up which sought to suppress the more outlandish beliefs of the wilder orders even at the expense of the brotherhood which was born of the dangers of life on the frontiers of Islam.

During the reign of Orhan's son, Murad I *Hüdāvendigār*—a title with significant pretensions to royalty—Sunni *medreses* or colleges were established and literacy in the sacred law was to win precedence for the *'ulemā* class. Yet Shi'ism and the heterodox sects of Islam remained important and a cause of conflict and rebellion in Anatolia down to the present day. These challenges to the conservatism of the *'ulemā* fertilized the empire. Their presence, loosely speaking, was reflected in the division of art into that of the court and that of the populace, whether it were the painting of carts or the making of amulets. The establishment of an orthodox judiciary which grew rich created a new level of patronage which underpinned that of the court, especially in respect of the calligraphers. From their early privileges, resulting from the duality of religious and legal authority, the power of the *'ulemā* grew until they became a second party in the state while escaping the demanding duties required of the Sultan's household. By the eighteenth century, their position had become as ideal as that of any ruling class. This power rested on the law that decreed that only a fiat of the Grand *Müftī* or *Şeyhü'l-İslām* could depose a Sultan and only a Sultan could depose the *Müftī*. Such power had grown gradually from tender roots planted in Bursa during the reign of Murad. As with all empires, however, the Ottomans were saddled with the perennial problem of trying to devise policies, on both secular and religious matters, that would be acceptable to all their heterogeneous subjects. Thus the orthodoxy of the *'ulemā* was set against the heterodoxy of the Anatolian populace.

Wealth also divided Ottoman society. An anonymous chronicler in the fifteenth century wrote nostalgically of the days before power corrupted and Sultans walked up and down the streets of Bursa. Murad II dined with ten noble companions but his son, Mehmed II, ate alone. This aloofness was inevitable, for the rulers were left stranded by the confluence of two majestic rivers: that protective exclusiveness common to central governments and the inheritance with Constantinople of Byzantine court procedures. Byzantine ceremonial and etiquette offered natural precedents for the new emperor, who shared with his immediate predecessors a sense of mission, a mission to establish in old Rome a universal theocracy in the manner of the Caesars.

These early sultans were not merely leaders in battle but had their visions, which could also be mystical, as with Murad II and his grandson, Bayezid II. To understand some Ottoman artifacts the symbolism and purpose of a rug or robe needs to be recognized, as with the extraordinary Shamanist kaftan of Murad III in the collection at Topkapı Sarayı. Murad II was even to retreat at the magic age of 40 to Manisa with his wine cup, only to be recalled when the boy Mehmed and his ministers were unable to control the Janissaries.

The latter were a professional infantry armed with accurate bows and, later, arquebuses and muskets such as no European monarch at that time commanded. At first the corps had been small and made up of prisoners-of-war, mercenaries and some children captured by coastal emirs. In the late fourteenth century, or soon after, children were recruited from Balkan villages and, after 1511, from peasant families in Anatolia.

The *devşirme* or Christian levy was to have influence on Ottoman art as well as the army. The best-looking and most intelligent boys were sent to the palace school within the walls of Topkapı Sarayı. There they were educated not only in horsemanship and arms but in languages, some mathematics, etiquette and music. The pages of the household were excluded from the city and this exclusiveness resulted in marriages with the girls of the harem, who were as assiduously trained in domestic graces as the youths were trained in public affairs with a view to a military or administrative career. The best recruits served their final year in the Sultan's chamber, where they were able to achieve office as sword-bearer, falconer or the like. They could hope for the highest offices in their master's gift.

The palace also housed design studios and workshops where, for example, the designs were drawn for the İznik tiles executed for the royal mosques and the brocades of the imperial kaftans. There was therefore a concentration of wealth and favour within a selected class, which inherited, through its intensive education, an awareness of a style in every aspect of living which was uniquely Ottoman. Such patrons were imbued with the tastes of the court, especially since the grandest officers were habitually married to princesses who were often as wealthy and gifted as they were themselves, as in the case of the remarkable Mihrimah Sultan.

When these former pages became viceroys and governors they carried with them, along with their household, a baggage train of Imperial appurtenances in the style to which they had been bred. From their miniature courts flowed provincial patronage, whether in Buda, Damascus or Cairo, where they built their own garden suburb at Bulaq. Their taste selected tiles for mosques or, when the great *Tekke* of Süleyman I was being built, sent for designs in the İznik style for local craftsmen to imitate. This common visual training gave a unifying quality to an art which was Ottoman, as opposed to Turkish, throughout the Empire. Only at its extremities such as Tunis or Algiers, where the ruling class had never been trained in the palace school, was the influence of the capital so slight as to be easily overlooked.

The conquest of Constantinople by Mehmed II in 1453 intensified Ottoman trade. The period that followed saw velvet designs travelling to and fro between that city and Venice and the flowers of Chinese porcelain reborn on the side of an İznik jug. Designs were absorbed and regurgitated with characteristic Ottoman robustness and exuberance. Occasionally a direct influence like that on the mosque of Murad I can be seen, or the Egyptian work in the complex at Gebze. But these examples show how exceptional such direct borrowings were. Like the royal cypher or *Tuğra*, Ottoman artists possessed a vitality that fed on other art forms, whether Christian or Islamic. They were never as exclusive or conservative as Persian miniaturists, who reached decadence when symbolism became a substitute for sensitivity: at such a juncture the Ottoman draughtsman broke the stems of his tulips.

The Ottoman love of the open air was rewarded with carefully tended gardens and choice rides and walks. Thus Evliya Çelebi, when describing the Okmeydanı or sacred archery ground above the Horn, writes as much about the byways in the vicinity as the marks and kiosk. His preference was for the old Greek Spring of the Mirror, known to lovers. At Beşiktaş he claims that there were one hundred and sixty gardens filled with fragrant roses, narcissus and odoriferous herbs, while shaded in a recess of the hills lay the walk of Yahya Efendi, luxuriant with plane, cypress, willow, fir and nut-trees. In death, too, the Ottomans preferred a view and liked to lie among trees.

Credulity was a force in Ottoman society, as it is still all over the world. Entangled with a myriad superstitions which were sometimes contradictory was the Sufi concept of the fool, akin to the jester of the West, whose idiotic manner of expressing wisdom concealed a message for princes. Indeed, this long-established Muslim respect for the insane made it possible for mentally sick princes to accede and their dismissal was difficult to achieve. Nonetheless, it was superstition exploited by the *ulemā* that destroyed the observatory built by Sinan for Sokollu Mehmed Paşa at the end of the sixteenth century, a destruction symbolic of a decline which was to sap every aspect of secular learning.

Credulity is related to the ritual important to all societies. Some ritual is designed to enhance the prestige of a government and such were the great processions of İstanbul: there was the Friday ride of the Sultan to noon prayer to show the populace that he lived, and there was the rare procession of the guilds, an obeisance by the traders to their Sultan sovereign who watched them from a specially constructed kiosk opposite the Porte, or gate of government. There was the procession to Eyüp, where the Grand Master of the Mevleyi Order of dervishes girded a new Sultan with the sword of his forebears, and the annual progresses to and from Edirne. All these were formal displays of Ottoman splendour with the horsetail standards of the vezirs, the banners and the plumes of crane and heron on the headgear of the officers, the glittering costumes of the grandees and pages, the clamour of the *Mehter* or military bands and the groomed horses, carefully reared on selected plains in Asia and Thrace, which were the envy of European visitors. There were also displays for the sheer delight that displays afford. The jollifications celebrating the circumcision of his sons won popularity for Murad III, because the crowd, unlike the ambassadors of the French king, who were embarrassed by his invitation, could enjoy pantomime and parade without thinking. The floats, the cardboard castles attacked and captured, the tumblers and jugglers, the fireworks and the feasting had a touch of buffoonery and fun that was the reverse of the dignity of bearing usually observed. However, religious ritual in Islam is simple and the elaborate ceremonial of the court was no more exaggerated than it was elsewhere. The formal kaftans were effectively a series of uniforms and this was true of the less ostentatious garments of humbler classes which, by the colour of their sandals and other marks, differentiated each man's trade and religion.

The *hammām* was the centre of social life and the bathing process was all the more relaxing because of its ritual from start to finish. Each bath had its special clients, whether the lawyers at Aya Sofya or the libidinous apprentices at Kılıç Ali Paşa. The ritual of disrobing modestly, of depilation in private, and of massage was matched by the scrubbing with rough gloves and the froth of the special soap or the dowsing with water from a silver bowl, filled, if one were rich, from a marble basin. The domed halls or the hot-rooms were places for conversation where women might pass the whole day, with their children and friends bringing baskets of food for refreshment.

Cooking was also an Ottoman art which was enriched by the products of a widespread empire: the honey of Egypt or the coffee from the Yemen. But neither *hammām* nor kitchen could sap the hardiness of a society which lived so much in the open, however bitter the weather. It was through the cultivation of their senses that they called for the peaches of Amasya, or the virgin vegetables of the extensive kitchen garden of each palace, the surplus of which was sold in order to keep the Sultan supplied with handfuls of gold. In keeping with this was a love of music—the last Sultans produced family orchestras—and of conversation, even if in the great age it was mainly theological, as it was in puritan Britain or Catholic Spain. That the Sultans were poets of varying merit is less interesting for the visual arts than that they were craftsmen trained for the good of their souls, for they could judge workmanship with the experienced eye of a goldsmith like Süleyman I, or of a master gardener like Mehmed II.

A striking difference from the European world was the right of merit to ride over the claims of rank and heredity, for the Ottomans sought to be rid of the old aristocracy as efficiently as any Tudor. Even if Busbecq, the Habsburg ambassador, exaggerated, nonetheless Piyale Paşa, that most successful of admirals, really was the son of a Croatian cobbler, and Sokollu Mehmed, the son of a priest, helped the rebirth of Serbian nationalism by restoring the patriarchate to Peć. For him, or for his royal wife, the finest achievements of Ottoman art were commissioned: as good an example of joint Ottoman patronage as can be imagined. But to read Ottoman history, particularly that after the death of Süleyman, is to find ourselves in the midst of a perpetual family row, intermingled with the bellows of the İstanbul mob, a row stoked by implacable economic forces that harassed the graduates of the palace school who were less slaves than members of the imperial family, a truly household brigade. They risked their lives for magnificent stakes—power and transient splendours. Their wealth was, at least in theory, returned to the state when they died, and their palaces were so ephemeral that few remain: two rooms of a hunting-lodge above a pool in a garden here or overbuilt foundations there. There are no Stokesays or Hatfields or Chenonceaux.

Some of the imperial tents have survived in captivity, but none of the personal pavilions of the monarch, which took ten years to embroider and were exhibited in the Hippo-drome. Ideally, life was a picnic in the spring; if it rained seriously festivities continued indoors with meadows of tiles to contemplate instead of the day's reality. In springtime, too, when candles lit the fountains and the flowers and tortoises wandered with lights upon their backs, banks of buds and blooms invaded the threshold and the garden spread through the Saray where the court came to disport in their fantastic plumage and brocaded robes, creating an intense luxury on a modest scale that was the antipathy of Versailles: things durable belonged only to God. This was the world with which this book is con-cerned, or with what remains of it after the fireworks are spent, embers of the golden rain.

Metalwork

James Allan & Julian Raby

Ottoman textiles and ceramics have had an established part in the European collecting tradition for over a century, for they appealed to both aesthete collectors such as Salting and artists enthused with the Orient, such as Lord Leighton. Ottoman metalwork, on the other hand, has enjoyed no such collecting popularity, either in Europe or the East, and it is consequently difficult to imagine that there was ever a metalworking tradition as inventive and impressive as those of the ceramics and textile industries. Yet there is evidence that Ottoman culture had less of a ceramic bias —be it towards İznik pottery or imported Chinese porcelains—than has been assumed, and that in many instances it was metalwork that took pride of place.

SILVER & GOLD

'And he filled the Treasury with tears'

A glance at the list of contents of Bayezid II's Inner Treasury indicates at once the importance of gold and silver, for before the textiles and ceramics come four columns of gold and silver items including objects from Europe, Hungary and Trabzon.[1] The early importance of precious metals at the Ottoman court comes as no surprise when we remember that the Venetian ambassador, Alvise Gritti, reporting back to the *Serenissima* on Bayezid II's character, singled out his love for 'worked silver'.[2]

Bayezid's father, Mehmed the Conqueror, whose passion for European bronze medallions is well known, was sufficiently interested in other metals for his Grand Vizier, Mahmud Paşa, to request in 1465 the Ragusans to send 'copper, silver and gold'—and here unfortunately the phrase is obscure—'curved combs (?), of which the Sultan is fond'.[3] What previous interest there had been at the Ottoman court in such things is difficult to say, but, at the wedding-feast for Murad I's son, Evrenoz Gazi's gifts included ten silver and ten gold trays, filled with coin, plus silver chalices and ewers; such coin-filled presentation pieces were evidently an early Ottoman custom.[4]

At his audience in Edirne in 1433 Bertrandon de la Brocquière noted that Murad II was served from two great 'gilded' plates, and the Burgundian was impressed by a large silver chalice.[5] Nevertheless, Murad's table hardly compares with the gold, silver and be-jewelled splendours of the Timurid feasts described by Clavijo.[6] This was, however, to change, so that by the second decade of the sixteenth century Spandugino could describe the Ottomans as having 'the greatest pomp in the world'. The question is when this change occurred.[7]

It is tempting to view Mehmed II's reign as the cardinal point, since it saw both the conquest of Constantinople and the acquisition of the productive silver and gold mines of the Balkans, in particular the auriferous silver mines of Novo Brdo in 1455. Turkish booty at the fall of Constantinople was so considerable it became a legend in East and West. Even if the Palaeologues had long since replaced their gold and silver secular plate with humbler metals there were numerous church treasures plundered.[8] Mehmed also seized the imperial Akkoyunlu booty after the battle of Tercan in 1473, and gold vessels are expressly men-tioned by one contemporary present on the campaign.[9] Despite these windfall riches and the steady output of the Balkan mines, Mehmed's reign, with its incessant campaigns, saw an increasing pressure on state finances and the debasement of the silver coinage. Never-theless, we find that, according to Iacopo de Promontorio, one of the Sultan's chief mer-chants, Mehmed's *grand sommelier* or *kilercibaşı* had in his charge a vast array of gold and silver washbasins, drinking cups and bowls, *tazze* and candelabra, many inset with balas rubies. According to another Italian at the court, Mehmed ate from a silver or on occasion gold dish, but Iacopo refers to what might be thought of as a principle of court etiquette—a metallic hierarchy, with the Sultan eating from gold, his Viziers from silver and the soldiery from base metal.[10]

The only person said to be privileged to eat from gold at this time apart from the Sultan was the *Kadıasker* or chief judge of the army and traditional though this hierarchic principle may have been, it contradicted the *Ḥadīth* or tradition of the Prophet which states: 'Do not drink in vessels of gold or silver and do not dress in silks and brocades, for they belong to them, the infidels, in this world and to you in the next.' The same *Ḥadīth* records the warning that whoever drinks from a cup of silver imbibes the fire of Hell.[11] Yet a Sultan like Selim II not only dressed in silks but had a notorious taste for 'firewater'; gold and silver cups should therefore come as no surprise.

The attested use of precious metal utensils at Mehmed's court belies a claim in the late sixteenth-century chronicles of Mustafa Ali and Solakzade to the effect that such items were only introduced in AH 916/1510-11 AD or alternatively AH 914/1508-9 AD.[12] Neverthe-less, the claim reflects the view that it was not Mehmed's reign, as one might assume, but the reigns of Bayezid II and Selim I which witnessed a marked increase in the *luxus* of the Ottoman court. That imperial pomp did in fact grow significantly during these reigns is confirmed by a contemporary, Spandugino, whose intimate knowledge of the situation was probably derived from his Cantacuzene relations in the Saray. Spandugino goes so far as to say that 'pomp' *began* under Bayezid and *grew* under Selim, particularly with the appropriation of the Safavid treasures in 1514 and the Mamluk in 1516-17.[13]

The contradiction between imperial *luxus* and the ascetic strictures of the *Ḥadīth* ensured an ambivalence towards the use of gold and silver tableware. This ambivalence explains why Menavino, a former page in the Saray during the reigns of Bayezid II and

Selim I, wrote, on the one hand, that the Sultan 'never eats from gold or silver, even though he has many of the most superb services (*credenze*), which he has laid out for Ambassadors when they come'; and why he refers, on the other, to the Sultan's beverages being served in vessels of silver.[14] The ambivalence explains why Ottaviano Bon, the Venetian ambassador, in his report of 1608, describes the Sultan's tableware as gold, with gold covers, and claims that it was replaced—for obvious reasons of piety—during the holy month of *Ramazān* by highly prized 'yellow porcelains'.[15] Indeed, the importance of Chinese porcelains in general at the Ottoman court cannot be divorced from the problem of orthodox disapproval of precious metal utensils.

In the final analysis, however, it appears that gold and silver vessels were interchangeable with porcelain, both for the Sultan's personal table and the reception of foreign dignitaries. Tavernier, for example, writing in the first half of the seventeenth century, and relying on the account of two former pages in the Imperial Treasury, claimed that the Sultan was brought water 'sometimes . . . in a Cup of Gold, sometimes in a vessel of Pourcelain, placed upon a large Server of Gold, about two foot diameter, and enrich'd with Precious Stones within and without. That is look'd on as one of the richest pieces of Plate belonging to the Seraglio.'[16]

The Sultan's golden tray had its pendant in a silver salver which was specially brought out for ambassadors; it is frequently referred to in European descriptions of audiences in the Saray and there is an extant document of 1567 in which Piyale Paşa orders the tray to be taken out of the Treasury. Precious metal occurred at the same time in the most private of contexts—the Sultan's bedchamber—where the felicitous bed was said to be flanked by a pair of gold or silver candlesticks.[17]

The prevalence of precious metal objects at the Ottoman court can also be gauged from the fact that they were frequently used as gifts. At the circumcision feast for the Princes Mustafa and Ahmed in 1675 the Grand Vizier Ahmed Köprülü gave the Sultan a golden goblet complete with lid, while the Beylerbey of Erzerum—a city Evliya Çelebi noted as one of the leading centres of precious metal working—gave nine silver bottles and nine silver drinking cups to Prince Mustafa, and two of each to Prince Ahmed. It is interesting that at the same feast the Greek Patriarch presented the Princes with two silver bottles, four silver cups, one silver basin and jug, two silver candlesticks and one silver box.[18] Gold and silver items are recorded among the *bayram* presents given by the court artists to the Sultan in the mid-sixteenth century; and prominent among the gifts which Sultan Süleyman sent to Shah Tahmasp in 1560—in gratitude for executing Süleyman's rebellious son Bayezid—were a gold tray, gold water-bottle, gold belt (*kemān*), gilded silver jar and a silver tray.[19] Ottoman princes, moreover, at least at the beginning of the sixteenth century, were equipped with a silver table service when they departed to take up a provincial governorship.[20]

'Jewellers' are mentioned among the royal companions (*müteferrika*) in the fifteenth century, and jewellers and goldsmiths appear on the palace payrolls that survive from the sixteenth century on. In one, datable to the late 1530s or early 1540s, there is a record of thirty-five goldsmiths (*kuyumcıyān*) and two gold-inlay workers (*zernişān*); there are also references to a certain Ustad Ahmed, the retired head of the goldsmiths, to Muhiddin, a

4. *Tombak* tankard, 16th century. H: 13.2 cm;
w: 589 gm. Walters Art Gallery, Baltimore 54.512

silversmith from the time of Sultan Bayezid, and to the head of the gold-inlay workers, Emir Hasan and his two apprentices who are described as 'slaves of the Sultan' (*hünkār kulları*).[21] Referring to the situation at the beginning of the sixteenth century, Menavino claims that there were seventy goldsmiths (*'ciumgeler cioè orefici'*) who made all the silver and gold objects for the *Grand Signor* and who consisted of a mixture of Persians and slaves; they received piece-work payments in addition to their salary and their shops were 'in the middle of Constantinople', which must refer to the jewellers' quarter of the *Bedesten*, formed by Mehmed the Conqueror.[22] By the last quarter of the sixteenth century the number of *orefici* and *gioielleri* had risen enormously if we are to credit the word of one of Murad III's former private physicians, Domenico Hierosolimitano, who claims that they totalled 500 persons in all, including master craftsmen and apprentices.[23]

The court's taste for luxury and patronage on an imperial scale must have ensured a large production. To these we must add another factor which must have helped promote the goldsmith's art both quantitatively and qualitatively—imperial participation. It was a custom of the Ottoman House for princes to learn a manual skill, and the trade chosen by Selim I and Süleyman I was that of the goldsmith. According to Evliya Çelebi, the seventeenth-century traveller and writer, the goldsmiths attained a high degree of prestige as a result of Selim's and Süleyman's training in their art. Evliya is an author notorious for his whimsy but he deserves credence in this context having been a goldsmith himself and the son of the guild's head. The princes received their training in Trabzon, Süleyman's pupil-master being a Greek by the name of Constantine. Süleyman, Evliya notes, built a factory and fountain for the goldsmiths, while Selim established an assay-office.[24]

At present, little appears to survive as proof of all this activity. Yet once it is recognized that there was a significant Ottoman tradition objects will surely be identified. All the same, losses must have been enormous. The imperial treasury, although spared the depredations of a foreign enemy, was 'raided' on several occasions by the Sultans themselves, usually in an attempt to bolster their military finances. Murad III melted the silver and gold objects into coin and removed the jewels from items such as swords, amassing them in one pile.[25] And a register survives cataloguing the gold and silver objects—well over 300 silver and 50 gold—which Selim III had members of his court consign to the Imperial Mint in AH 1204/1790 AD.[26] By this late date probably much of the sixteenth- and seventeenth-century material had already succumbed to the melting pot. Murad IV, Evliya Çelebi relates, entered the treasury on his accession in 1623, accompanied by Evliya's father among others; when the young Sultan saw that the treasury contained only six purses of money, a bag of coral and a chest of china, and that 'there were no gold vessels', he 'filled the empty treasury with his tears.'[27]

The 'Bejewelled Aesthetic'

Despite the ravages of time, enough objects survive to allow the identification of several aesthetic traditions, even if it is too early to attempt a sequential history of Ottoman precious metalworking. One of these traditions was for jewelled objects in which the emphasis on surface coruscation and preciosity entailed negation of the form and texture of the matrix material. Jewels were applied with equal lavishness to arms and armour and to domestic objects, examples being the armour of Murad IV and two gold candlesticks in the Türk ve İslam Eserleri Müzesi.[28] The jewels were set either into the metal or onto jade plaques, as on the gold flask illustrated on plate 28.

The characteristic method was to set the stone, usually semi-precious, into a bevel raised out of an elliptical plaque of gold foil whose edges lay on the surface of the matrix material; the edges were often worked to look like petals, and the gold plaque thus served as the calyx of the jewel flower. Each inset was linked to its neighbours by a floral stem, but any organic appearance was contradicted by the rigid and symmetrical—grid-like—arrangement of the jewels. Identical bejewelling occurs on Ottoman jade jugs and mugs and on Chinese porcelain in the Saray, in total disregard of the object's material or decorative virtues.[29]

This method of insetting jewels was distinctly Ottoman, but the principle—the 'bejewelled aesthetic'—was by no means unique. Mention has already been made of Timurid jewelled gold and silver; a few Safavid objects survive;[30] and of course there are numerous later examples from Mughal India. Similar traditions occurred in Europe and Byzantium, and even in China, as the treasures of Emperor Wan Li's tomb prove. It is therefore difficult at this stage to isolate any specific influences on the Ottoman tradition.

Crowns played no part in Ottoman court ceremonial although one now in the Schatzkammer in Vienna was presented by Sultan Ahmed I to Stephen Bocskay of Transylvania in 1605.[31] A similarly decorated object that was of ritual importance however is the jewelled flask illustrated in plate 28. It is frequently represented in sixteenth-century Ottoman miniatures being carried by one of the two pages standing behind the Sultan, the other page bearing the imperial sword (plate 207). The flask was for boiled drinking-water and its unlikely shape is explained by the fact that it is a metallic derivation of a leather drinking-flask, Ottoman examples of which have also survived.[32] Such bejewelled flasks were not confined to the Sultan, and Evliya Çelebi refers to one carried by the Paşa of Erzerum's head musketeer or *tüfenkçi başı*, which indicates the way in which metropolitan tastes were disseminated through the provinces.[33]

The 'bejewelled aesthetic' was admirably suited to the *Schatzkammer* mentality of imperial courts, and it enjoyed a long life. A datable example of Ottoman court work is the round gold tray, with a flanged rim studded with turquoises and an octagonal jade centre-piece which is inlaid with gold arabesques and a six-pointed star, and the accompanying gold-studded jade cup, presented by Mustafa II to the voivode of Poznań in 1699, on the occasion of the treaty of Karlowitz.[34] Also from the very close of the seventeenth century we find a matching ewer and basin given as a present by the mother of Peter the Great in 1692; it was inventoried a decade later as 'Greek work', and has on this basis been attributed to İstanbul. The use of transparent enamels for the cypress trees is of interest here because Evliya Çelebi claimed that the best enamellers in the Ottoman Empire were non-Turks.[35] The origins and evolution of Ottoman enamelling have never been studied, but an example of its variety is the opaque cloisonné enamel disc on the silver bowl illustrated in plate 5.[36]

Decorated silver: engraving, repoussé and hammering

The bejewelled tradition combined the arts of the jeweller and the goldsmith. This second group was the province of the goldsmith. The material for the body of the objects is usually sheet silver, often with gilding which can be total or partial. The decoration can be engraved on a flush surface, but the design is frequently in relief, produced in a combination of repoussé and hammering. The most usual tool for the process of hammering was a ring punch; consequently, when we find ring-punch backgrounds in Ottoman base-metal objects we should perhaps view it as a technical derivation from precious metalworking rather than, as has been suggested, a *retardataire* decorative borrowing from fifteenth-century Persia.[37]

5. Silver bowl, parcel gilt and enamelled, mid-16th century. Priv. Col. London

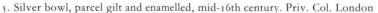

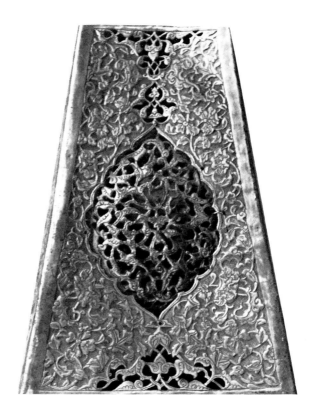

The designs consist of lotus palmettes, trilobed leaves and petalled rosettes on scrolling stems, and are Ottoman variants of the so-called 'International Timurid style', which developed, as its name implies, in fifteenth-century Persia. It is essential, however, to distinguish between species and genus, and it is possible to identify an Ottoman species which developed its own morphology in the second half of the fifteenth century and which reached its most characteristic form in the 'Abraham of Kütahya' style. Whatever the associations of its name, the 'Abraham of Kütahya' style was not, it must be emphasized, unique to pottery; it can be paralleled on Ottoman woodwork, book-bindings and decorative drawings. It was, in other words, a Court style originating in the royal ateliers or *nakkāshāne* and common to a variety of media.

There are no known metal examples of the classic 'Abraham of Kütahya' style. This must, however, be a fortuitous lacuna for several reasons. In the first place, one of the finest specimens of early Ottoman silver, the mosque lamp from the mosque of Mehmed II, has an early form of the style (plate 6); the motifs are less dense and introverted than on the full-blown versions associated with ceramics some twenty years or so later.[38] Nevertheless, we see the beginnings of the characteristic tendency for tendrils and leaves to curl in on themselves. Secondly, there are numerous sixteenth-century objects, notably a series of jugs of which the finest is that in the Victoria and Albert Museum (plate 18), which carry a simplified version of the 'Abraham of Kütahya' style, in that the motifs are less fulsome and the structure less tense.

Variants exist, then, of the 'Abraham of Kütahya' decorative style in metalwork before and after the ceramics which gave their name to the style. However, the ceramics enable

7a. İznik dish, 16th century. Diam: 30.6 cm. MMA
1970.30

7b. Silvered brass bowl, 17th century. Diam: 37.9 cm;
w: 870 gm

one to visualize fully the missing period in the metalwork. Their shapes show a clear
derivation from metalwork.

Torus mouldings, moulded upturned rims and sharp articulations betray a metallic
origin, while the band of thin lozenges in the cavetto of a dish in the Topkapı Sarayı or on
the upper body of the mosque lamps from the *türbe* of Bayezid II suggest a fluted or
gadrooned metal prototype. Similar lozenges occur in several Ottoman silver bowls.
The 'Abraham of Kütahya' jug at Sèvres amply illustrates the point: the sharply angled
joint of neck and body, and the slight moulding at this juncture are technically redundant
features in ceramics, a medium which enabled the potter to produce a fluent outline. By
the mid-sixteenth century the İznik potter had fully realized the potential of his medium
and created jugs with sensuous, sweeping curves. At the outset, however, he must have
derived his inspiration from a jug of the Victoria and Albert type where the torus moulding
was a structural necessity to link two separate metal sheets.[39]

Further evidence that the potters copied metalwork is apparent in the disposition of
the decoration. This is compartmented in a manner appropriate to highly articulated
metalwork.

This style of decoration was admirably suited to metalwork, because its motifs were of
varied size and its structure expandable; it could therefore be adapted to almost any two-
dimensional shape and three-dimensional surface. It thus continued in metalwork long
after it had gone out of fashion in ceramics. It occurs on a silver jug in the Hermitage
(plate 7c) which is closely related to the one in the Victoria and Albert Museum but which,
to judge from its tapering neck and weaker decoration, is somewhat later.[40] By the 1540s a
miniaturist variant of the style had been developed with floral elements of a reduced size

7c. Silver jug, 16th century. H: 13.5 cm. Hermitage N.T. 358

7d. İznik jug, 16th century. H: 17.5 cm. B M 90-3-20 1

and complexity, and greater emphasis on arabesques. This can be seen on a bowl in the National Museum of Hungary dated 1537, on two daggers with European crests, one dated 1543 (plate 8a), the other 1549, while a late but fine example occurs on an evangeliary binding dated 1593 from the monastery of Petkovica.[41]

The Balkan provenance of this binding raises the problem of the Balkans' role as a precious metalworking centre under the Ottomans. As we have seen, the Balkan gold and silver mines, especially those at Novo Brdo, Srebrnica and Rudnik but many others too, maintained their importance, and numerous Ottoman documents relating to these mines have survived.[42] Mining development in the Balkans in the later mediaeval period is known to have greatly encouraged the gold- and silversmiths of the area, although little of their work has actually survived.[43] There is no reason, then, to presuppose a total break in production under the Ottomans. The independent city-state of Ragusa, present-day Dubrovnik, relied on the Balkan mines for its precious metals and had a thriving goldsmiths' quarter. Forty-four goldsmiths are documented, for example, in the second half of the fifteenth century, several of them of Jewish origin.[44] One renowned fifteenth-century goldsmith, Ivan Progonović, was from Novo Brdo, indicating that Ragusa drew not only raw materials but manual expertise from the hinterland.[45] The Ragusans are known to have sent worked silver to the Ottomans; in 1458 they presented 'silver plates' to Mehmed the Conqueror and the Grand Vizier Mahmud Paşa, himself of Serbian extraction; and at the great circumcision festivities of 1582, which are so vividly portrayed in the miniatures of the *Sūrnāme*, the Ragusan authorities made a gift of fifteen silver cups.[46] Ragusan workmanship in the fifteenth century was evidently prized by the Ottomans, to judge from Mehmed II's request for metal objects referred to earlier, and in

8a. Silver dagger dated 1543. Nat. Mus. Hungary 341/1934

1494 there is a surprising record of the Sultan, Bayezid II, ordering a gold inlaid sword from Ragusa.[47]

From the central Balkans metalworkers are said to have fled over the Sava and Danube to escape the Turkish invasions, settling in Hungary and Transylvania. One group from Chiprovac in Bulgaria settled in Wallachia in the seventeenth century.[48] Yet the exodus cannot have been total, because there are numerous references in Hungarian documents, particularly from the turn of the eighteenth century, to South Slav goldsmiths who had learnt their profession under Turkish rule and eventually moved north.[49]

Under the Ottomans, Balkan goldsmiths continued to produce liturgical artifacts in a Byzantine manner, occasionally modified by Ottoman decoration.[50] Their most numerous productions were small bowls of flattened hemispherical shape. The size of these bowls is not large and rarely exceeds 15 cm. The majority rest on a flattened base without a footring and have a raised central boss or disc. In some examples, the boss consists of a roundel which rotates on a pin; in others the boss is again a separate sheet which has been riveted to the body. A number of them include a small sculpted animal, presumably cast, as a finial for the central pin, the favourite animal being a sejant stag. Their decoration ranges from the floral arabesque, under the influence of the Ottoman court style, to the figural, which remained loyal to the Byzantine saintly and Balkan teratological traditions. Bowls of both types are known with Slavonic and Greek inscriptions. Several are dated and state that they were made in the reign of Selim II and that they were made for drinking the honour of God and the Virgin Mary. One is inscribed as the work of a Sofia craftsman in 1578.[51] It is thus to the Balkans or at least Balkan influence that we may attribute the fine bowl illustrated on plate 21, since it is comparable to the Balkan series in shape, size and aspects of the design, such as the gadrooned lozenges, the raised print which swivels on a pin, and the border cartouches which contain animals more western than eastern in appearance, such as the wyvern, a form of dragon rarely encountered in Islamic art.[52]

It is frequently claimed, even in works on Balkan and Byzantine art, that the ultimate origin of this bowl type was mediaeval Persia. Confusion has been caused because a typical example of these Balkan bowls was mistakenly published in the Persian exhibition of 1931 as 'Persian 13th or 14th century', a mistake compounded by Kurt Erdmann who attempted to attribute several such bowls to eleventh-century Iran.[53]

By contrast, the shape of the second substantial series of Ottoman sixteenth- and seventeenth-century 'repoussé' silver is of certain Eastern origin. This is the dragon-handled jug of a form customarily associated with Timurid Persia.[54] Nevertheless, the Ottoman examples are decoratively distinct, and certain design features they share with the

8b. *Tombak* dagger, 17th century. L: 55 cm; w: 790 gm.

earlier of our Balkan bowls point to a common, Balkan, manufacture.[55] One jug from the Serbian monastery of Dečani has a frieze of animals in the Balkan teratological style on its lid.[56] Similar animal representations are also found on ceramics (plate 67).

It is a curious feature, then, of this second group of Ottoman metalwork that an Ottoman style of decoration was often applied to foreign shapes, whether Timurid, as the jugs, or Mamluk, as the silver mosque lamp from the mosque of Mehmed II.

The Plain Tradition

Both the 'bejewelled aesthetic' and the 'repoussé' tradition subjected in their different ways the entire surface of the object to decoration. The Ottomans persevered with the 'bejewelled aesthetic' until at least the mid-eighteenth century (a fine example being the gold chalice made in İstanbul in 1749 for the Armenian Patriarch Gregory the Chainbearer[57]), while a descendant of the 'Abraham of Kütahya' style was still in use in the last decade of the sixteenth century, and other expressions of the 'repoussé tradition' doubtless continued into the seventeenth century. There was, however, a concurrent tradition that was the complete aesthetic antithesis.

Here the emphasis was on form, and on the texture and reflective values of the undecorated silver, rather than on surface elaboration. The objects were economical in structure and decoration (plates 23, 29–33). Yet their bold simplicity stems not from 'primitive' ignorance or inability, but from a total disregard for the virtuoso art of the goldsmith. Their success lies in their proportions, and the balance between substantial volumes and sweeping outlines, in a clear parallel to the exterior forms of Ottoman architecture. Structural necessities, such as the knop of the water-bottle or the plaque where the body and handle of the ladle are joined, are turned into telling elements in the design; this tectonic 'honesty' recalls the constructivist approach of Ottoman architects.

This 'plain tradition' is totally unexpected in an Islamic context. Islamic metalwork from the twelfth century on is characterized by elaborate inlaid decoration. More sober decoration prevailed, it is true, in silver attributed to twelfth-century Balkh, but here too colour contrast was achieved with the use of niello. Niello is used for the inscription on the ladle, but the lines are arranged to form a decorative medallion rather than a frieze as on most Islamic metalwork. It is also difficult to point to Islamic metalwork or ceramics that give outline such priority over decoration except the solitary plain red İznik bottle on plate 88.

Even more striking is the contrast with the Ottoman 'bejewelled aesthetic'. This dichotomy was not confined to metalwork, however; compare, for example, the restraint of the crescent silk from Lyons or the *saf* (plates 115 and 157) with the exuberance of the embroidered carpet (plate 130). Ottoman taste for the 'minimal' is sufficient, then, to explain the development of the 'plain tradition' in metalwork; this does not, though, exclude the possibility of external influence. The closest metalwork parallel is to be found in Hungary; for example the four Gothic beakers from Budapest or the hemispherical bowl from the Körmend hoard. A feature which links these plain Hungarian objects to Ottoman silver is a horizontal canelure just below the rim similar to that on the ladle on plate 23.[58]

At present it is impossible to say how early the *plain tradition* began. It must surely, though, have been in vogue by the 1520s because in pottery—in the 'Abraham of Kütahya' and so-called 'Damascus' İznik footed bowls especially—we discover a comparable volumetric sense, whatever the emphasis in these ceramics on decoration. Whenever it began, the 'plain tradition' continued until the mid-nineteenth century, as is proved by a hemispherical bowl, illustrated in plate 31, which bears the assay mark of Selim III (1789–1808).[59]

More difficult to date is the *sürāhī* or water-bottle illustrated in plate 30 because it carries no inscription or assay mark. Nevertheless, it can be assigned to the sixteenth century by comparing its shape with datable ceramic equivalents. The comparison underlines the argument that precious metal objects enjoyed priority—chronological, if not also qualitative—over ceramics. The standard pottery *sürāhī* of the sixteenth century had a knop midway up its elongated neck. This knop is a structural requirement in goldsmithing, since a tall neck made out of a single sheet of silver would be unmanageably weak; it is, however, redundant in the plastic medium of pottery and does not occur, for instance, in contemporary Safavid bottles. Its appearance in Ottoman pottery must therefore reflect the influence of metalwork, which is confirmed by another redundant feature in ceramic *sürāhīs* of the first half of the sixteenth century, namely the step at the junction of neck and body. Later pottery versions tend to dispense with this break in contour, but often retain a decorative articulation, in that the body is distinguished from the neck by a painted band. This band can therefore be seen as a vestigial 'step'.

Another ceramic shape, which was popular in the second quarter of the sixteenth century, confirms the influence of metalwork. This is the flat dish with shallow sides and a flat narrow rim, illustrated on plate 79. A silver version, which still awaits publication, exists in the Topkapı; its centre is elaborately engraved with a radial design of 'Abraham of Kütahya' flowers and arabesques. The decoration suggests a date in the first quarter of the sixteenth century, but this can only be corroborated when the assay seal has been read. An earlier example of the same shape is a finely decorated tinned copper piece in the Victoria and Albert Museum, which is dated AH 902/1496–97 AD. It has recently been attributed to Khorasan rather than Anatolia, an attribution one might question in view of the Mamluk character of its cavetto pattern.[60] Interestingly, the rim of this dish is engraved with a z-band, which seems to have been one of the commonest types of decoration for İznik pottery examples of this shape (plate 79) and for the silver bowls on plates 5 and 21.

One of the most striking representatives of the 'plain tradition' is the mosque lamp which bears the control stamp of Osman II (1618–22). Its shape too finds an echo in ceramics, notably in the İznik lamp in the Kuyaş collection, which is datable to the last quarter of the sixteenth century and is peculiar for its Hebrew inscription.[61] From the same period too is the silver and parcel-gilt mosque-lamp dedicated to the shrine of Eyüp by Osman II in AH 1027/1618 AD. It has a much taller foot than any known İznik lamps, and differs from the other Osman II silver lamp in its additional decoration, which consists of gilded lobed medallions; on the foot they are plain, while on the body they are engraved with floral and arabesque motifs which also appear on the neck in openwork. This decoration leads us into our final group, but before we leave the 'plain tradition' it is worth noting that the Eyüp lamp bears Sultanic inscriptions. What is striking is that these are only thinly engraved, or to be more precise, traced, and that, although well formed, they play no role in the design. They illustrate the tendency for inscriptions on Ottoman metalwork to be purely documentary rather than decorative—a feature which distinguishes Ottoman from other types of Islamic metalwork.

Saz leaves and rosettes

Midway—typologically but not chronologically—between the nakedness of the 'plain tradition' and the rampant designs of the 'repoussé' group is a style which aims to contrast decorated and undecorated areas. The decoration is envisaged in terms of accents, and the design motifs are clearly demarcated from the plain ground by confining them within lobed medallions, which are usually ogival in shape. The contrast is heightened by the use of gilding, which tends to be restricted to areas of decoration. The resulting emphasis on examples such as the exterior of the silver bowl on plate 5, the incense burner (plate 51) and the hexagonal casket (plate 9), is less on the individual floral motifs in the medallion than on the medallion's overall impact. It is understandable, then, that we find a simpler range of floral forms—usually *saz* leaves, rosettes and palmettes—and less differentiation in the size of individual motifs. A similar process of simplification and standardization of size took place, however, in metalwork in the later sixteenth-century derivatives of the

9. Silver casket, circa 1600.
H: 11.3 cm; w: 260 gm. Priv.
Col. London

10. *Tombak* ewer, 16th century.
H: 28.4 cm; w: 1,119 gm. MMA
1975.41

'Abraham of Kütahya' style. The quasi-naturalism and elaboration of the '*saz* leaf and rosettes' style suited it most to painting, ceramics and textiles, media which could enhance the details in colour. It was not primarily conceived in terms of metalwork and the metal versions are insignificant cousins by comparison. This group of metalwork sees a change not just in motifs but in pattern and composition. 'Abraham of Kütahya' dishes tend to have radial patterns, pivoted on a central rosette. The '*saz* leaf and rosettes' style prefers rotational patterns, often without a clearly defined centre. As regards composition, the innovation in metalwork must be viewed in connection with structural changes.

Sheet silver, unless extravagantly thick, is too fragile to be made into large flat surfaces without either ribbing or internal support. One alternative that faced the goldsmith was to produce rounded forms which had an inherent tensile strength; this was the solution so successfully employed in the 'plain tradition'. Another was to create a wooden frame onto which the silver was pinned; this was the method used for the Qur'ān case in plate 39. A third solution was to facet objects, such as the incense burner in plate 51 or the hexagonal casket in plate 9, both of which have a very different tectonic character to the 'plain tradition'.

The adoption of rectangular facets, combined with decorative medallions, resulted in a composition identical to the standard formula used on Ottoman bookbindings, that is, a central ogival medallion with quadrant medallions in the four corners. The same scheme is translated on a grander scale in carpets, but the connection between this group of metalwork and bookbinding is not solely decorative. It is also technical, because leather binding designs were stamped—with a metallic die. Of necessity the die-cutters were metalworkers, whatever else they may have been. However, on the die the floral or arabesque motifs were countersunk *intaglios*; vice versa, in the medallions on the incense-burner (plate 51), the socket of the axe (plate 3) and the exterior of the silver bowl (plate 5), the designs are isolated in relief by the background being chiselled away. This technical difference may be misleading, though, because the result the die-cutter intended was a stamped leather medallion with embossed floral elements; both goldsmith and binder, in other words, aimed at reproducing relief designs, but whereas the goldsmith could achieve this directly, let us say, positively, the binder was obliged to use an indirect, negative, process. One should emphasize that the favourite motifs on these binding medallions were arabesques or '*saz* leaves and rosettes'.[62] This relief effect was only possible when the vessel had thick walls. On an object such as the hexagonal casket (plate 9) the '*saz* leaves and rosettes' designs were engraved flush with the background.

It is a curious phenomenon that the most axiomatic of Ottoman decorative styles—the so-called '*quatre fleurs*' which typifies polychrome İznik ceramics, and textiles, of the second half of the sixteenth century—found little favour in metalwork. The style appears with regularity only in arms and armour and particularly on the horse chamfrons (plate 16d), which afforded an extensive surface suited to directional decoration. Of other objects illustrated only the gilt copper, *tombak*, ewer (plate 34) belongs to this style, but it uses an elementary abbreviation, directly derived from textiles (plate 145), namely a single carnation in a drop repeat. While the '*quatre fleurs*' style appears, then, on *tombak* objects, it seems to have been ignored in precious metal.

Why? Again the relationship with bookbindings may be instructive because that medium made almost no use of the '*quatre fleurs*' style. An emphasis on medallion compositions on bookbindings and small-scale precious metal objects perhaps precluded the use of '*quatre fleurs*', because there was a difficulty in reconciling directional designs with ogival medallions unless these were of substantial size, as on the silks (plate 147).[63]

Before we leave the goldsmith's art, a word is needed on the silver stamps. In principle

11. Silver Qur'ān stand, inscribed with the name of Ahmed I, early 17th century. TVİEM

all silver objects were officially tested for purity, but in practice many went unstamped, as is evident from the silver bowl on plate 5 and the bottle on plate 30. A firman of AH 1000/1592 AD which insisted that all silver items sold in the İstanbul bazaar were to be stamped, is a further indication that the system was far from fully effective.[64] The earliest stamp so far identified is that of Bayezid II on the small bowl (plate 21) and as we have seen, Selim I is said to have built an assay house.

Stamps are not a feature of earlier Islamic silver, and one wonders therefore how the idea came to be adopted by the Ottomans. The Byzantines used silver stamps, but the practice appears to have lapsed at the end of the seventh century, which makes it difficult to argue a Byzantine influence.[65] Marks were, however, employed in Western Europe, Hungary and Ragusa-Dubrovnik by the fifteenth century. Alternatively one might argue that the practice was a function of a highly structured, centralized Empire, and that the Ottomans required no precedent for the idea.[66]

It is not known if control stamping was limited to İstanbul or if the system extended to provincial centres in the Balkans and the East, the latter including Aleppo, Baghdad, Cairo, Diyarbakır, Erzerum, Gümüşhane, Kayseri and Trabzon, all of which are known to have had goldsmiths' quarters.[67] Indeed as yet we have few criteria by which to identify regional products or specialities.

It was a truism among Western scholars in the last century and the early part of the present that all Ottoman art was the creation of either displaced Persians or subject Christians. The role of both groups can certainly be documented in metalwork. As we have seen, Menavino specifically mentions Persians and according to Gerlach, the chaplain of the Imperial Habsburg mission to the Porte, who was writing in 1576, numerous goldsmiths were Armenian.[68] At the beginning of the seventeenth century the head jeweller in Cairo, Koca İbrahimşah, was an Armenian from Diyarbakır, while two of the most famous enamellers and engravers singled out by Evliya Çelebi were also Armenian.[69] Little Armenian work has yet been published, except a group of seventeenth-century repoussé silver bindings from Kayseri, to which can be added a gold reliquary from the same town.[70] It is interesting that in the eighteenth century, when repoussé was so common in Ottoman silver, the Armenian family of Duz provided several of the most eminent court jewellers.[71]

It is evident that the Greeks too were active goldsmiths.[72] Not only did Süleyman the Magnificent learn the art from Constantine, a Greek from Trabzon—the city where Süleyman's father, Selim, had been trained as a goldsmith—but the humble Evliya claimed to have been taught Latin and Greek by a Greek goldsmith called Simeon. In Evliya's eyes the most famous of all enamellers was a Greek by the name of Michael Simitçioğlu.[73]

The final enameller mentioned by Evliya was an Albanian, Osman Çelebi, who was master of the mint in Cairo in the late sixteenth century.[74] Evliya says little about the Jewish contribution, but the Jews are known to have had a hand in the jewel trade. Via Jewish ladies who were confidantes in the harem but also had access to the outside world, Jewish jewel merchants gained access to the important female patrons of the court. One famous example is Kiratza, whose son traded in jewels in Venice during the reign of Murad III.[75] Jewish goldsmiths are mentioned in Cairo and Aleppo, and there is evidence of some leaving Rhodes for Salonica and İstanbul.[76] Finally, there were European metalworkers in the Ottoman Empire.[77]

Until more Ottoman objects have been published and detailed studies undertaken of the metalworking traditions of the various minorities, it will be impossible to identify their technical or stylistic contributions. One needs, however, to distinguish between the Christian religious tradition, which tended to be conservative and often Byzantinizing in character, and the Ottoman secular tradition which emerged from the Court styles. It can therefore be misleading to stress the identity of each minority; in the secular arts ethnic diversity was offset by a unity of style that had its ultimate origin in the Court ateliers.

COPPER, BRASS AND STEEL

Silver and gold objects are but one aspect of Ottoman metalwork. Of equal importance to our understanding of Ottoman metal is the hitherto largely unpublished and unknown body of objects made of base metals consisting almost exclusively of steel, copper and copper alloys, the latter primarily brass.

Anatolia is rich in copper; not surprisingly, therefore, the brass is of two types: a copper-zinc alloy suitable for raising and beating (plate 43) and a copper-lead-zinc alloy suitable for casting (plates 22 and 41).

Tin, on the other hand, which in combination with copper is the basis for bronze, seems to have come from Europe. The shortage of tin, however, is corroborated by many references to imports from England of lateen dishes—that is dishes made of tinned copper or possibly bronze. It, therefore, emerges that in the main, the Ottomans used either relatively pure copper or brass for their base metal objects.

Even if tin was little used for the body of Ottoman base metal objects, it was commonly used for plating copper. There are two reasons for this; the first was utilitarian, since tin formed a protective layer against the poisonous effects of pure copper in cooking and eating utensils, and the second was decorative since it provided a cheap way of emulating silver.

Both in mediaeval Europe and the Islamic world, craftsmen tinned objects by rubbing over them tin and *sal ammoniac* on a very hot pad. The vapourizing *sal ammoniac* cleans the surface of the copper and enables the melting tin to form a thin covering layer over the object.

Gilding, a technique widely used in Ottoman metalwork, is not applicable to all metals. After silver (plates 18, 21, 39, 51, 52 and 53), the most suitable material for gilding is copper. It is therefore no surprise that the *tombak* objects analysed are all of relatively pure copper (plates 19, 32, 33, 34 and 50). Mercury gilding was used in Iran and probably elsewhere in

12. Brass door-post, 15–16th century. H: 458 cm. V & A 34.1890

the Middle East from early Islamic times. Al-Hamdani in the tenth century, Al-Biruni in the eleventh and Abu'l-Qasim Kashani in 1300 all describe or mention the process. While gilding is better known on silver objects, the Nishapur excavations brought to light a number of gilt copper objects, especially belt-fittings and horse harness plaques. Horse-leathers and other horse trappings were embellished in the same way under the Ottomans, witness the booty captured in the seventeenth century from the Turks and now housed in Karlsruhe, Dresden, Cracow and elsewhere, suggesting a continuous tradition. A Seljuk Anatolian gilt copper plaque bearing precious stones, and a late fifteenth-century Syrian Mamluk dish in the Ashmolean Museum,[78] provide links in this continuity. Adding to this the existence of gilt copper in Byzantium, perhaps we do not need to look westwards to Venice for the origin of its use in the Ottoman empire as has been suggested elsewhere.[79]

However, the material shown here demonstrates amply that gilding had a wider use under the Ottomans than earlier on in the Islamic world. They evidently delighted in golden objects and the mosque lamp, ewers, candlesticks, bowl, flask, jug, rose-water sprinklers (plates 19, 10, 34, 33, 32, 13a, b, c, d) indicate the wide range of utilitarian objects in their gilt copper repertoire. Other types of *tombak* work include door plaques in the Süleymaniye mosque and the Topkapı Palace, as well as chimney-pieces in the latter such as that in the Vestibule of the Hearth[80] and in the room adjoining the kiosk of Murad III.[81]

The techniques used for the manufacture of base metal objects published here include both casting and raising from sheet metal but the concentric rings on certain pieces suggest that they might also be spun (plates 46 and 43).

The techniques of surface decoration include fluting, incising, piercing and openwork casting. The fluting on the qum-qum or rose-water sprinkler (plate 13a) at first calls to mind early Islamic *repoussé* work such as is found on the famous Herat ewers of the late twelfth and early thirteenth centuries. Comparison, however, with Ottoman silver such as the small bowl (plate 21) indicates that this type of work is more probably derived from the contemporary Balkan silversmithing tradition discussed earlier. Spiralling flutes such as

Tombak rose-water sprinklers, *qum qum*, 16th–17th century

13a. H: 15.3 cm; w: 195 gm
13b. H: 14.2 cm; w: 170 gm

13c. *Tombak* flask, 16th century. H: 19.7 cm. British Museum 97-3-20 1

13d. *Tombak* jug, 16th century. H: 14 cm; w: 310 gm

those in plates 7b, 32 and 48 are uncommon elsewhere in Islamic metalwork, while closely related to Byzantine silver, for example a large sixth-century dish in the Hermitage[82] and Syrian Raqqa ceramics of the thirteenth century. The pattern, however, found great favour with the Ottomans who used it on domes[83] and on the decoration of helmets and shields. It is worth noting here that a cursory examination of metal objects represented in miniature painting always shows them to have a fluted surface. Such a convention may indicate the wide use of the technique and its identification with metal vessels.

Piercing or openwork decoration is found particularly on Ottoman religious or military standards—*alem*—and on dome finials. These occur in a large variety of shapes and forms most of which are strikingly different from their Mamluk or Iranian counterparts. The technique is also used, however, as a decorative device in other Ottoman objects such as on the foot of the Ashmolean ewer in plate 48, the central ring on the body of the poly-candelon/incense-burner in plate 44 and on the base of a large brass candlestick with calligraphic and arabesque decoration in the stores of the Topkapı museum. Decoration and function, however, are often combined as is the case with the hemispherical lids of the incense burners in plates 49 and 50.

Incised decoration was also widely used, as attested here by plates 19, 20 and 22. One particular characteristic of this technique demands comment: the use of a ring-punched background in the same plane as the incised designs, as seen on the candlesticks in plates 22, 15a and 15b. Most incised designs from other areas of the Islamic world consist of re-moving the ground from around a design, thus leaving the design itself standing in low relief against a hatched or cross-hatched ground. Here, however, the leaves of the arabesque are in the same plane as the ring-punched ground. In an earlier publication,[84] Melikian-Chirvani suggested that this is an archaism going back to Soghdian and Khurasanian silverwork of the eighth to thirteenth centuries, while admitting that there are no known examples from the fourteenth century onwards. However, given the hierarchical system in metalworking, whereby objects in the more precious metals are copied in the less precious, it is in the more precious metalwork of the candlestick's own culture that the origin of this form of decoration should first be sought. And that is exactly where such designs are to be found—in the silver bowls attributed to the Ottoman Balkans, exemplified by plate 21. Here, on the base of this bowl, we find a single plane design with incised arabesques against a punched ground, just as on the candlesticks, even though the actual form of the arabesques is quite different.

Such background ring-punching, however, is not found on all Ottoman incised metalwork. Thus the designs on the gilt copper jug with a dome lid in plate 13d are set against a plain ground. The dense floral decoration of this piece, unusual in Ottoman metalwork, is typical of Ottoman embroidery patterns (plate 143). Interestingly enough, the inscription it bears around the neck is identical to that on the tapestry woven rug in plate 154. The designs on this jug are so close to those on the British Museum gilt copper flask in plate 13c that the two pieces must surely have been incised by the same artist, a rare example of survival indeed. The British Museum flask has in the past been attributed to Iran. Filiz Çağman, however, has recently demonstrated the Ottoman origin of the form which was also discussed here (page 21 and plate 28).

One of the more intriguing questions about Ottoman metalwork is whether the fashion for inlaid brasses, so popular in Egypt, Syria and eastern Anatolia in the fourteenth and fifteenth centuries, spread to İstanbul. There is only one inlaid object so far published which was definitely destined for the Ottoman court—a bowl in the Hermitage Museum bearing the name and certain tiles of Sultan Murad II (plate 14).[85] Whether Murad's bowl was made in a Mamluk or an Ottoman city is at present unclear. In style it is certainly Mamluk, but Melikian-Chirvani[86] has ascribed a related bowl in the Victoria and Albert Museum to Venice, on the basis of the shape of shield it bears, and a bowl identical in shape to Murad's, now in Naples,[87] is of equally uncertain origin. It is, however, perfectly conceivable that a group of Mamluk craftsmen set up a workshop in Bursa in the reign of Murad II and continued to produce inlaid objects in a Mamluk style which were destined for export as well as for Ottoman consumption. That would certainly be the implication of another object relating to the fifteenth-century Mamluk style, though this time apparently bearing no inlay—the bowl in Cairo signed by Ahmad al-Faqih al-Istanbuli.[88] Further objects may well have reached the Ottoman court through Selim II's capture of Cairo. Al-Siddiqi's *Al-Rauḍa al-Ḍāhīya* reads as follows: 'And when our Lord the Sultan Selim Khan went out from Egypt, there were with him a thousand camels laden with gold and silver, besides what he looted, consisting of rarities, weapons, porcelain (*ṣīnī*), copper (vessels), (*naḥās*), encrusted things (*mukaffāt*), horses, mules, camels etc.'[89] However, the word *mukaffāt* is perhaps more likely to mean gold, silver, or gilt plates attached to leather harness or belts, rather than objects inlaid with silver and gold.[90] Be this as it may, the total lack of sixteenth-century inlaid brasses makes it apparent that such objects did not conform to Ottoman taste, and that the art of inlaying base metal with precious was not a technique encouraged by royal patronage.

14. Silver inlaid bowl inscribed with the name of Murad II, 15th century. Hermitage N.T. 359

Turning from decoration to form, among the most striking base metal objects shown here are the candlesticks. No fourteenth- or fifteenth-century Ottoman candlesticks have yet been identified and the only indication of their form which has come down to us is the depiction of a pair in the *miḥrāb* tiles of the Yeşil Cami in Bursa (plate 58a). These follow the form associated with central and eastern Anatolia in the thirteenth and fourteenth centuries, particularly with the town of Siirt.[91] Given that the tiles are signed by a Tabrizi artist, the use of this form in Bursa circa 1420 is not conclusively proven. However, a solitary early İznik ceramic candlestick (plate 70) demonstrates its existence at the end of the century. It is from the middle of the fifteenth century onwards that the most typical Ottoman candlestick emerges (plates 22, 33, 38 and 42), probably deriving from earlier or contemporary South Anatolian and North Syrian forms.

If the standard Mamluk candlestick form[92] did not influence Ottoman taste, a Mamluk lighting system which was taken up by the Ottomans is the chandelier. In the late fifteenth century this was commonly a large faceted conical brass object, the base of which had numerous holes for cylindrical glass oil-lamps.[93] A number of magnificent Ottoman versions have survived in the store rooms of the Turkish and Islamic art museum in İstanbul. Among them is one of gilt copper dating from the reign of Bayezid II (plate 20) and another of silver (plate 6 and page 23). The similarity of shapes between these chandeliers and their Mamluk cousins is obvious and extends to the incised decoration of the gilt copper example and pieces dating from the reign of Qaitbey,[94] although the pierced and *repoussé* work is typically Ottoman and akin to that found on plates 18 and 51. These Ottoman chandeliers are decorated with inscriptions as well as arabesques, an identifiably Mamluk feature but atypical of Ottoman work.

Also in the Mamluk tradition but in this case a replacement or deliberate copy is the *tombak* mosque lamp in plate 19. Apart from the lack of a foot, which may in any case be missing given the structural similarities with the Eyüp silver mosque lamp (plate 52), it follows one of the most common glass mosque lamp forms of the fourteenth century. Various features of epigraphy and decoration, however, make a Mamluk attribution highly unlikely—for example, the combination of blazon and sultanic titles within the same roundel and the form of the arabesque incised into the object's surface. While there is no available evidence of Egyptian copper gilding, it is conceivable that the lamp may have been made in sixteenth-century Ottoman Egypt and it should stand apart from the typical Ottoman Turkish mosque lamp form found in silver (plates 29 and 52).

Returning to Ottoman candlesticks, a chronology is at present impossible owing to the absence of available published material. Certainly numerous examples have survived in Turkish mosques and museums as well as scattered throughout private sources. This potentially enormous body of material, however, has yet to be gathered and studied. For the time being, suffice it to say that the form found in plates 22, 33 and 36 was current in the sixteenth century, as demonstrated by two examples in Cairo[95] which were manufactured almost certainly in İstanbul in AH 947/1540-1 AD and from plate 15d bearing the date AH 984/1576-7 AD.

Another candlestick type with uniquely Ottoman overtones is the tulip candlestick. Here, the elaborate, elongated tapering neck reminiscent of architectural forms, culminates in a tulip-shaped candleholder.

Dating is equally problematic here since the form continued to be made, albeit with a gradual degeneration in both elegance and workmanship, until the present century. The early date AH 905/1499-1500 AD found on the piece illustrated in plate 40 is corroborated

Four Ottoman brass candlesticks

15a. H: 22.5 cm; w: 1141 gm. V&A 411f 1880

15b. H: 23.8 cm; w: 1610 gm

15c. H: 19.5 cm; w: 717.5 gm. V&A 931 1884

15d. H: 28.0 cm; dated AH 984/1576 AD. Priv. Col. Kuwait

15e. Timurid candlestick. Priv. Col.

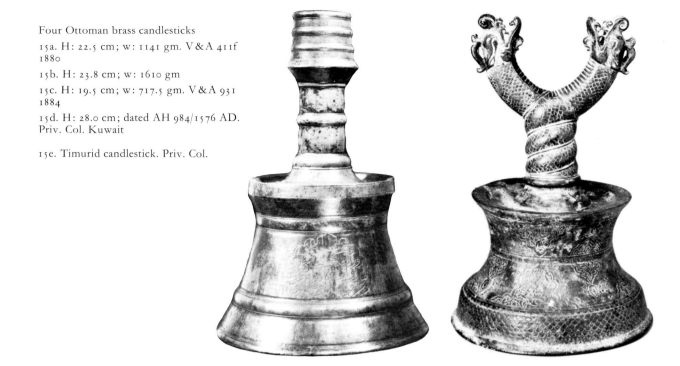

by the representation of such candlesticks on a fragmentary tile panel in the Hazret-i Süleymān in Diyarbakır[96] dating from the second half of the sixteenth century, and the appearance of a pair at the foot of a *miḥrāb* tile panel at the Darwishiya mosque in Damascus (plate 58b), dating also from that period.

The form with a long slender neck, standing on a large flat dish-shaped tray in plate 47, also deserves a mention. Although oil-lamps surmounting a small dish-like drip-tray standing on a central column are well known in the Islamic world, it seems unlikely that there is a direct connection between the two. Perhaps a style of late classical silver goblet on a baluster stem and flat dish base is the ultimate source—through Byzantine intermediaries.

Incense-burners are another type of object related to the Islamic tradition. Ottoman examples, however, such as the gilt copper piece illustrated in plate 50, and the silver one in plate 49, are distinct from earlier or contemporary Islamic incense-burners made elsewhere. They stand apart by the massiveness of the ovoid body, the curious hollow handles and the form of the foot. The latter is close to that of the polycandelon/incense-burner on plate 44, an object of unprecedented shape, and to that of the *tazza* in plate 45, a form of object better known in İznik pottery and also in Ottoman Greece and the Balkans.[97]

As to the identity of the centres which produced all these metal pieces nothing can be said. The only documented Ottoman copper-making centre is Tokat, from which comes a quantity of copper objects now in the Armenian patriarchate of Jerusalem.[98]

No discussion of fifteenth- to seventeenth-century Ottoman metalwork would be complete however without mention of steel, an alloy used primarily for weapons and tools.

The mass of Ottoman steel weapons and armour in the Topkapı Sarayı armoury includes many objects made for the Sultans themselves among which pride of place goes to the swords such as those made for Osman I, Mehmed the Conqueror, Bayezid II, Selim I and Süleyman the Magnificent.

More impressive than these perhaps are the bejewelled suits of armour of Mehmed II and Murad IV, both of which consist of mail adorned with gold, silver and precious stones such as rubies and turquoises. Examination of this material brings to light two techniques of particular interest. The first and more unusual is setting thick gold wires into an under-cut area of steel so that the gold design stands proud of the surface of the steel. The actual method used can be seen where a gold rosette has fallen out of one of Topkapı's richest helmets.[99] This use of thick gold inlay is found too on the finest swords, where it is used for dedicatory inscriptions, but it is not confined to steel. Intriguingly it is also found on silver, as for example on the two locks made in AH 1002/1593–4 AD and AH 1003/1595 AD which are illustrated in plates 24 and 26. Silver inlaid with gold is extremely rare in the Islamic world and the origin of its Ottoman use is at present uncertain, as also is the origin of the thick gold inlay on steel. A more typical Islamic use of gold and silver inlay is to be found on a steel lock for the Ka'ba made for Sultan Ahmed I (plate 25).

Gold *Kūft-gārī* work is much more common. In this technique, gold wire is shaped to a particular design and hammered onto the rough surface of the steel. Use of this technique is not confined to the Ottoman empire in the fifteenth and sixteenth centuries, and the earliest examples so far published are all Mamluk. Thus, there is a decorated steel helmet in the Louvre made for Sultan Barsbay (1422–38),[100] and a similarly ornamented shield boss in the Musée de l'homme in Paris bears a blazon associating it with Sultan Jaqmaq (1438–53).[101] Given the possibility that certain armourers bearing the *nisbat* al-Misri were actually working in İstanbul it would be no surprise to discover that the technique was imported direct from Cairo.

The scarcity of surviving objects makes it impossible to speculate on the origins of *Kūft-gārī* work. But comparison of Ottoman steel with more easterly products does bring to light one interesting fact. With the exception of Bayezid's helmet, the majority of published turban helmets appear to be Akkoyunlu objects. These are usually overlaid with silver not gold, although occasionally parcel-gilt. Hence, there seems little evidence that the *Kūft-gārī* technique was adopted from an eastern source by the Ottomans, but the form of Bayezid's helmet may well be due to contacts with the Akkoyunlu (plate 16b).

The less ostentatious Ottoman pieces are of course simply engraved rather than over-laid with gold, as for example the Arnhem, Munich, Berlin and Turin chamfrons.[102] This is typical too of less ostentatious Mamluk work such as Khayrbek's helmet[103] although there is no need to suggest that such a straightforward technique should also have been imported from Egypt.

Not all arms and armour manufactured by the Ottomans were of steel, nor presumably were they all designed for the battle field. Gilt copper with engraved decoration was also used, as in a helmet in the Metropolitan Museum of Art (plate 16a), a chamfron on plate 16d, and also in an enormous shield which belonged to Mehmed II's Grand Vizier, Mahmud Paşa. The softness of the copper and the gilding suggest such objects were parade ground pieces. The standard or field insignia in the Victoria and Albert Museum (plate 16e) is also of gilt copper, but since it is not protective, there is no reason why it may not have been

16a. *Tombak* helmet, 16th century. Diam: 23 cm; MMA 1974. 118.

16b. Inlaid steel helmet. 16th century. Nat. Mus. Florence, Carrand Col. 1645.

16c. *Tombak* helmet, 16th century. Diam: 21 cm; TKS 1/1465.

16d. *Tombak* horse chamfron, 16th century. H: 58.5 cm

16e. *Tombak* battle standard, *'alem*, 17th century. H: 36.4 cm; w: 1219 gm. V&A 933 1884

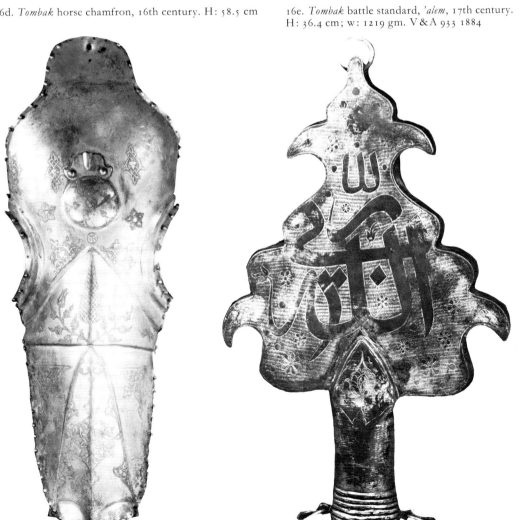

used on campaign. To what extent an Ottoman sultan or vizier would be willing to use richly decorated objects in battle, is difficult to decide. The suits of armour of Mehmed II and Murad IV have already been mentioned. A richly ornamented coat of mail which did actually see battle was that made for Mustafa Paşa in 1682 which bore clasps, neck triangles and breast roundels of gilt silver inlaid with niello.

The most famous of all sixteenth-century goldsmiths, Benvenuto Cellini, offers in his autobiography an important contemporary comment on Turkish inlaying of steel. He writes:

'About this time there fell into my hands some little Turkish poniards; the handle as well as the blade of these daggers was made of iron, and so too was the sheath. They were engraved by means of iron implements with foliage in the most exquisite Turkish style, very neatly filled in with gold. The sight of them stirred in me a great desire to try my own skill in that branch, so different from the others which I practised; and finding that I succeeded to my satisfaction, I executed several pieces. Mine were far more beautiful and more durable than the Turkish pieces, and this for diverse reasons. One was that I cut my grooves much deeper and with wider trenches in the steel; for this is not usual in Turkish work. Another was that the Turkish arabesques are only composed of arum leaves with a few small sunflowers; and though these have a certain grace, they do not yield so lasting a pleasure as the patterns which we use.'[104]

Ottoman metalwork offers a fruitful field for future research, for there are numerous surviving archival and historical documents, and, in an Islamic context, an unusual number of surviving precious metal objects. The documents will undoubtedly throw light on the organization of metalworking guilds, on the economy of the industry and on the relationship between artists and the court. Further study of the objects will clarify the role of different metals within a single tradition, in a way that is not possible for other Islamic dynasties, and the relationship too between metalwork and ceramics and other media. On the other hand the objects themselves are often less informative than their Islamic predecessors. There is in particular an almost total lack of makers' names. Thus the documents will provide us with the names of artisans, yet there may be little hope of relating names to objects. It is perhaps indicative that two precious metal products whose makers are recorded—the bejewelled cover made for the *Dīvān* or Collected Poems of Murad III by his chief jeweller, Mehmed, in 1588, and the *Bayram* throne given by İbrahim Paşa to Murad III, which was the work of İbrahim Bey and Derviş Bey in 1585—are both extraordinary commissions which prove the virtuosity and range of Ottoman goldsmithing but tell us nothing about the making of more mundane objects.[105]

The general lack of makers' inscriptions is paralleled by a striking absence of the inscriptions normally associated with Islamic metal objects. Owners' inscriptions occur, often in ornamental, *tuğra*-like cartouches, but they are lightly traced and are rarely conceived as part of the decorative scheme. Inscriptions of good luck are occasionally found, but the bold friezes of self-glorificatory titles so typical of the Mamluks, or the mystical verses characteristic of the Safavids evidently had no appeal.[106] Equally atypical is the taste for undecorated objects, both in precious and base metal, a taste which perhaps explains the restricted use of inlay.

What has been viewed in negative terms—the absence of decoration—leads us to the most positive quality of Ottoman metalwork: its emphasis on form. Traditional Islamic objects such as mosque lamps and candlesticks are no longer treated as assemblages of separate units; they are conceived as coherent structures with bold volumes and fluent outlines. Form triumphs over decoration.

For analysis of the metalwork examined here see page 217.

17. *Tombak* water spout, 16th century. H: 32.7 cm. Edwin Binney 3rd collection

THE PLATES

3
Ceremonial Silver Axe

Second half of 16th century

Cast silver and parcel gilt, this ceremonial axe is mounted on a solid ivory handle. The blade is decorated with openwork arabesques punctuated with engraved details, while the socket contains a lobed medallion with *saz* leaves and rosettes. (See p. 29.)

Published: *Art Treasures of Turkey*, Smithsonian Institution, Washington D.C. 1966, no. 240

Topkapı Sarayı Müzesi, İstanbul, no. 1/2404

18
Gilt Silver Jug

First quarter of 16th century

Sheet silver, gilded, with a cast handle. The body is decorated with flowers and arabesques on intertwining stems, the neck with a band of arabesques. The decoration is worked from both sides against a ring-punched ground. The lid appears to be a later replacement, possibly early seventeenth-century.

Published: Hayward, 1976, plate 163

Victoria and Albert Museum, London, no. 158—1894

Height: 12 cm (excluding lid); diam. of body: 11.5 cm; weight: 526.5 gm

19
Gilt Copper Mosque Lamp

Early 16th century

Gilt copper with engraved decoration and additional piercing on the neck. Inscriptions on the neck and body include the name of the Mamluk Sultan Qalaun (1280-90). On the lower body are three medallions containing an armorial cup within a Sultanic inscription. For epigraphic reasons, however, this lamp cannot be Mamluk. A more positive attribution is based on the arabesque decoration, which is strictly Ottoman in character, and on the pattern of the two bands at the base and rim of the neck which are identical to those on two İznik ceramic mosque lamps in the Godman collection (Lane *AO*, figs. 20 and 21).

Published: *Calligraphy and the Decorative Arts of Islam*, London 1976, no. 33

Height: 30.2 cm; diam. of rim: 25.4 cm; weight: 1,310 gm

20
Mosque Chandelier

c. 1480

An Ottoman version of the familiar Mamluk shape, this chandelier is made of gilded sheet copper which is embossed, engraved and pierced. The principal components—the finial, the gadrooned lid, the hexagonal body and the base tray with its seven tubular holders for oil lamps—are each made from individual sheets. The lid has twelve applied rosettes, and both lid and body are pierced and engraved with arabesques and flowers. Along the top and bottom of the body run bands of inscriptions in a style similar to the illuminated Qur'ān heading in plate 171.

Türk ve İslam Eserleri Müzesi, İstanbul, no. 170, formerly in the Bayezid Camii, İstanbul

Height: 69 cm; width: 36 cm; weight: 4,890 gm

21
Silver Bowl

Late 15th-early 16th century

This important early piece is made of parcel gilt thick sheet silver. The fluted body has been worked from both sides and subsequently engraved. The base is countersunk and decorated on the outside with an engraved arabesque pattern set against a ring-punched ground. The same pattern in repoussé appears on a disc rotating on a silver pin which covers the interior of the base. Along the rim, both on the inside and the outside, is a series of twenty cartouches with engraved animals and floral motifs on a ring-punched ground, each cartouche corresponding to one of the flutes of the body. The side wall bears the stamp of Sultan Bayezid II (1481-1512) and the base an assay test strip. The arabesque decoration is common to the 'Abraham of Kutahya' group of early İznik wares (plate 72) which are thought to be copies of metal objects.

Published: *Art Islamique*, Musée N. Sursock, Beyrouth 1974, no. 145.

Ex collection Ibrahim Beyhun

Height: 3.1 cm; diam: 10.8 cm; weight: 150 gm

22
Brass Candlestick

Late 15th-early 16th century

Brass, cast in two pieces, the neck and body joined by a reverse screw. The traced arabesques punctuated by small chintamani motifs are reserved against a ring-punched ground. This candlestick is comparable to plate 15 and is attributable to the reign of Bayezid II (1488-1512).

Freer Gallery of Art, Smithsonian Institution, Washington D.C., no. 80.19

Height: 26 cm; diam: 17.1 cm; weight: 1,770 gm

23
Silver Fountain Ladle

Dated AH 985/1577-8 AD

In the 'plain tradition' of Ottoman decoration, this fountain ladle is made of sheet silver and the handle is set with eight stones, possibly amethysts. The body sits on a countersunk ridge base and has a shallow flute around the rim. The interior of the bowl is lightly gilded. On the exterior, opposite the handle, in perfect counterpoint to the plain surface, sits a bold inscription in niello which reads:

'In the name of God, the Compassionate, the Merciful, and We made from water every living thing' (Qur'ān, XXI, 30), AH 985/1577 AD.

Height: 4.6 cm; diam: 16.4 cm; length (overall): 28.6 cm; weight: 360 gm

24
Silver Lock and Key

Dated AH 1002/1593-4 AD

In the form of a bolt, this lock made of sheet silver is inlaid with gold in high relief, a technique more common to the decoration of sword blades.

The key bears an invocation to God, the lock a *Besmele*, while the horizontal bolt states:

قفل باب روضه

حسب الله تعالى

اثر مصطفى اغا بواب دركاه عالى سر محضران مصر ناظر

خاصكى سلطان تابع غضنفر اغاى باب سعادت سلطان مراد

خان عز نصره .

سنة ١٠٠٢

'Lock of the garden gate ... The work of Mustafa Ağa, Gatekeeper of the Sublime Porte, Chief Summoner of Egypt, *Waqf*-Superintendent to Haseki Sultan, Client of Gazanfer, the Chief Eunuch. Sultan Murad Han ... AH 1002'.

Topkapı Sarayı Müzesi, İstanbul

25
Steel Padlock

Early 17th century

Decorated with split-leaf arabesques, this padlock is made of steel overlaid with silver and gold in the *kūftgārī* technique and is said to have been made for the Ka'ba in Mecca on orders from Sultan Ahmed I (1603–17).

Topkapı Sarayı Müzesi, İstanbul

26
Silver Lock and Key

Dated AH 1003/1595 AD

This is similar in shape and decoration to plate 24. The inscription on the horizontal bolt reads:

قفل باب اندر (و) ن

وحسب حضرت الله

اثر مصطفى اغاى مستحفظان قلعة مصر ناظر مرحوم

حاصكى سلطان تابع اغاى باب سعادت غضنفر اغا سلطان

محمد ...

سنة ١٠٠٣

'Lock of the Inner Apartments ... The work of Mustafa, Ağa of the Garrison of the Citadel of Egypt, *Waqf*-Superintendent to the late Haseki Sultan, Client of the Chief Eunuch, Gazanfer Ağa. Sultan Mehmed ... AH 1003'.

Topkapı Sarayi Müzesi, İstanbul

27
Gold Flywhisk

16th–17th century (?)

Sheet gold and horsehair. The handle has a spiral twist with plain gadroons; the knob finial twists in the opposite direction. The outward-curving head has twenty-four facets growing out of twelve palmette crests; the neck reproduces the same motifs.

Length: 31.7 cm; diam. of mouth: 6.9 cm; weight: 520 gm

28
Bejewelled Gold Water-Flask

Second half of 16th century

In the shape of a leather flask (see p. 21) this perfect exponent of the 'bejewelled tradition' in Ottoman metalwork is elaborately engraved on the gold ground with additional applied decoration of gold and jade plaques. The ground and plaques are inset with precious stones in gold mounts shaped like flower petals. A flask of this kind is depicted in a miniature (plate 207) being held by one of Sultan Süleyman's pages.

Topkapı Sarayı Müzesi, İstanbul, no. 2/3825

Height: 28.5 cm; width: 21 cm; depth: 12.5 cm; weight: '640 dirhems'

29
Silver Mosque Lamp

c. 1620

Similar in shape and proportion to a ceramic İznik mosque lamp in the Godman collection made a hundred years earlier (Lane 1957, fig. 20), this totally undecorated lamp is made of sheet silver with three faceted 'eyes' holding suspension rings with attached chains. There is a shallow gadroon around the rim, stamped with the *Tuğra* of Osman II (1618–22).

Türk ve İslam Eserleri Müzesi, İstanbul, no. 177

Height: 31 cm; diam. of body: 20 cm; weight: 1,290 gm

30
Silver Water-Bottle—'Sürāhī'

16th century

This is a potent example of the 'plain tradition' in Ottoman art where form and simplicity combine to produce works of unparalleled elegance in Islamic art. A familiar form in İznik ceramics, this *sürāhī* demonstrates the metal origin of the shape. Features which in pottery are purely decorative such as the knop in the middle of the neck and the torus moulding where the neck meets the body are here structural requirements. Made of totally undecorated sheet silver, this elegant bottle consists of six separate sheets soldered together; its lid, of four.

Height: 41 cm; diam: 14 cm; weight: 870 gm

31
Silver Bowl

Period of Selim III (1789–1808)

This bowl demonstrates the conservative trend in Ottoman art. At a time when Turkish 'baroque' was prevailing, the elegance of the 'plain tradition' still had its faithful followers. Made of sheet silver, this shallow hemispherical bowl is undecorated except for a double line with remains of niello inlay on the exterior, below the rim. The centre of the bowl bears the *tuğra* of Selim III (1789–1808) and the lower part of the same *tuğra* appears on the rim. There is an assay test strip on the base.

Private collection, London

Height: 4.5 cm; diam.: 13.9 cm; weight: 180 gm

32
Gilt Copper Basin

16th–17th century

This basin, in the form of a large hemispherical bowl, is made of gilt copper, raised from a single sheet. The perfect understatement, it is decorated with great economy by means of nine spiralling gadroons.

Height: 12.2 cm; diam: 29 cm; weight: 730 gm

33
Pair of 'Tombak' Mosque Candlesticks

16th century

Large *tombak* candlesticks of this type flank the *miḥrāb* of many Ottoman mosques such as those of Rüstem Paşa and Sokollu Mehmed Paşa. These two candlesticks resemble very closely a particular pair in the *türbe* of Sultan Süleyman the Magnificent. Totally undecorated, they are made of beaten gilt copper (*tombak*) in two pieces with a joint at the base of the neck.

Height: 70.5 cm; diam: 48 cm; weight: 7,250 gm

34
'Tombak' Ewer

A sheet copper body, foot spout and lid with a cast handle. The body, lid and lower spout are decorated with engraved carnations in a drop repeat pattern against a stippled ground. The leaves sprouting from the stems of the carnations create the impression of an ogival lattice. This floral style of decoration is more common in embroideries (plates 144 and 145) and its only other recorded appearance in metalwork is on gilt copper horse chamfrons.

Height: 33.5 cm; diam: 18 cm; weight: 515 gm

35
Brass Candlestick

16th century

One of a pair, this candlestick is made of cast brass. The unusual inverted baluster shaft sits on a flat drip tray similar to that in plate 22. The foot appears to have been cut down.

Private collection, London

Height: 77.5 cm; diam: 37.6 cm

36
Tinned Copper Candlestick

Dated AH 1068/1657–8 AD

One of a pair, this large, undecorated mosque candlestick is made of sheet copper in two separate pieces joining at the base of the neck. For a similar candlestick dated 1540 AD see G. Wiet, *Objets en Cuivre*, Cairo 1932, plate XXXV.

Height: 75.5 cm; diam: 52.3 cm; weight: 15,000 gm

37
Pair of Tinned Copper Candlesticks

Dated AH 1095/1683–4 AD

Sheet copper with traces of tinning, each of these candlesticks consists of two separate pieces joined at the base of the neck. An inscription on the body is contained in a *Tuğra*-like medallion with a tulip finial bearing the name of Hacci Mustafa, son of Hacci Hasan, and the date AH 1095.

Height: 59 cm; diam: 37 cm; weight: 5,500 gm

38
Brass Candlesticks

Probably first half of 16th century

Similar in size and form to the piece dated 1576–7 (plate 15d), this plain, undecorated candlestick is made of brass, cast in two pieces and joined at the base of the neck.

Height: 32.8 cm; diam: 20.4 cm; weight: 2,775 gm

39
Qur'ān Stand

Dated AH 1026/1617 AD

Eight-tiered rectangular base with pyramidal lid. Parcel gilt silver plaques are set into a silver surround riveted onto a frame. The inscriptions and floral arabesques are set against a hatched ground consisting of fine, long, parallel lines. The lid is decorated with verses from the Qur'ān and the six upper layers of the base with poetry. The cartouches at the two lower tiers are decorated with floral arabesques in a composition closely resembling that of the early ceramic tile in plate 85. The Sultan mentioned on the piece can be identified as Ahmed I (1603-1617).

Topkapı Sarayı Müzesi, İstanbul (not inventoried)

40
Tulip Candlestick

Dated AH 905/1499-1500 AD

Made of brass, cast and turned, the candle-holder is in the form of a faceted octagonal tulip. Two small snuffer rings project from the deep, concave drip-tray, which has a pierced rim. An inscription in a *tuğra*-like cartouche is traced on the body bearing the name of Hüseyin Ağa, *voyvoda* of Galata, and the date AH 905.

The Madina Collection

Height: 35.3 cm; diam: 18.4 cm

41
Tulip Candlestick

Late 15th-early 16th century

Similar in most respects to the previous piece except for the proportions of the neck, this candlestick is also cast in two pieces and joined at the base of the neck. The body and neck show marks of turning. For candlesticks of this type see p. 38 and plate 40.

Height: 41.1 cm; diam: 19.6 cm;
weight: 2,300 gm

42
Candlestick

16th-17th century

Cast and turned in one piece. The base of this candlestick is similar in shape and workmanship to plates 40 and 41 but the neck is closer to those on plates 33 and 38.

Height: 26.2 cm; diam: 16.3 cm; weight: 950 gm

43
Scalloped Dish

16th-17th century

The Ottoman understatement *par excellence*, this scalloped dish is made of a single sheet of beaten brass. It is undecorated except for three small concentric rings around the centre.

Height: 6.3 cm; diam: 29.6 cm; weight: 980 gm

44
Incense-Burner/Polycandelon

17th century

Cast brass with six cast tulips, this unusual object has a swivelling knop with openwork arabesques. Just above the foot there is a traced inscription bearing the name of 'The Late Ayşe Sultan'. The lady in question can perhaps be identified as one of the daughters of Ahmed I, half-sister of Osman II (plates 29, 52, 53). She died in 1656.

Türk ve İslam Eserleri Müzesi, İstanbul, no. 26

Height: 29 cm; diam: 18 cm; weight: 3,312 gm

45
Tazza

17th century

Brass, cast in one piece, its form is an amalgamation of a complete bowl with a foot-ring and a separate stand. On the outer side of the bowl is a lightly scratched name in Arabic characters, now illegible, probably that of an owner.

Height: 11.6 cm; diam: 19 cm; weight: 960 gm

46
Brass Casket

15th-16th century

An example of provincial Ottoman metalwork from south-east Anatolia, this casket has a cast body, lid, feet and fittings with twin hinges and clasps. The body bears bands of engraved rosettes, criss-cross ornaments and interlaces while the lid is decorated with roundels, medallions, arabesques and two forms of interlace of the type found on Diyarbakır border tiles (plates 113 and 114). All the designs are reserved against a hatched ground. The hinges and clasps are attached with copper rivets.

Height: 26 cm; length: 19.5 cm; width: 16.7 cm

47
Brass Candlestick

16th century

Cast in three pieces and turned. The long hollow baluster shaft joins the base above the knop by means of a reverse screw, a feature typical of Ottoman metalwork. The knop unit is soldered onto the raised centre of the drip-tray.

Height: 36.5 cm; diam: 34 cm

48
Brass Ewer

16th or 17th century

Cast brass with fluted spiral decoration on the body, spout and cup at the top of the neck, this elegant ewer has a splayed foot decorated in openwork. The handle is engraved with pairs of chevrons and the neck bears an inscription on a roundel which reads: 'Hacci Abdurrahim'.

Published: A. Pope, *A Survey of Persian Art*, London 1939, vol. VI, plate 1378A

Ashmolean Museum, Oxford, 1976.43

Height: 51 cm; diam: 19 cm

49
Silver Incense-Burner

c. 1600

Cast silver with a hinged openwork lid decorated with engraved arabesques. In common with all incense-burners of this type the handle is hollow. The body bears an indecipherable, badly rubbed seal and a traced inscription which reads: 'Sultan Mehmed Han'. The inscription probably refers to Mehmed III (1595–1603). A more crudely executed example with a curved handle similar to that of plate 50 bears a Rumanian inscription with a date equivalent to 1669–70 (Nicolescu 1968).

Türk ve İslam Eserleri Müzesi, İstanbul, no. 16

Height: 17.5 cm; diam: 11 cm; length of handle: 10 cm; weight: 640 gm

50
Gilt Copper Incense-Burner

c. 1600

Gilt copper, the body and foot cast in one piece, with a hinged openwork lid and a curved, hollow and faceted cast handle; the decoration of the lid consists of a central register of six trefoil palmettes interlacing with upper and lower registers of small trefoils.

Private collection, London

Height: 22.7 cm; diam: 11.2 cm; weight: 975 gm

51
Silver Hanging Incense-Burner

Probably second half of 16th century

The walls of the twelve-sided base are formed from a single silver sheet. Each facet is decorated in a style better known from bookbindings with engraved and parcel gilt lobed ogival medallions containing *saz* leaves and rosettes. The unusual cage-like canopy is made of twisted silver wires springing from six 'escutcheon' cartouches supported on cast silver baluster legs. The same style of decoration appears on plates 5, 128, 139. The assay mark on the body is indecipherable.

Türk ve İslam Eserleri Müzesi, İstanbul, no. 15

Height: 34.5 cm; width: 16.5 cm; weight: 2,260 gm (base filled with mortar)

52
Silver Hanging Mosque Lamp

Dated AH 1027/1618 AD

From the shrine of Ebu Eyyub, this lamp bears a remarkable similarity to one shown hanging at that same shrine in a miniature depicting Sultan Süleyman going there on pilgrimage (plate 207). It is made of sheet silver, partially gilt on the decorated areas. The chains and faceted 'eyes' are similar to those in plate 29. The body is decorated with two offset rows of engraved, lobed, ogival cartouches containing floral motifs. A band of three similar medallions executed in openwork goes around the neck, while those on the foot are plain and undecorated. The lamp bears the assay mark of Osman II (1618–1622) and on the body are three incised inscriptions which give the name and titles of Osman II, state that the lamp was the *waaf* of this Sultan to Ebu Eyyub, and give the weight of the object (950 dirhems) and the date (AH 1027). This suggests that the lamp was a gift from the Sultan to the shrine on his accession.

Türk ve İslam Eserleri Müzesi, İstanbul, in trust from the shrine of Eyüp. Eyüp inv. no. 293

Height: 49 cm; diam. of body: 29.5 cm; weight: 2,850 gm (950 dirhems)

53
Silver Incense-Burner

Dated AH 1033/1624 AD

An unusual object, this parcel gilt silver incense-burner has the same basic cup and foot as those on plates 49 and 50. Here, however, the hinged lid is in the form of a tall cone and the foot rests on a flat dish supported on three cast legs. The form of the lid is reflected in the decoration which consists of three engraved cypress trees and openwork arabesques. The assay marks are all indecipherable. The inscriptions on the body and the dish give the name 'Sultan Osman dayası Havva Kadın' (Havva Kadın, nurse of Sultan Osman) and the date AH 1033. This object came from the tomb of Ahmed I where Osman II was buried. It was exhibited at the New York World's Fair in 1939.

Türk ve İslam Eserleri Müzesi, İstanbul, no. 18

Height: 45 cm; diam. of dish: 27 cm; diam. of body: 14 cm; weight: 1,200 gm

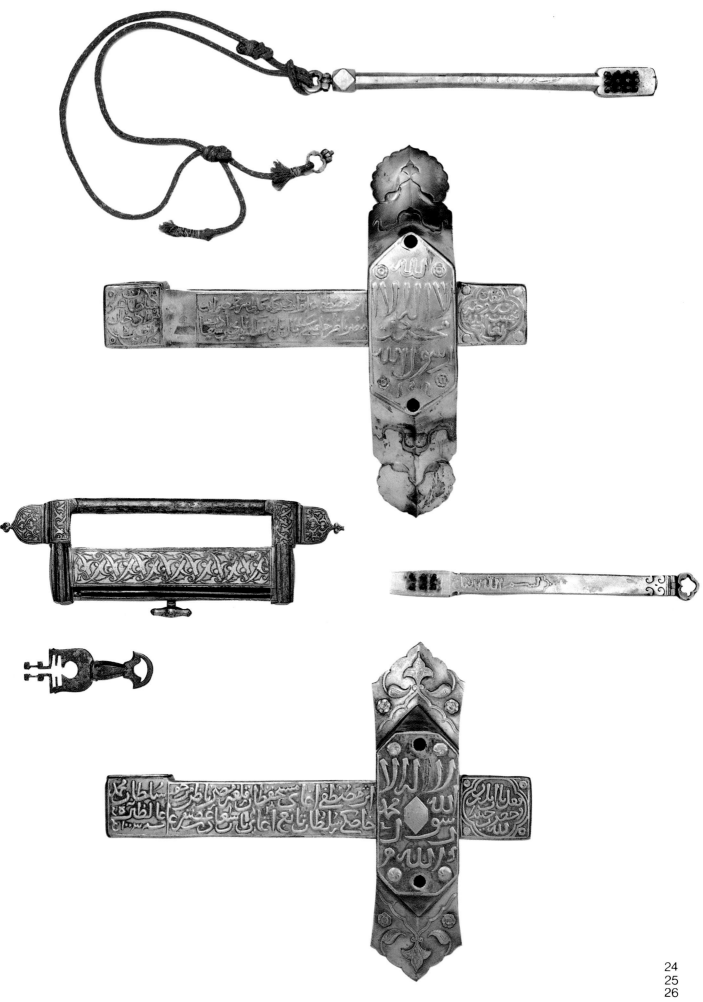

29

32·33

33 34

35·36
37·37·38

40·41·42
43

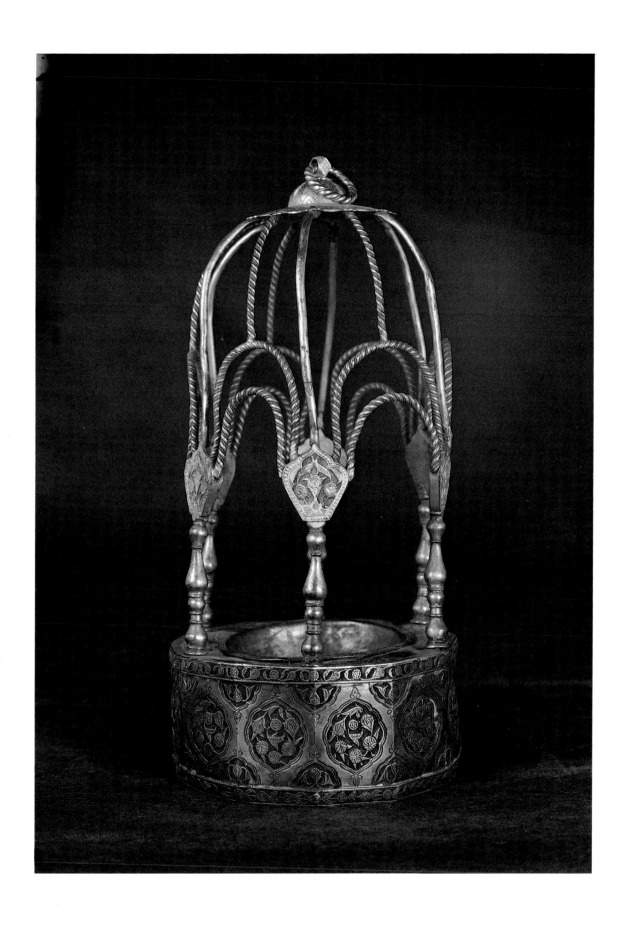

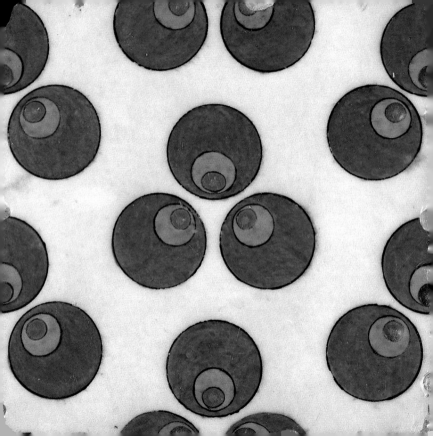

Ceramics

John Carswell

Any study of Ottoman ceramics should start with a perusal of the works of Arthur Lane. Lane was a pioneer, and it was he who laid down the broad lines of the subject creating general categories of material and establishing the fundamental chronology, defining the technical characteristics and the pattern of stylistic change and influence. Since he wrote, his text has gained universal acceptance, and the mastery of his synthesis remains undisputed. Simplicity, as someone once remarked, is balanced complexity, and this is exactly what he achieved.[1]

In recent years new evidence and a fresh scrutiny of some of the material already known has suggested some slight modifications of his conclusions. This is exactly what he would have wished—no one was more eager to learn of new discoveries—and it is no criticism of his earlier work that the subject is now seen as more subtle and elusive than it once appeared. The essence of Lane's approach is contained in a long article, 'The Ottoman Pottery of Isnik', contributed by him to *Ars Orientalis* in 1957.[2] Here he developed in detail his views on the evolution of İznik ware, beginning with a discussion of the antecedents that led to the emergence of this extraordinary industry. It is a recurring phenomenon in the history of ceramics that some of the greatest technical and aesthetic achievements appear to spring fully formed on to the stage, with no obvious ancestry; one thinks, for instance, of the earliest Neolithic painted pottery, or fourteenth-century Chinese blue-and-white porcelain. At first glance İznik pottery of the late fifteenth to early sixteenth century also seems remarkably assured, with no immediate precedent. But there are a number of pointers to suggest that this is not entirely so, and Lane rightly rehearses the evidence for an earlier ceramic tradition. To this we may now add some new facts.

As Lane pointed out, in the twelfth and thirteenth centuries under Seljuk rule there was a hard, white composite ware available, applied to great effect in the tile mosaic decoration of a number of buildings, particularly in Konya. This white ware was also used for pottery vessels, and the body material is similar to that found in northern Mesopotamia and Iran. Sherds of this type have been excavated at Kubadabad, a Seljuk palace on the shores of Lake Beyşehir in southern Anatolia. The production of this white ware appears to have lapsed in the thirteenth century, for there is no further development. Instead, it is succeeded in Anatolia by a crude red earthenware, covered with a white slip and painted under a lead glaze in blue-green, purple or black. This is the misnamed 'Miletus' ware, so called after

55. Miletus ware dish, late 15th century. Diam: 31.5 cm.
Berlin-Dahlem I 1362

the town of Milet in south-western Turkey where many examples were found. More recently, Professor Oktay Aslanapa's excavations at İznik have proved that the ware was actually made there, thus establishing İznik as a centre for the manufacture of pottery long before the classical sixteenth-century wares more usually associated with that town.[3]

The early İznik 'Miletus' pottery was an unsophisticated product, rightly classified as a peasant ware (plate 55). The designs show a passing familiarity with Chinese export ware, particularly on some rim patterns based at one remove on the Chinese 'breaking-wave' design. At the same time, radiating panels to be seen on a dish in the museum in İznik, a waster with a triple spur still adhering to its centre, are more likely to derive from an engraved Mamluk metal piece than any painted prototype. This transference of motifs from metal to ceramics is common enough in Islamic pottery. There is even one example where the same phenomenon can be observed on Chinese porcelain, a piece in the British Museum whose shape and painted decoration are clearly inspired by an engraved Mamluk metal stand. Another 'Miletus' dish has a diaper pattern at the centre, which can be traced to the moulded patterns found on Chinese celadon plates. And other Chinese features of early İznik ware include flowers of the chrysanthemum type with cross-hatched centres, birds, classic scrolls, and the use of ogival panels filled with tight scrolls. This lead-glazed earthenware appears to have been common currency in Turkey during the fourteenth and fifteenth centuries, the tastes of the more affluent no doubt catered to by imported Chinese porcelain and celadon.

If this early İznik ware represents the first pottery made there, the existence of three major buildings of the same period with ceramic decoration in Bursa and Edirne, the first two capital cities of the Ottoman Turks, must surely be taken into consideration.

In Bursa, in the ceramic decoration of the Green Mosque (Yeşil Cami) and the Green Tomb (Yeşil Türbe), there is a new and fully-developed style with a strong Timurid

56a. Underglaze and *cuerda seca* tiles, early 15th century. Green Mosque, Bursa

56b. Underglaze tiles, mid-15th century. Murad II
mosque, Edirne

56c. Underglaze tiles, mid-15th century. Tawrizi
mosque, Damascus

flavour. Both buildings employ extensive schemes of ceramic decoration, with elaborately
designed *miḥrābs* of moulded tiles, executed in the *cuerda seca* technique, and tile mosaic
(plate 58a). The Green Mosque, built between 1419 and 1424 AD, has walls panelled with
plain turquoise, blue or green hexagonal tiles with unfired gold decoration, separated by
turquoise triangles (plate 56a). The *miḥrāb* and the three recesses at the rear of the mosque
including the Sultan's gallery are decorated with moulded tiles of great intricacy, repeating

forms familiar from carved stone and wooden prototypes. The complexity of the designs and the skill with which they are executed suggest a firm controlling hand; and this is confirmed by an inscription painted in the Sultan's gallery recording the fact that the decoration was completed in 1424 by Ali ibn Ilyas Ali, or Nakkaş Ali, a native of Bursa carried off by Timur in 1402, as a result of which he no doubt became familiar with the Timurid style. The tilework itself is signed twice, once on the *miḥrāb* by 'the masters of Tabriz' and again on the gallery by 'Muhammad al-Majnun'.

In the Green Tomb, circa 1421 AD, the mausoleum of Mehmed I (1413–21), the walls are also panelled with plain hexagonal tiles. Again, the *miḥrāb* is composed of moulded *cuerda seca* tiles. It should be noted that the tiles both in the Green Mosque and the Green Tomb are of a red earthenware body.

Subsequent to the capture of Edirne in 1361 and the establishment of a new Ottoman capital, the mosque of Murad II was built in 1435 on the outskirts of the town. For ceramic decoration, the mosque must rank as one of the most interesting in Turkey, in its variety of techniques and styles. The mosque is T-shaped in plan, and decorated with a great *miḥrāb* of moulded tiles, with friezes of tiles on the *qibla* and two flanking walls. The material for the tiles is not red earthenware like that at Bursa, but an off-white ware. Spectrographic analysis of two of the tiles has shown that they have a very high silica content.[4] Apart from the ware, there is another innovation, in the decoration of the Edirne *miḥrāb*. Similar in design to the two *miḥrābs* at Bursa, the majority of the moulded tiles are executed in *cuerda seca*. But the vaults and part of the borders are painted in blue and turquoise under a clear glaze, some with designs in black under a transparent turquoise glaze (plate 56b). The tiles are decorated with lotus and camellia-like flowers, which combined with thin

57. *Cuerda seca* sarcophagus, early 15th century. Green Mosque, Bursa

58a. Cuerda seca tiled *miḥrāb*, early 15th century.
Green Mosque, Bursa

58b. Underglaze tiled *miḥrāb*, 17th century. Darwishiya
mosque, Damascus

and sometimes spiralling stems would suggest they owe their inspiration to early fifteenth-
century Chinese porcelain. But those familiar with fourteenth-century Chinese blue-and-
white will also recognize the lobed, spiked leaves which are only found on Chinese ware of
that date. The apparent stylistic contradiction between the monochromatic underglaze-
painted designs on the stalactite vault of the *miḥrāb* and the *cuerda seca* spandrels in the
Timurid style might lead one to suppose that they could not be contemporary. That this
was not so can be seen from the borders to the right and left of the *miḥrāb*; side by side with
the *cuerda seca* tiles, part of the moulding is painted in underglaze blue, in what must have
been an experiment.

The underglaze-blue decoration reaches its climax in the frieze of hexagonal tiles round
the three sides of the mosque (plate 56b). Here is the further development of the concept
of hexagonal tiles set with intervening triangles, noted a few years earlier at Bursa. The tile
frieze is capped with a crest of moulded palmettes each with a raised white pattern reserved
on a dark blue ground, with the sloping sides glazed turquoise. The hexagonal tiles,
numbering 479 in all, are of fifty-three distinct types. They provide an extraordinary repertoire of Chinese and Islamic designs, with the former predominating. There is a freedom
and precision of touch, combined with sinuous rhythm, which is the precursor of the
future İznik style. Besides elements of early fifteenth-century Chinese inspiration, the
fourteenth-century spiked, lobed leaf also occurs.

The mosque was founded in 1435/6, and it has been the custom to ascribe these tiles to that date. But a close inspection of the walls above the tile frieze reveals that under successive coats of plaster, the walls were once painted (plate 59). Patches of plaster have fallen away to reveal not one, but two layers of decoration. Even without further work, to reveal the wall-paintings in their entirety, it is clear that all the walls of the mosque were once painted, and that the hexagonal tile-frieze was a later addition. How much later, it is of course difficult to ascertain. That the first series of paintings was not simply a temporary measure to decorate the walls whilst the tiles were being prepared is evident from the complexity of the designs still visible, which covered not only the body of the mosque but the interior of the dome above as well.

To summarize so far, at Edirne we have the evidence for a transition from *cuerda seca* to the underglaze technique, and the substitution of white ware for the reddish earthenware at Bursa. It was suggested by Lane that the Edirne tiles might have been the work of Syrian craftsmen, because of their similarity to the tiles in the tomb chamber of al-Tawrizi in Damascus (d. 1430). But a comparison with the Syrian tiles shows that the resemblance is quite superficial; the Damascus tiles are smaller and set horizontally, and are far inferior in design and execution to those at Edirne (plate 56c). They are also painted in a dingy cobalt blue, under the thick, crackled glaze typical of Syrian pottery.

The dado of hexagonal tiles in Edirne has a border of narrow rectangular tiles decorated in underglaze blue and white with a running floral scroll. This scroll can be compared to the border of a tile panel in the courtyard of the Üç Şerefeli mosque, also in Edirne (plate 60). Riefstahl pointed out many years ago that the same band of potters who worked on the Muradiye must have been responsible for the two surviving Üç Şerefeli panels.[5] Murad II was the patron of both mosques; indeed the inscription on one of the Üç Şerefeli

59. Wall paintings above tiles, mid-15th century. Murad II mosque, Edirne

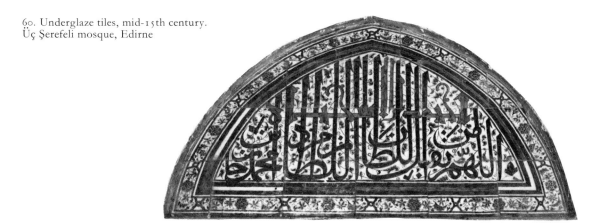

60. Underglaze tiles, mid-15th century.
Üç Şerefeli mosque, Edirne

panels reads: 'O my God, accept from the Sultan, Sultan Murad son of Muhammad Khan'. An abbreviated form of the same inscription occurs in the Muradiye in a cartouche at the bottom of the great inscription framing the *miḥrāb*, and is repeated again in mirror script at the bottom left of the *miḥrāb*. It is worth noting that one of the Üç Şerefeli tympana, while similar in design, extends the underglaze palette to include turquoise and manganese purple.

Thus, some time between 1435 and the death of Murad II in 1451, tiles were installed in both these buildings, painted in underglaze blue, turquoise, and black, and in the Üç Şerefeli mosque, in purple as well. It would seem highly probable that the tiles were manufactured in Edirne itself. The history of Near Eastern ceramics shows that it is usually the potters that move, rather than the pottery. It was certainly within the resources of the court to arrange for the import of pottery materials, to be fired in kilns close at hand. Indeed, later Turkish records document just such orders for the transportation of potters' materials. The experimental nature of the tiles, with the switch from *cuerda seca* to underglaze techniques in the Murad II *miḥrāb*, would also seem to confirm that they were made on the spot.

This now leads to the next question, which is: how does the work at Edirne dovetail, if at all, into the origins of sixteenth-century İznik ware? As a hypothesis, I would suggest that after the completion of the work at Edirne, the potters moved closer to the new capital and settled at İznik. İznik would have been a logical choice, for there was already a tradition of making pottery. Following the success of the new white-bodied ware and underglaze decoration at Edirne, the potters would surely have wished to perpetuate their discovery. This would account for the changeover at İznik from red earthenware to a finer white material.

But here we encounter a snag, for we do not know what the potters produced during the fifty years that elapsed after the completion of the Edirne tiles, and the beginning of the classic phase of İznik pottery, traditionally dated towards the close of the fifteenth century. The only extensive ceramic revetments from this interim period are the tile mosaic decorations of the Çinili Kiosk (1473), in İstanbul. Possibly these years represent the changeover from tile-making to the manufacture of pottery at İznik, and the appearance of a white-bodied ware at İznik may be earlier than previously thought. If one studies the early İznik monochromatic underglaze-blue group as a whole, with its formal designs and unspontaneous decoration, often with pious inscriptions unrelated to the forms, it could well represent the efforts of craftsmen attempting to master the production of three-dimensional objects alien to anything they had produced before (plates 70, 72 and 63a).

At this point it is worth considering why İznik should have become the centre of the ceramic industry, instead of a site nearer the capital. Admittedly there was an early ceramic tradition, but this is hardly enough to explain the later development. A more obvious answer would be that the necessary materials were in abundant supply nearby, and recent research indicates that this is indeed the reason. First of all, the clay itself: Dr John Covel, a seventeenth-century traveller, noted that the 'whitish, very fine and mealy not gritty' earth was obtained at Hormarcui [Ömerli Köy] about an hour and a half from the town; elsewhere he says that a fine white sand comes from the same locality, about 6 to 8 miles from İznik.[6] Wood for firing the kilns and fresh water were in abundant supply, and one suspects that the necessary minerals for preparing the glazes were to be found not far away as well. Added to this, Covel notes that İznik was on the main road from 'Aleppo, Damascus, Brussia, and Smirna to Stambol',[7] so that it was by no means a backwater. He also remarks that, with the exception of the sale of the local pottery, the market of İznik is largely concerned with furnishing travellers with provisions, a fact which may have led to the widespread dispersion of İznik ware throughout the Ottoman empire.

An absolute date for the beginning of the new phase of İznik ware is hard to determine, and the first positive evidence is contained in an inventory of goods at Topkapı Sarayı dated AH 901/1495 AD which mentions *ibrīk* (spouted jugs), *liğen* (water-bowls) and other İznik products. A later inventory dated AH 911/1505-6 AD mentions an *ibrīk-i izniki* (a spouted jug from İznik), a *liğen-i izniki* (an İznik water-bowl) and *İznik çīnīsinden ayak tası* (bowls on feet of İznik China-ware).[8] The last item is of special interest as it invites a direct comparison with Chinese porcelain, examples of which must have already

Early underglaze tiles:
61a. Tomb of Mustafa Paşa, Gebze, 1528
61b. Tomb chamber of Şehzade Mahmud, Bursa, 1511
61c. Berlin-Dahlem I 5614, early 16th century

62. Underglaze tiles, Yeni Valide,
Mosque Manisa,
1522-3.

been in Ottoman possession. Besides these references, actual examples of this ware are
contained in several of the royal tombs at Bursa. The tomb of Cem Sultan (1459-95)
contains three graves besides that of Cem himself, the latest being that of Alemşah who
died in 1510. Most of the tiles in the tomb are dark blue or turquoise hexagons, with additional gold decoration; but the border tiles are of interlacing palmette design, painted under
the glaze in light and dark cobalt, and purple with dark green outlines. Above the windows
are five hexagons painted in underglaze blue and pinkish-grey, in designs which are inferior examples of patterns seen originally in the hexagonal underglaze tiles at Edirne.

In two other tombs commonly attributed to Mustafa (d. AH 879/1474-5 AD) and
Mahmud (d. AH 913/1507-8 AD), there are border tiles of two types, painted in shades of
underglaze cobalt blue, which fit in well with the current style (plate 61b). There are problems, however, in deciding exactly who was buried in each of the eleven mausolea in the
garden of the Muradiye mosque at Bursa. Final evidence for the dating of the early İznik
style is provided by two panels of tiles in the Yeni Valide mosque at Manisa dated AH
929/1522-3 AD (plate 62). Although somewhat ungainly in overall design, the exuberant
use of interlocking palmettes, plaited stems and floral motifs in Chinese style is clearly linked
to İznik pottery decorated in the same manner.

Finally, any attempt to date the first monochromatic phase at İznik has to take into consideration a famous piece in the Godman Collection, which I shall refer to as the *birinci
kırmızı uskumru*.[9] This spouted ewer (plate 63a) is rather boldly decorated in the early
İznik manner, and bears a spiralling Armenian inscription on the base, dated 1510. This
piece may be convincingly ascribed to the emergent Armenian pottery at Kütahya, about
as far away again from İstanbul as İznik, and here its only function is to amplify the
evidence for the early date of this style in Turkish pottery.[10]

What, then, are the characteristics of the early monochrome İznik ware? First of all,

63a. Ewer, dated 1510, Godman collection, Horsham   63b. Bottle, dated 1529, Godman collection, Horsham

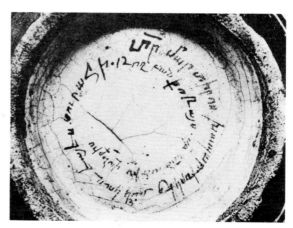

the shapes include large vases, dishes with flattened rims (some with foliate edges), large, deep bowls (some with a tall pedestal foot), mosque lamps, pilgrim flasks, pen-boxes, ewers with rectangular, angular bodies, tankards, and a magnificent candlestick (plates 63a, 70 and 72). Lane has already noted the extreme angularity of the forms and the tight, manuscript-style of the decoration, with motifs drawn from Chinese and Islamic sources but with none of the spontaneity of the earlier hexagonal tiles at Edirne. Inscriptions are often in a painstakingly angular style, meticulously drawn, rather than fluently painted. The divisions of the bodies of the pieces into bands of contrasting design, often with the pattern reserved on a blue ground, is again very Chinese in inspiration. There is a taut assurance in the execution of the patterns and an intellectual density in their concept which suggests the designer/draughtsman in control, rather than the potter/artist. All the wares have a hard white body, masterfully painted in varying shades of underglaze cobalt blue under a technically perfect, transparent, colourless glaze.

To the monochrome cobalt blue, a second additional colour was added (or rather, revived), a brilliant turquoise blue. This turquoise was the first step in the expansion of the İznik palette, to culminate in the brilliant polychrome wares of the second half of the sixteenth century.

These blue and turquoise wares bring up the subject of the *ikinci kırmızı uskumru*.[11] This is the so-called Golden Horn group of Turkish wares. With little resemblance to other İznik products except for the body material, they were at first explained away as being the work of a group of potters settled in İstanbul on the Golden Horn. The shapes consist of large bowls with tall pedestal bases, dishes with and without rims (plate 74), vases with tall necks (plate 73), mosque lamps, tiles (plate 61c), a little ink-pot and a very strange, angular ewer with a lid, once in the Kelekian Collection. Common to all of them is their decoration of fine spiral stems bearing rosettes and cusp-like leaves and bands of plaited ornament. The similarity of the elegant scroll work with patterns found in illumination such as those on the *Tuğra* of Sultan Süleyman (1520–66) in plate 185 suggests the hand of the *nakkāşhāne* artists in the designs of these ceramics. Their dating rests on a series of tiles in this style at Gebze in the mosque of Çoban Mustafa Paşa dating from 1528–9 AD (plate 61a).[12] This is also the date on a cut-down vase in the Godman Collection (plate 63b) on which appears an Armenian inscription. In this instance the Armenian text states unequivocally that it is 'an object of Kütahya' and this would suggest that this piece at least was made by Armenian craftsmen in that town.[13] Whether the whole group should be assigned to Kütahya is arguable; for the moment, given the court origin of the decoration, it is more prudent to use the Kütahya piece as evidence for the general date of this style in the wider context of Ottoman pottery.

A puzzling survival dating probably from the same period is a number of blue and turquoise tiles with 'stencilled' decoration (plates 82, 83 and 85). Despite the considerable variety of shapes, sizes and patterns none appear to have been found in situ. Their decorative repertoire includes lotus palmettes, split-leaf arabesques, elegant scrolls and an assortment of small blossoms.

Unlike the earlier monochrome İznik products which derived their shapes from metalwork and their decoration from illumination, the typical blue-and-turquoise İznik ware seems to rely for both shape and decoration on Chinese ceramic prototypes from almost a century earlier. Sparingly applied on some pieces, the turquoise occupies a larger place on others, particularly on a series of dishes decorated with bunches of grapes and a border of 'breaking waves' (plates 75, 76 and 77). The cavettos of these dishes, like the Chinese originals, are painted with tight little floral bouquets, and again like the Chinese prototypes, the rims are often carved with a foliate edge. The development and gradual degeneration of the 'breaking wave' pattern from its fourteenth-century Chinese origins can be traced in sixteenth- and seventeenth-century İznik pottery (both in blue-and-white and polychrome pieces) where it becomes progressively simplified and abstract. The earlier examples would seem to be those with looser drawing, the waves overlapping to give a fish-scale effect as in plates 75 and 77. On later equivalents, the waves consist of tightly packed but not overlapping circlets as in plate 76. The most common designs for the decoration of the centre are clusters of grapes and leaves, although the Chinese inspiration is

64a. İznik dish, mid-16th century. Diam: 39 cm. Freer

64b. İznik dish, mid-16th century. Diam: 42 cm. Antaki collection

equally apparent on pieces with lotuses, camellias and paeonies.[14] These appear on some early examples (circa 1520) as in plate 64a and in a more stylized form later on (plates 97, 98 and 99).

Lying somewhere in between the blue-and-turquoise group and the later polychrome style is a further group of İznik ware, again with a misnomer, this time erroneously referred to as 'Damascus' ware. Its two salient characteristics are the use of sage green, grey and manganese purple, as well as cobalt blue and turquoise and a looser style of design of tremendous sweeping assurance, showing once again the unmistakable hand the *nakkāş* had in formulating ceramic designs (plates 80, 81 and 86). Known as the '*saz* leaf and rosette' style, it marks the introduction of naturalism in Ottoman art and is characterized by curving long serrated leaves, fleshy rosettes, lotus palmettes and other blossoms elegantly inter-connected by means of undulating tendrils, and often combined with the familiar cloud-bands and arabesques. As to form, the variety of surviving objects includes many earlier shapes: both those of the monochrome wares which were inspired from metalwork and those of the blue-and-turquoise pieces deriving from Chinese porcelain. They include large dishes, bowls with pedestal feet, mosque lamps and a larger number of tiles in the Yeni Kaplıca baths at Bursa. These baths, a Byzantine foundation, were redecorated, according to a tile inscription above the entrance (plate 65) by the Grand Vizier Rüstem Paşa (d. 1561). Although they have badly deteriorated due to the sulphurous atmosphere of the hot springs supplying the baths, there are numbers of elegantly painted hexagonal tiles in eight basic designs, combining geometric and floral motifs with a charming delicacy (plate 78). To date this group, we are dependent on a famous mosque lamp in the British Museum decorated in cobalt blue, green, turquoise and a rich black (plate 87). This is from the Dome of the Rock in Jerusalem, and is dated 1549. Furthermore, besides Qur'ānic and

Ḥadīth inscriptions painted on the body with a relaxed calligraphic assurance, on the foot is a series of little panels referring to 'Eşrefzade of İznik' (d. 1469), a local saint. The style, like the dishes, is altogether looser, while losing none of the precision of the earlier manner.

This now leads to the classic period of İznik ceramics, of the second half of the sixteenth century. Not only in the great tile schemes for the capital, but also in the associated pottery, there is a freedom and exuberance seldom equalled in the history of ceramics. Technically, the refined white body was now decorated with flawless underglaze cobalt blue, turquoise, green, black and a brilliant red slip in relief which has been rightly compared in effect to sealing-wax, all under a perfect transparent glaze. Aesthetically, the designs, however closely related they might be to other Ottoman crafts, and the work of court designers, were executed with complete assurance. The subjects, mostly floral, achieve a super-realism which has little to do with nature and whose hybrid style has become associated with Ottoman imperial art at its height (plates 89, 96, 100 and 105).

In İstanbul, there begins a series of buildings with tiled ornament, each one of which marks a new departure in initiative and innovation. The first of these is the Süleymaniye Mosque (1550-57), where the new red makes its appearance. The tiny but exquisite mosque of Rüstem Paşa (1561) is decorated with tile panels of extraordinary diversity of design. This is followed by the elaborately tiled mosques of Sokollu Mehmed Paşa (1571), and Piyale Paşa (1573), to name only a few of the major buildings. Outside the capital, the Selimiye mosque in Edirne (1567-74) was also decorated with İznik tiles. Doubtless the collaboration between architect, court designer and artisan was close; but this would hardly be enough to explain the mastery of these tiles, which must ultimately have been dependent on the extraordinary sensitivity and skill of the painters who executed them. This skill is even more evident on the contemporary vessels, in which the designs are much more likely to reflect the predilections of the potters rather than court orders from the capital.

65. Underglaze calligraphic tile, mid-16th century. Yeni Kaplıca baths, Bursa

66a. Ka'ba tile panel, dated AH 1085/1674–5 AD.
Bursa Museum

66b. İznik dish dated 1670 AD. Priv. Col., London.
Diam: 26.2 cm

That the İznik factories achieved a more than local esteem we know from various documents. The Austrian ambassador David Ungnad spent a considerable amount between 1573 and 1578 on İznik pottery and tiles, to be shipped home via Venice.[15] İznik ware in European collections with European sixteenth-century metal mounts testifies to the esteem in which the Turkish ware was held—and this in competition with imported Chinese ware of the finest quality. Fragments of İznik ware have been found as far afield as Nubia, Essex, London, Budapest, the Crimea, and Jerusalem.

Nor were mosques the only buildings tiled. The interior of the harem section of the palace at Topkapı Sarayı was extensively tiled, with work of different periods, and the salons and private apartments of the various sultans were also decorated. It is recorded that even the Sultan's royal barge was furnished with tiles. Indeed, the royal demand for İznik products exceeded the supply, and a series of firmans reflects the apprehension of court officials unable to produce the goods, issuing strict injunctions that the imperial orders were to assume first priority. The İznik kilns continued to be fully active until well into the seventeenth century, as can be seen in the decoration of such buildings as the Blue Mosque, finished in 1617. Indeed, the Turkish traveller Evliya Çelebi claims that there were more than three hundred workshops at İznik at the beginning of the century.

By the middle of the seventeenth century, the İznik factories were in decline, the victims of economic and social upheavals. Most important was the collapse of central Ottoman authority itself, and the beginning of a preoccupation on the part of the Turks with keeping the empire together, rather than engaging in expansionist enterprises. This was reflected in a diminution of building activity from the grand scale of the sixteenth century. With the withdrawal of official patronage, the number of potters declined and those that were left began to seek other sources of employment and developed an increasing interest in the export market. By the middle of the century, Evliya Çelebi records that the workshops were reduced to nine.[16] About this time the production began of large numbers of plates in a rather coarse manner, often decorated with sailing-ships and sometimes with Greek inscriptions (plate 66b), which were destined for foreign clients. They have survived in such quantities in Greek houses in Rhodes that they erroneously led to an identification as 'Rhodian' by earlier scholars. A pierced panel with a Greek inscription dated 1667, and probably made for a *sebīl*, or wall fountain, is a typical example of such export ware. And a series of tiles made for various monasteries on Mount Athos falls into the same category.[17] Those in the Grand Lavra monastery are inscribed in Greek and dated 1678, recording that they were the gift of the Patriarch of Constantinople. They are of special interest as they are still decorated in a reasonable sealing-wax red, in contradiction to the theory that the İznik ware of the mid-seventeenth century had reverted to the limited blue-and-turquoise palette of a hundred years earlier. Such blue-and-turquoise tiles are to be seen in quantity on the mosque of İbrahim Ağa, in Cairo, dated 1652. In mosques in the Ottoman capital, such as the Yeni Valide mosque (1663–72) and the Çinili mosque at Üsküdar (1640), a similar limitation is to be detected in the colour-scheme, and the designs have an increasing tendency to be confined to single tiles, rather than conceived in terms of a comprehensive scheme. Also dating to the second half of the seventeenth century are picture-tiles with stylized depictions of the Muslim holy shrines of Mecca and Medina, such as the Ka'ba (plate 66a). These are related to similar illustrations in manuscripts of the period, and are interesting as they show an increasing awareness of aerial perspective.

By the turn of the century the İznik industry appears to have been in a state of virtual collapse, and the craft only survived in the eighteenth by the transference of a group of potters to the capital, to be settled at Tekfur Sarayı near Eyüp. This revival does not concern

67. İznik polychrome dish painted in the animal style, c. 1600. Diam: 30.2 cm. Priv. Col., London

68a. 17th-century underglaze tiles:
Darwishiya mosque, Damascus

us here, and was responsible by and large for technically inferior tiles with debased İznik designs. At the same time, the Armenian potters at Kütahya flourished, based on an industry whose origins date at least to the late fifteenth century and whose sixteenth and seventeenth-century products (apart from the famous Godman ewer and water-bottle) have yet to be clearly defined. The Kütahya potters in the eighteenth century produced a wide range of gaily-decorated little vessels and dishes, and a number of specially commissioned tiles. The most famous of these are the pictorial and decorative tiles in the Armenian Cathedral of St James in Jerusalem, dated 1718/19.[18] Other tiles also found their way into Turkish mosques, a neat reversal of the situation at the end of the seventeenth century when Muslim potters had taken to working for Christian clients.

The pottery of the Ottoman provinces

No study of Ottoman ceramics can ignore the production of the provinces. The most substantial industry is that which was based in Syria, and Syrian/Damascus pottery, with its close stylistic relationship to contemporary İznik ware, has in the past often tended to confuse the picture and has led to a number of misattributions. The Syrian industry itself predates the Ottoman conquest, and Syrian pottery and tiles were produced in quantity in the early fifteenth century, such as those in the tomb-chamber of Ghars al-Din al-Tawrizi (d. 1425) in Damascus (plate 56c).

It has long been considered that there was a gap in the history of Syrian glazed ceramics from the first half of the fifteenth century until the Turkish conquest, but recent research has shown that this is not so.[19] However, the Ottoman campaigns and the construction of new buildings did lead to an intense revival; between 1550 and the end of the century a number of buildings in Damascus were decorated extensively in the new style, with colours now including cobalt blue, turquoise, black, purple, rose-pink and a very characteristic green, ranging from apple green to olive in shade.[20] Besides this distinctive green, Syrian tiles are also easily identifiable by the complete absence of the 'sealing-wax' red and by a thick 'vitreous' glaze which develops a wide crackle never seen on İznik ware but typical

68b. Sulaymaniya mosque, Damascus

of Syrian pottery, and by three cockspur marks on the centre of the dishes, another feature never encountered in İznik.

. But it is in the conception and execution of the Syrian tiles that their greatest interest lies. Unlike the hybrid, court-orientated İznik product, the Syrian tiles show a lively independence and are much more easily identifiable as the work of individual artists (plates 68a and 68b). The floral motifs, in particular, are treated with far greater naturalism, and painted in a very spirited and spontaneous manner (plates 106 to 110).

It has been suggested that the Syrian revival was the result of the transfer of a band of potters from Jerusalem, where they had been previously engaged on the redecoration of the exterior of the Dome of the Rock. The Dome of the Rock tiles, sheathing the exterior and forming part of a programme of renewal initiated by Sultan Süleyman, are of particular importance (plate 69). Like the mosques at Bursa and Edirne of the fifteenth century, they also combine in the same scheme tile mosaic, *cuerda seca* and underglaze tiles. The exterior of the Dome of the Rock was apparently first tiled with a great mosaic inscription below the drum, dated AH 952/1545–6 AD. On the upper walls of the octagon was an underglaze-painted inscription, removed in the 1870s but still surviving in the Islamic Museum store-room in the Haram, and various panels of *cuerda seca* and underglaze painted tiles, including a few imported İznik specimens. An inscription above the north porch is dated AH 959/1551–2 AD and signed Abdallah of Tabriz. Again, recent study has shown that the Dome of the Rock tiles were almost certainly produced in the vicinity of the building itself.[21] The unlikely suggestion has been made that the craftsmen came from İznik, but there are no comparable Turkish buildings at such an early date. The octagonal inscription, however, is very Turkish in concept; maybe this was the execution of a design supplied from the capital. A more likely origin for the workers would appear to be Iran, and the number of tiles which can be technically shown to be some way between *cuerda seca* and true underglaze in technique strongly argues that they experimented successfully with underglaze on the spot. At any rate, extensive exterior tiling was a Persian fashion whose only appearance in İstanbul—in the Çinili Kiosk mentioned above—was associated with a Persian style of architecture. The exterior tiling of the Dome of the Rock belongs to a Persian rather than Ottoman aesthetic. The last enterprise in Jerusalem was the tiling of the little Qubbat al-Silsila, next to the Dome of the Rock which appears to have been clothed with tiles left over from the main building, and a date on the *miḥrāb* gives a clue to the termination of the work.

The Jerusalem-Syrian connection is most evident not in the Damascene mosques of the second half of the sixteenth century, but in a mansion in Aleppo. The Bayt Jumblatt has a great tiled *īwān*, the tiles of which can be directly linked to those on the interior of the Qubbat al-Silsila. What this implies as far as the Syrian industry is concerned has yet to be examined in depth.

Finally mention must be made of a minor tile industry in eastern Turkey, at Diyarbakır. In a recent and succinctly argued study by Julian Raby,[22] it was shown that Diyarbakır was producing its own tiles in the mid-sixteenth century, like İznik, Jerusalem and Damascus, and that the tiles themselves were of an identifiable and distinct style. Again related to the court products of İznik, Diyarbakır tiles of the first half of the sixteenth century include both underglaze and *cuerda seca* specimens. The tiles of the second half of the century are more closely related to İznik underglaze tiles, with a bright blue, and an unsuccessful attempt at red under a crackled heavy glaze (plates 111 to 114). The designs are somewhat overwrought and crowded, and examples of these tiles may be found in Erzerum, Sağmanbahçe, and Van, as well as at Diyarbakır, to which latter centre Julian Raby convincingly ascribes their manufacture.

THE PLATES

54
Tile

Third quarter of 16th century

A square tile painted in cobalt blue, emerald green and 'sealing wax' red on a white ground. Part of an endless repeat pattern, the decoration consists of *chintamani* motifs in a drop repeat formation (see p. 126 for discussion of this design). Similar tiles can be seen in the Apartments of the Mantle of the Prophet in the Topkapı Sarayı.

Height: 22 cm; width: 22 cm

70
Candlestick

Late 15th–early 16th century

A candlestick with concave sides and a short neck rising from the shoulder and capped with a metal ring. The shape, and particularly the use of a torus moulding on the neck point, correspond as with much early İznik to a metal prototype of the kind seen in the fifteenth century *miḥrāb* panel in the Yeşil Türbe (plate 58a). It is decorated with Chinese-inspired motifs in cobalt blue, reserved in white on the sides of the body. In the lower band, the characteristic lotus blossoms and stems are overlaid with an inscription. A frieze of cloud bands lies on the foot ring and a chain pattern decorates the neck.

Published: Musée des Arts Décoratifs, *Exposition d'Art Musulman*. Paris 1903, plate 45

69. The Dome of the Rock, Jerusalem

71
Tazza

First half of 16th century

A large dish with outcurved rim and foliate edge on a high splayed foot, painted in shades of grey with cobalt blue outlines on a white ground. The interior is decorated with all-over patterns of stylized serrated leaves and blossoms with fine curling tendrils, while clusters of flowers decorate the exterior.

Private Collection, Cologne

Height: 12.5 cm; Diam: 39 cm

72
Pilgrim's Flask

Late 15th–early 16th century

A flat circular flask with a metal neck (possibly later). Painted in a blackish blue on a white ground, this is probably one of the earliest pieces of İznik pottery. It is decorated with spiralling split-leaf arabesques and flowers of Chinese inspiration in a pattern which echoes the design of the silver bowl illustrated in plate 21.

Published: Lane, 1957, Fig. 5

Sèvres, Musée National de la Céramique, 15472

Height: 31 cm

73
Bottle

1510–1540

A bottle with a bulbous body and tall slender neck divided midway by a knop and flaring at the mouth. It is painted in cobalt blue and turquoise on a white ground with an all-over pattern of tightly spiralling stems forming concentric circles joined together by small trefoil cartouches. A plaited motif decorates the mouth and the knop, while a simplified form is found at the foot. For the metal origin of the shape see p. 28 and plate 30 and for a similarly shaped ceramic bottle see Rackham, plate 21 no. 59.

British Museum 78 12–30

Height: 43 cm

74
Dish

Second quarter of 16th century

A large dish with outcurved foliate rim painted in two shades of cobalt blue and touches of turquoise on a white ground. The centre is decorated with tightly spiralling stems studded with tiny flowers forming concentric rings, joined together by small trefoil-shaped cartouches. On the rim, a fine undulating stem is dotted with similar flowers, while in the cavetto is a frieze of confronting cloud bands. The decoration resembles strongly that of the *tuğra* of Süleyman the Magnificent (plate 185) dating from the same period.

Private Collection, Kuwait

Diam: 45 cm

75
Dish

First half of 16th century

A large dish with outcurved rim and foliate edge painted in shades of cobalt blue and turquoise on a white ground. The rim is decorated with an early version of the stylized 'breaking wave' pattern and, in the cavetto, an exceptionally large number (12)

of small shrubs. Lying in the centre and springing from a flaming sun disc is an undulating vine tree from which hang clusters of grapes. The shape of this dish, the grapes and 'breaking wave' motifs are all derived from fourteenth- and fifteenth-century Chinese porcelain.

Antaki Collection

Diam: 45.5 cm

76
Dish

Mid-16th century

A large dish with outcurved rim and foliate edge painted in shades of cobalt blue, touches of sage green and turquoise on a white ground. The 'breaking wave' on the rim has attained the typical format of juxtaposed circlets, found on dishes of the middle and second half of the sixteenth century. Unlike plate 75 the cavetto and back have the conventional eight symmetrically disposed floral sprays. A comparable grape dish is in the Victoria and Albert Museum, Lane, 1971 32B.

Diam: 42 cm

77
Dish

Early 16th century

A large dish with outcurved rim and foliate edge painted in pale cobalt blue with darker outlines on a white ground. It is decorated on the rim with a stylized 'breaking wave' motif, in the cavetto with a variety of floral sprays and in the centre with clusters of grapes. The early 'fish-scale' version of the 'breaking wave' pattern on the rim (as on plate 75), the absence of an outline between the cavetto and centre, the drawing of the floral sprays on the cavetto and the grape clusters, all point to this being one of the earliest examples of this group of grape dishes.

Diam: 39 cm

78
Tile

Mid-16th century

A hexagonal tile painted in blue, sage green and manganese purple on a white ground, decorated with tulips, hyacinths and carnations. It is contemporary with similar tiles in the Yeni Kaplıca Baths in Bursa discussed by Lane (1957 p. 267). Another tile decorated in a similar way is in the Musée des Arts décoratifs (Paris 1977 no. 587).

Private Collection, London

Height: 20.7 cm; width: 18.6 cm

79
Plate

1530–1550

A shallow plate with a narrow flanged rim suggestive of a metal shape, painted in a dark greenish black on a white ground. It is decorated with a symmetrical arrangement of stylized tulips and hyacinths radiating from a central rosette. Related plates are in the Victoria and Albert Museum. One published by Lane (1971 pl. 33B) is similar in design and colour and the other (Lane 1957 fig. 40) is identical in shape and has the same 'Z' band on the rim, a motif also found on the two silver bowls (plates 5 and 21).

Private Collection, London

Diam: 27.6 cm

80
Dish

1530–1550

A large dish with outcurved rim painted in shades of cobalt blue, turquoise, sage green and manganese purple with darker green outlines on a white ground; a palette typical of 'Damascus' ware. It is decorated on the rim with small rosettes alternating with stylized sprigs of blossoms. A large tree with undulating branches culminating in pomegranate flowers covers the entire interior surface of the dish: a feature typical of İznik dishes from the 'Damascus' group onwards but atypical of earlier examples. A comparable dish in the Victoria and Albert Museum is illustrated by Lane (1957 plate B).

Private Collection, London

Height: 6.5 cm; diam: 36.5 cm

81
Dish

1530–1550

A large dish with outcurved rim and foliate edge, painted in shades of cobalt blue, manganese purple, sage green and turquoise with black outlines on a white ground. It is decorated on the rim with a 'breaking wave' motif. In the cavetto and centre, two sprays of hyacinths enclose a large blossom from which spring two outcurving stems with rosettes and serrated leaves typical of the 'saz leaf and rosette' style common on metalwork (plate 5), textiles (plate 122) and illumination (plate 202).

Private Collection, London

Height: 14.5 cm; diam: 35.5 cm

82
Tile

1530–1540

A rectangular tile from a border frieze, 'stencilled' in shades of cobalt blue and turquoise on a white ground. From a lobed ogival medallion in the centre spring spiralling tendrils onto which are attached stylized lotus flowers, rosettes and curved serrated leaves reserved on a blue ground.

Height: 17.5 cm; width: 27.2 cm

83
Tile

1530–1540

A hexagonal tile 'stencilled' in shades of cobalt blue and turquoise with darker blue outlines on a white ground. It is decorated with a radial pattern of stylized lotuses alternating with arabesques around a central rosette. A narrow outer band is filled with similarly stencilled flowers. Part of a repeat pattern. A dish with a similar pattern is in the Godman collection (Lane 1957 fig. 37).

Edwin Binney 3rd Collection

Height: 27.5 cm; width: 24 cm

84
Tile

1530–1540

A hexagonal tile painted in shades of cobalt blue and turquoise with darker blue outlines on a white ground. The radial pattern consists of 'Chinese' cloud-bands alternating with arabesque medallions enclosing stylized lotus flowers. The rest of the ground is covered with smaller blossoms, split-leaves and rosettes attached to thin tendrils. Similar tiles are in the Fogg Art Museum and the Victoria and Albert Museum.

Edwin Binney 3rd Collection

Height: 24.3 cm; width: 21.5 cm

85
Tile

1530–1540

A rectangular border tile 'stencilled' in shades of cobalt blue and turquoise on a white ground. It is decorated with a central medallion filled with symmetrically arranged lotus blossoms and split-leaf palmettes reserved on a blue ground. A similar composition appears on the lower panels of the Qur'ān stand in plate 39.

Height: 17.5 cm; width: 27.6 cm

86
Pair of tiles

Mid-16th century

A pair of arched tiles painted in shades of cobalt blue and turquoise with thin black outlines. They are decorated in the '*saz* leaf and rosette' style with fleshy lotus blossoms, rosettes and serrated leaves connected by elegantly curving stems. A similar pattern is found on the exterior of a bowl in the Godman collection (Hayward 1976, plate 413), on illuminated pages (plate 202) and on royal kaftans (plate 123).

Height: 31 cm; width: 26.3 cm (each tile)

87
Mosque lamp

AH 956/1549 AD

A mosque lamp, part of a set ordered by Süleyman the Magnificent for the Dome of the Rock, Jerusalem. It is painted in shades of cobalt blue and turquoise with black outlines and decorated with cloud bands, cartouches and Qur'ānic inscriptions at the mouth, neck and lower part of the body. Just above the foot is an inscription in the name of Esrefzade—a saint associated with the town of İznik—and mentioning the date AH 956/1549 AD.

Published: Lane (1971) p. 54 pl. 36

British Museum 87-5-16-1

Height: 38.0 cm

88
Vase

Second half of 16th century

The bulbous body with high sloping shoulder and flaring neck sits on a narrow splayed foot. A unique occurrence of the 'plain tradition' in Ottoman cermics, this vase is covered in 'sealing wax' red typical of polychrome İznik ware. The absence of any decoration except for the white and blue lines painted on a vestigial form of torus moulding at the neck and footring is suggestive of metalwork.

Türk ve İslam Eserleri Müsezi

Height: 25 cm

89
Dish

Mid-16th century

A large dish with outcurved rim painted in shades of cobalt blue, black, emerald green and 'sealing wax' red in relief on a white ground. The 'breaking wave' border contains a bursting arrangement of tulips, roses and rosebuds, the sweeping stems of which spring from a leafy cluster. The back is decorated with alternating pairs of tulips and rosettes.

Diam: 33 cm

90
Dish

Second half of 16th century

A large dish with outcurved rim and foliate edge painted in cobalt blue, emerald green and 'sealing wax' red in relief on a white ground. It is decorated on the rim with a 'breaking wave' pattern while the interior is divided into four compartments, each consisting of a bouquet of carnations enclosed by pairs of floral sprays springing from a central rosette.

Antaki Collection

Diam: 35.5 cm

91
Tile

1560-1580

A large octagonal tile painted in 'sealing wax' red, shades of cobalt blue, turquoise and green, outlined in blackish blue on a white ground. The pattern consists of a cruciform arrangement of lobed ogival cartouches containing arabesques flanked by floral sprays which spring from a central rosette.

Antaki Collection

Height: 39.5 cm

92
Moulded tiles

Second half of 16th century

Tiles, part of a moulding, painted in cobalt blue, 'sealing wax' red in relief and touches of emerald green on a white ground. They are decorated with a chain pattern in the centre running between a crenellated border above and below.

Length: 28 cm; width: 7 cm (each tile)

93
Tile panel

Second half of 16th century

A panel of four tiles painted in rich cobalt blue, 'sealing wax' red in relief and emerald green on a white ground. Part of a large-scale repeat pattern, they are decorated with bold split-leaf arabesques enclosing palmettes filled with flowers.

Antaki Collection

Height: 51 cm; length: 48 cm

94
Pair of tiles

Second half of 16th century

Rectangular tiles painted in shades of cobalt blue, 'sealing wax' red in relief and touches of emerald green with black outlines. They are decorated with intertwining split-leaves and foliate edges reserved on a blue ground. Part of a repeat pattern.

Antaki Collection

Length: 26 cm; height: 15 cm

95
Jug

Second half of 16th century

A jug with a bulbous body and a short flaring neck. In an attempt to emulate a fluted metal shape on a flat round surface, the decoration consists of narrow white lines running vertically down the body and joined at horizontal intervals by thin scalloped parallel lines. Bands at the neck and foot are suggestive of torus mouldings.

Published: Lane 1971 plate 44 A

Victoria and Albert Museum C2003-1910, Salting Bequest

Height: 29.3 cm; diam: 14.2 cm

96
Tile panel (fragment)

End of 16th century

Two tiles painted in shades of cobalt blue, dark green, dark purple and 'sealing wax' red in relief with dark blue outlines on a white ground. In the centre, under an elegant arch, is a base with tulips surrounded by sprays of plum blossoms, king flowers and smaller tulips. The composition is enclosed by a crenellated frieze. Part of a three-tile panel of which only the lower two tiles remain. This is an unusually small version of the splendid tile panels in İstanbul and especially those in the Takyeci İbrahim Ağa mosque built in 1592 (Öz ceramics plate LIII).

Philippa Scott Collection

Height: 38.2 cm; width: 29.6 cm

97
Dish

Third quarter of 16th century

A large dish with outcurved rim on a small footring. It is painted in shades of cobalt blue on a white ground. The decoration is of Chinese inspiration and consists of a 'breaking wave' border which contains undulating tendrils forming a six-pointed star onto which are attached paeonies and thin serrated leaves, the inner ones of which spiral around a central rosette. This dish is contemporary with the grape dish on plate 76.

Ex. David Stirling Collection

Diam: 35.5 cm

98
Candlestick

Middle of 16th century

A candlestick with a hollow conical base flaring at the top to form the sides of the drip tray. The slender neck tapers at the middle into a knop. It relates closely to Ottoman metal examples except for the top of its damaged neck. It is painted in shades of grey and cobalt blue on a white ground. Two narrow fret bands separate the scrolling floral designs of the body and the 'breaking wave' border at the bottom, a design normally associated with the rims of dishes. The neck has a series of panels scalloped at the ends and interrupted by a guilloche band around the knop. The interior of the drip tray bears the inscription in Arabic: *Ṣāḥibuhu Ḥājjī Muḥammad ibn Sulaymān*, 'its owner is Haji Muhammad son of Sulayman'.

Published: Rackham (1959 plate 24, no. 56), Denny (1977 plate 27)

Metropolitan Museum of art No. 66.4. 1

ex Adda, ex Homberg Collections

Height: 23.8 cm; diam: 19.3 cm

99
Jug

Third quarter of 16th century

A jug with a bulbous body, narrow neck, straight handle with a torus moulding at its base and low splayed foot. It is painted in shades of cobalt blue on a white ground and decorated at the neck and body with a frieze of curling tendrils onto which are attached small flowers and serrated leaves in a pattern closely resembling those of plates 97 and 98.

Height: 23.5 cm

100
Dish

Mid-16th century

A large dish with outcurved rim and foliate edge on a small footring, painted in shades of cobalt blue, black, emerald green and 'sealing wax' red in relief with thin black outlines on a white ground. A typical example of the 'quatre-fleurs' decorative repertoire of the second half of the sixteenth century, it is decorated with a 'breaking wave' pattern on the rim; this encloses a composition of tulips, carnations, hyacinths and other flowers swaying along curving stems which spring from a leafy shrub.

Private Collection, Cologne

Diam: 33 cm

101
Tankard

Circa 1600

A cylindrical tankard with a flat vertical handle (possibly a copy of a leather prototype), painted in shades of cobalt blue, emerald green and 'sealing wax' red in relief with thin black outlines on a white ground. It is decorated with a central row of crested birds lying amongst vine leaves and tendrils with crenellations above and below. At the mouth and foot, a zigzag pattern is formed of narrow leaves and half rosettes, a possible stylization of the tiger stripes and dots pattern (*chintamani*).

Published: Rackham 1959 plate 82A no. 198

Antaki Collection

Ex Adda, ex Wallis Collection

Height: 23 cm; diam: 11.5 cm

102
Tankard

Circa 1600

A gently tapering cylindrical tankard with a flat vertical handle painted in cobalt blue, turquoise and 'sealing wax' red in relief with thin black outlines. It is decorated with lateen-rigged ships and stylized rocks or vine leaves. This is one of the most popular designs in late 16th- and 17th-century Ottoman ceramics of the 'Rhodian' type and it was subsequently often copied in the 19th and 20th centuries. For other examples of tankards with lateen ships see Miller, D., *Turkish Ceramics* (Leningrad 1972), p. 105 and Atil, E., *Ceramics from the World of Islam* (Washington D.C. 1973), no. 86.

Philippa Scott Collection

Height: 22.5 cm; diam: 11.5 cm

103
Tile

Mid-16th century

A square tile painted in stippled cobalt blue, emerald green and 'sealing wax' red in relief with dark blue outlines. The pattern consists of two intertwined spiralling leafy tendrils springing from

floral cartouches around the edges and terminating in large serrated '*saz*' leaves. In the centre a series of 'S' shaped cloud bands is superimposed on the pattern. The same pattern is found on tiles in the room of Murad III (circa 1578) in the Topkapı Palace (Öz ceramics plate XLIX).

Private Collection, Bonn

Height: 25 cm; width: 25 cm

104
Tile

Circa 1560

A square tile painted in shades of cobalt blue, turquoise and 'sealing wax' red in relief on a white ground. It is decorated with a pattern of split-leaf arabesques; the arrangement of the intertwined stems forms four clockwise swastika-like patterns with a branch from each joining a central rosette to form an anti-clockwise swastika. Tiles with the same pattern are on the rear wall of the mosque of Rüstem Pasa (completed 1561) (Denny 1977, plate 2).

Private Collection, Bonn

Height: 25 cm; width: 25 cm

105
Tankard

Second half of 16th century

A cylindrical tankard with a flat vertical handle painted in cobalt blue, emerald green and orange-red in relief with thin black outlines on a white ground. The thin wall is decorated with life-like carnations on undulating, broken stems contained within narrow crenellated bands at the top and bottom. The carnations and border are almost indistinguishable from those on the flat rimless plate in the J. Homaizi collection (published: Sotheby's, London 23.4.79, lot 217).

Height: 18.5 cm; diam: 11.5 cm

106
Tile

Damascus, late 16th century

A square tile painted in shades of cobalt blue, turquoise and sage green. A central cartouche contains a floral cluster surrounded by serrated leaves reserved against a blue ground with rosettes, tendrils and leaves at the four corners.

Published: Papadopoulo, *L'Islam et l'Art Musulman,* Paris 1976, plate 454

Antaki Collection

Height: 27 cm; width: 27 cm

107
Tile

Damascus, second half of 16th century

A hexagonal tile painted in cobalt blue, sage green and manganese purple with black outlines on a white ground. The decoration consists of three dot clusters and wavy bands, a pattern known as *chintamani*. Part of a repeat panel.

Height: 27 cm; width: 24 cm

108
Tile

Damascus, circa 1540

A fragmentary hexagonal tile cut at the top and side, painted in cobalt blue, manganese purple and pale sage green with thin black outlines. It is decorated with flowers springing from a leafy shrub.

Private Collection, London

Height: 22.5 cm; width: 22 cm

109
Tile

Damascus, late 16th century

A large square tile from a border frieze, painted in shades of cobalt blue, sage green and touches of manganese purple with black outlines on a white ground. The repeat border pattern consists of blue trefoil cartouches containing arabesque motifs, the spaces between which form reciprocal white trefoils. A similar tile is published in *Céramique Orientale*, plate 7.

Height: 33 cm; width: 33 cm

110
Border tiles

Damascus, second half of 16th century

Two narrow rectangular border tiles, painted in shades of cobalt blue, turquoise and sage green with black outlines on a white ground. A series of undulating pale turquoise serrated leaves containing cloud-bands is intertwined with a similar series of split-leaf palmettes. Along the sides are stylized lotuses on thin stems.

Private Collection, London

Height: 14.5 cm; length: 30 cm (each tile)

111
Tile

Diyarbakır, second half of 16th century

A rectangular tile painted in shades of cobalt blue, dark green, 'sealing wax' red in relief and yellow tinged with red. It is decorated with a central ogival cartouche containing a vase of symmetrically arranged tulips and roses. In the four corners are compartments containing closely-knit serrated leaves and flowers reserved on a blue ground. Part of a repeat pattern. Tiles with a similar pattern are in the Hazret-i Süleyman mosque in Diyarbakır, a building dating from the eighteenth century with re-used tiles (Raby 1977–8, Plate 156/3). Another example is in the Victoria and Albert Museum, 1018–1872.

Antaki Collection

Height: 35 cm; width 32 cm

112
Tile

Diyarbakır, second half of 16th century

A square tile painted in shades of cobalt blue, dark green and 'sealing wax' red in relief with dark blue outlines on a white ground. It is a segment of a large panel with floral motifs arranged in an ogival grid formed by undulating bands filled with juxtaposed small flowers. İznik tiles with a similar pattern are in the mosque of Piyale Paşa in İstanbul (Raby 1977–8, Fig. 159/3).

Antaki Collection

Height: 35 cm; width: 35 cm

113
Tile

A border tile painted in shades of cobalt blue, blackish green and dull red in slight relief. It is decorated with a central arabesque medallion flanked by two trefoil cartouches. There is a chain pattern along the top and a plain guard stripe at the bottom. Tiles with the same pattern are in the tomb of Hazret-i Süleyman in Diyarbakır (Raby 1977–8, plate 156/1).

Height: 15.3 cm; width: 33.3 cm

114
Tile

A border tile similar to the last, painted in shades of cobalt blue, turquoise green and touches of 'sealing wax' red in slight relief with thin black outlines. It is decorated with an elaborate central trefoil cartouche to which are attached bold intertwining stems with split-leaf palmettes. There is a chain pattern along the bottom and a plain guard stripe at the top. Tiles with the same pattern are in the tomb of Hazret-i Süleyman in Diyarbakır (Raby 1977–8, plate 158/1).

Height: 15.5 cm; width: 33.2 cm

71

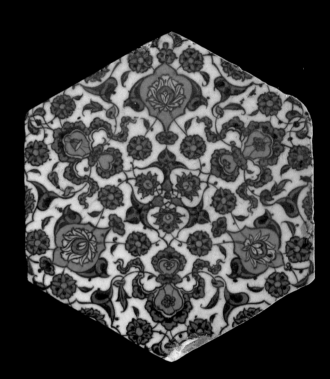

92
93
94

95

97
98·99

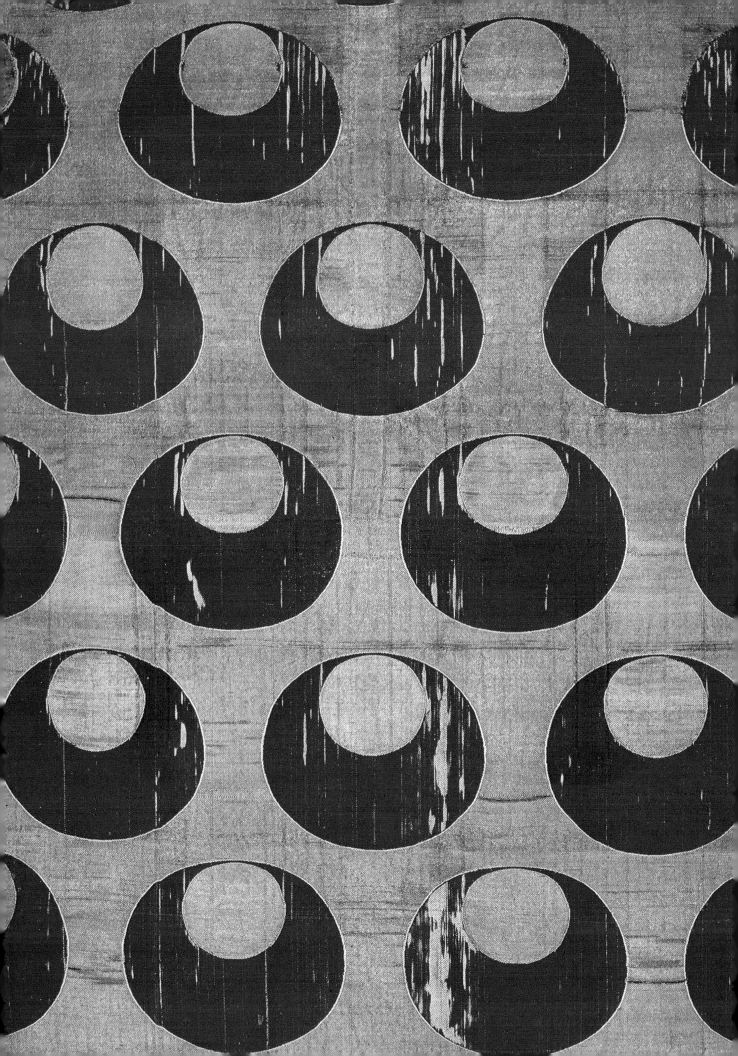

Textiles
Walter Denny

The production of hand-woven textiles represents both a craft industry distinguished by the physical processes of spinning and weaving, and an artistic endeavour characterized by the close co-operation of artists, technicians and skilled workers. Every age sees the production of simple fabrics designed to provide basic clothing and at the same time witnesses the production of special, more elaborate and more expensive textiles which move well beyond the requirements of warmth and modesty, into the realm of luxury, political and religious symbolism, thus raising complex questions about artistic influence and interchange.

During its long historical course, the Ottoman Empire was the scene of both types of textile production. Ordinary cloth, made from linen, cotton, or from animal fibres, by its sheer quantity, frequently figured prominently in matters of taxation, international trade policy, and the employment of large numbers of workers. When we think of Ottoman textiles today however, our focus quite naturally falls upon the more complex fabrics, those in which the levels of artistry and technology reached great heights. The history of weaving of such textiles in the Ottoman Empire is also one of economic importance, and because the silk, brocaded cloth, silk velvets and embroideries produced in the Ottoman dominions were major items of trade, they served as the vectors whereby styles and symbols travelled within the Empire itself, and across land routes and sea lanes to the West as well.

The basis for our knowledge of the history of Ottoman textiles deserves some scrutiny before we embark upon an outline of the development of style and technique. The administrative system of the Ottoman Empire was one of the most efficient and meticulous of its time, and the civil servants charged with levying taxes, protecting consumers, and overseeing labour organizations, kept written records with a zeal which today gives great joy to those historians fortunate enough to be able to read the perfunctory *siyākat* script in which such records were usually written. Records of imports and exports, guild registers, tax and revenue rolls, and legal records have survived in quantity into our own time in the various Turkish archives.[1]

The East-West commerce in textiles is also well-documented in Western sources. The Italian city-states whose ships provided the means for a thriving commerce in the eastern Mediterranean from late mediaeval times, and whose advanced banking system created the economic climate by which such commerce was sustained, kept trading records of their

116. Detail, silk brocade, *kemhā*, 16th century. Musée Historique des tissus, Lyons

dealings in the silk trade. The focus of this trade was the old Ottoman capital city of Bursa in Bithynia, set against a mountain range on a fertile plain to the south of the Sea of Marmara. There, weaving and trans-shipment of silk originating primarily from the province of Gilan on the south Caspian littoral of Iran created a vigorous commerce and one of the richest classes of entrepreneurs of the fifteenth century. Trade, which attempted to assuage the voracious appetite for oriental rugs and silks on the part of the European nobility and rich merchants, was not the only way Ottoman textiles found their way into Europe. From the late seventeenth century onward, the growing Habsburg power in eastern Europe began to push the Turkish empire back, acquiring considerable military booty in the process including many textiles. But unlike the remarkable record of the history of Turkish carpets existing in European painting, European artists have produced little in the way of pictorial evidence bearing upon the history of Ottoman textiles.

According to historical records, Ottoman silk weavings fell into three major groups: *kadīfe* or velvets, *kemhā* or figured brocaded silks, and *tāfta* or *atlās*, terms used to describe monochrome silk satins of light weight. Various subgroups among these basic categories were delineated by terms which both defined techniques and implied values and prices. For example, *çatma* was an especially tightly-woven and lustrous velvet woven according to very high standards in Bursa in the later part of the fifteenth century. Among the many different kinds of *kemhā* were the ordinary *serenk*, a multicoloured brocaded fabric; *serāser*, which utilized silver thread and grey silk for an overall silvery effect; and the most opulent of all Ottoman textiles, the heavy *zerbāft* brocaded with large quantities of gold thread.

These fabrics were produced in a number of formats, from the small velvet panels suitable for the facing of one large cushion or *yastık* (plate 117) to larger bolts of cloth in various dimensions which could be used as decorative panels or cut and tailored into garments (plate 131). A definitive history of Ottoman textiles has yet to be written, and consequently we cannot yet trace fully the ebb and flow of production in Bursa and İstanbul, the two main centres of the weaving industry. The government took an active role in regulating the production of goods, in order to ensure the quality of exports and thus provide a steady source of tax revenues. Changing its policy from time to time for political considerations, availability of precious metals, and the conflicting claims of various pressure groups in the silk industry, the government sought to play a positive role while often taking measures which had the opposite effect to that intended. Then as now, officials of the state, known as *muhtesib*, who were appointed to look after standards of quality and to prevent profiteering, found themselves in opposition to groups of entrepreneurs seeking higher profits, or to the weaving guilds, who were often caught between rising costs of raw materials and labour, and the fixed selling prices decreed by law.[2] At the same time the market for silk appears to have been very volatile. In the fifteenth and sixteenth centuries, when the weaving industry of the Ottoman empire depended almost totally on the import of cocoons from Iran, the numerous Ottoman-Iranian conflicts often played havoc with supplies of raw silk. To free themselves from dependence on Iranian silk, the Ottomans encouraged local production. The earliest record of production of cocoons in Bursa itself dates from 1587, steadily increasing after that date, so that by a century later a traveller's account mentions the plain of Bursa as being covered with mulberry orchards.

In later times the weaving of Ottoman silk textiles gradually declined in both quality and quantity. Whereas in the early sixteenth century the Ottoman silks were avidly sought in both East and West, by the nineteenth century the industry was a shade of its former self. Yet the much higher level of cocoon production and the introduction of mechanized spinning mills still served to supply European weavers with silk thread.[3]

In dealing with what is indeed a major art form in Ottoman tradition, the reasons for paying so much attention to economic factors lying behind silk manufacturing go beyond

117. Velvet cushion cover, *yastık*, 16th century. Antaki collection

the mere assessment of quantity of output. Economic factors underlie the gradual coarsening of Turkish silks over the centuries; the number of 'teeth' on a loom which determined the density of warp threads declined over time. Similarly, there were periodic prohibitions in the use of precious metal thread in textiles, and wars or changes in trade patterns sometimes interrupted the availability of certain dyestuffs; all these factors can be of great help to art historians in the search for a definitive chronology of Ottoman weaving.

The Ottoman textile industry was organized along a complex system of guilds. These were responsible for recruitment, training, setting of standards, wages and prices and generally all aspects of textile making except the growing of cocoons. This, until the seventeenth century, lay beyond the boundaries of the Empire. Before then, raw silk imported from northern Iran was brought by caravan to the central market of Bursa, the *bezzāzistān* or cloth hall, where members of the guild of silk dealers purchased loads of cocoons on which transport fees and transit and customs levies had already been paid. The silk dealers of Bursa were often very wealthy, and in the latter part of the fifteenth century the private fortunes of the most successful dwarfed the capital of the largest Florentine banks then underwriting the textile trade in western Europe. The silk dealers then sent the silk to be spun into two types of thread: the tightly spun warp (*meṣdūd*) and the lighter, less tightly spun weft (*pūd*), a process undertaken by members of the spinners' guild. The spun thread then passed to the *boyacı* or dyer, who dyed it the required colours according to quality standards set by his guild. The silk-dealer would then sell the dyed thread to the weaver or *dokumacı*. Weavers were divided into many groups, according to the type of textile in which each specialized. In İstanbul, the weavers of brocaded silks (*kemhācıs*) appeared to have been the most numerous, but in Bursa it was the guild of velvet-weavers or *kadīfecis* which was the most important in numbers and prestige, and whose products had made the city of Bursa famous. Each of these guilds had its own rules and organization, with elected officials responsible for the recruitment and training of apprentices, for the examinations which qualified members to become journeymen or masters, for maintaining standards of quality and for ensuring fair prices and profits. The election of guild officials and the regulations of the guilds were subject to state control, and thus became part of the general economic regulations (*ihtisāb*) administered by the *muhtesib*, whose office inspected the final product, taxed it and stamped it with official government seals. The finished fabric then passed on to the warehouses of exporters or to shops in the Bursa and İstanbul bazaars, where specialized sellers, again organized in guilds on the basis of the type of fabric they sold, undertook to distribute each bolt of cloth to the wholesale or retail market.[4]

The silk was unwound from the cocoon by hand on simple filiatures, and the spinning was done according to regulation for both the warp and weft threads. The dyer used a fairly simple range of colours together with alum and other simple mordants. A dark red derived from lac was the most common colour, with imported indigo providing blue hues. Valonia or acorn-husks were the preferred sources of yellow, and the primary colours were mixed to give a dark maroon and bright green hues. Undyed silk of a creamy colour was used in both brocades and velvets, as on occasion was black and grey. The looms used by weavers were of a standard width, generally under a metre, but some of them could weave bolts

118. Detail, silk and gilt thread brocade, *zerbāft*, 16th century. Textile museum 8.10.73.

of cloth up to eight metres in length. The warp density was set by law and was determined by the number of 'teeth' on the warp beam, a matter of enormous legal importance as the transcripts of early trials before the provincial judge indicate.[5] Metal thread used in Ottoman velvets was purchased from the guild of *sīmkeş*, the bulk of whose activities appears to have been undertaken in İstanbul. With the exception of the luxurious *zerbāft* (plate 118) and certain heavily-embroidered items using solid gold threads, Ottoman fabrics incorporating precious metals show an ingenious maximization of the visual effect from a minimal use of metal. A silver thread wound around a dove grey silk core provides the effect of silver, while the same metal wound around a dull yellow silk core creates the impression of gold. Gold thread is also used in the same manner but much more rarely.

The designs used by the silk weavers adhered to a basic standard repertoire which was occasionally supplemented with patterns produced by professional designers (*nakkāş*) from İstanbul. Some of the earliest Ottoman textiles used simple striped designs[6], but documents from the early fifteenth century onwards suggest a variety of designs were in use which were modified by weavers in response to changes in taste and techniques. The most remarkable creations of Bursa weavers were those which reflected the latest trends in court art and which were created following paper cartoons by the *nakkāş*.

There is also ample evidence that Ottoman weavers were capable of executing orders according to European taste in an effort to encourage exports. But although they adapted their patterns, Turkish weavers appear to have stayed with their basic techniques as stipulated by law. The traffic however was in both directions; thus, velvets utilizing looped-pile as well as cut-pile technique, although showing Ottoman designs, are now thought to have been woven in Europe according to the prevailing Turkish taste.

When we attempt to formulate a history of the art of Ottoman textiles, we are hampered by the fact that unlike buildings and manuscripts, textiles rarely bear the date of their manufacture, and almost never an indication of the names of artists or weavers. Our evidence for constructing a chronology from the surviving examples is therefore based instead on a series of comparisons, inferences from documents, and deductions, buttressed where possible by technical and documentary evidence of other kinds. Resources for textile dating have focused primarily on the collection of kaftans or royal ceremonial garments kept in the Topkapı Palace Museum in İstanbul, where linen or cotton wrappers bore inscriptions giving the name of the sovereign to which a particular garment supposedly belonged. It was this collection of garments which formed the basis of the chronology developed by the Turkish art historian Tahsin Öz, in his pioneering work in two volumes entitled *Turkish Textiles and Velvets*, the first attempt at a comprehensive overview of Ottoman Turkish woven silk textiles.[7] Unfortunately, the 'wrapper' system of the İstanbul collections proved unreliable, most probably because these inscriptions were not actual contemporary records. A second possible source of dating information is the descriptions of designs found in written sources. Unfortunately, these rarely go beyond the rudimentary level of 'cloth with crescents' or 'striped cloth'. Such evidence is not accurate enough for the art historian. A third possibility, already mentioned, is the use of documents specifying density of warp fibres; while this may bear fruit some day, there is not enough evidence at present to use the system to date fabrics with much confidence; we can however speculate on the identity of the legendary fifteenth-century Bursa *çatma* held up again and again in sources as the ultimate standard of technical excellence, because a small number of surviving velvet fragments clearly demonstrates a density of weave of a much higher level than that found in other groups of surviving velvets (plate 134).

It is style, the fourth category of evidence, which in conjunction with technique gives us the best chance of constructing a reliable chronology. The participation of the *nakkāş* in the textile-making process as well as in most other forms of Ottoman art is probably the single most important reason for the remarkable degree of stylistic homogeneity found in Ottoman art as the illustrations in this book will testify. Thus the stylistic influence of other more dateable art forms on textiles and conversely the influence of textiles on them in terms of patterns, designs and colours provide often, if not always, the best information about when the textiles were woven.

What were the designs used in Ottoman textiles? The earliest examples seem to have employed striped designs, or the ball-like forms referred to as *benekli* in the literature. The design of three balls or spots, known as *chintamani*, which is found in almost all of the velvets now thought to be examples of fifteenth-century Bursa *çatma*, remained for many centuries one of the favourite Ottoman textile designs, sometimes used in characteristic groups of three with wavy stripes, and occasionally as individual crescent or globe-like forms of impressive grandeur and simplicity as in plate 115. The origins and symbolism of the form appear to stretch back to China in Buddhist times; the three balls and the wavy lines apparently represent pearls borne on the waves of the sea, an auspicious symbol associated with good luck and power.[8] By a curious series of adaptations, this symbol developed two other associations in the course of the fifteenth century. First, the three dots. Although they

119. *Serāser* brocade, c. 1600. Kunstgewerbe
Museum, Cologne

120. *Serāser* brocade, 18th century. TKS No. 4643

121. *Kemhā* brocade, late 16th century. Textile
Museum 1.57

122. *Kemhā* brocade, 16th century. Keir Collection

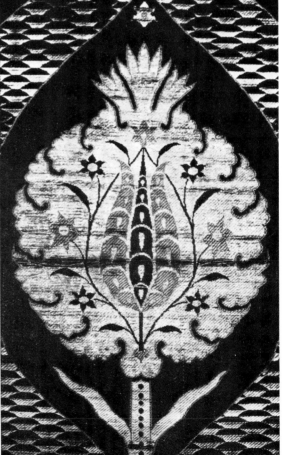

appear in Islamic art as early as the ninth century in Iraq, they effectively became the blazon of the Timurid dynasty in the latter part of the fourteenth century, and thus acquired a general significance of power and importance beyond their original associations. Second, the stripes and dots combined, were associated with tiger and leopard pelts, which in turn were associated with the costume of Rustam, the greatest of Iranian mythical heroes from the *Shāhnāme* or 'Book of Kings'.[9] Thus the motifs also seem to have acquired a specifically masculine and heroic connotation. By placing a smaller ball inside each larger one as in plate 115, the form of a crescent was created; the crescent, although originally a part of both Byzantine and Sassanian symbolism, became associated from the fourteenth century onward with the Ottoman Turks, and was found on their war flags, their military standards (*sancak* or *alem*) and of course on the domes and pointed roofs which crowned Ottoman secular and religious buildings.

Ogival patterns (plates 119–22), which the Ottomans may have acquired either through exposure to Egyptian Mamluk textiles,[10] Chinese or Chinese-inspired Iranian silks, or from European sources, represent one of the most common patterns found in *kemhā* or brocaded silks, but are more rarely found in velvets. Indeed, the separation of weavers into distinct guilds according to the technique of the fabric woven appears to have ensured that although the various guilds shared a common repertoire of motifs, such as the *chintamani* and the stylized flowers, the patterns and combinations in which these motifs were used, and the scale of the designs, were specific to the various types of textiles and rarely intermixed, thus further complicating any attempt at chronology.

Stylized flowers, especially the beloved tulips, carnations, and hyacinths, combined in a multitude of patterns, represent the most common forms encountered in Ottoman textiles (plate 132). Since the decorative repertoire of stylized flowers sometimes referred to as the '*quatre-fleurs*' style did not develop until the middle of the sixteenth century, and underwent a definable series of mutations after that time, it is possible to derive a limited amount of dating information for textiles by looking carefully at the evolution of floral forms, and comparing them to similar forms in book illumination or the ubiquitous dateable building decorations executed in ceramic tiles.[11]

Those rare examples of brocaded silk textiles which show the direct participation of a *nakkāş* in the design can be even more positively dated, since the court designers practised in the mid-sixteenth century and beyond, a particular decorative style known either as the *saz* style (from *saz*, 'reed pen') or in Turkey as the *hatāyī* or Cathayan style, which employed a repertoire of curving, sinuous leaves, and vines bearing complex lotus-blossoms, rosettes, floral sprays, and even small birds (plates 123a and b). While Ottoman textiles apparently never followed the Iranian example of using figural designs taken directly from narrative miniature paintings, and depicting recognizable historical or mythical figures, they did closely follow the ornamental styles popular in the court, and often seem to have employed designs made specifically for the purpose at the court painting atelier in İstanbul.[12]

The meanings attached to these floral forms are determined only with some difficulty. We do know that certain flowers, in the context of being given by one individual to another, carried conventional symbolic meanings ranging from unrequited passion to erotic satisfaction. The simplest and probably the most sensible explanation for the abundance of

123 a & b. Details of mid-16th-century brocaded silk kaftans with 'saz leaf and rosette' decoration, formerly attributed to Bayezid II. TKS 2/164 and 13/529

124. Brocaded silk panel, late 16th century, Benaki museum 3897

flowers appearing in Ottoman textiles is that the designs are attractive, the culture from which they came was and is still extremely fond of the growing of flowers, there was no stereotyping of flowers as 'feminine' in Turkish society, and flowers were appropriate to the bright colours of the silk textiles.

Among them, pride of place goes to the tulips and carnations. The tulip appears in a multitude of forms, sometimes in conjunction with curly Chinese cloud bands taken from book binding and illumination, sometimes with bunches of carnations or hyacinths, and sometimes as a dominating motif all by itself (plates 96, 122, 147 and 155). The carnation, the most loved of all flowers on textiles, is found in great abundance in Ottoman velvets. It is arranged in blossoms, the petals of which are sometimes decorated with small tulips, hyacinths and rosebuds. The hundreds of such repeat pattern carnation velvets surviving in the world's collections exhibit a superficial similarity. A closer look, however, shows them to have an almost endless spectrum of subtle variations which bring constant delight to the viewer as the comparison between plates 1 and 131 will testify.

The complex *hatāyī* designs appear combined with floral motifs in examples of *zerbāft* (plate 118) and other rather expensive patterned silks, among which are to be found some

125. *Nuzhat al-Akhbār* of Feridun Paşa, 1598, detail
showing dress. TKS H. 1339

126. Melchior Lorichs engraving of Süleyman I,
circa 1558

of the most exquisite textiles produced in the Islamic world. Two kaftans in the Topkapı
Palace Museum (plates 123a and b), once attributed to Sultan Bayezid II (1480–1504) but
now thought to have been woven for the future Murad III while that prince was still heir-
apparent around 1570, show the most brilliant application of the *saz* style to the art of
the loom, recalling the designs on pen and paper where the design must have originated
(plate 202). The later part of the sixteenth century saw such *hatāyī* motifs adapted to progressively more symmetrical and repetitive designs (plate 124), but the magic of the style
often referred to as the '*saz* leaf and rosette' style was such that the curved leaves and
palmettes continued to appear in silk weaving even after a decline in fineness of weaving
and abased dye quality had robbed them of their fire and fury.[13]

The evidence from Ottoman miniature paintings (plate 125) suggests that simpler,
repetitive designs in *kemhā*, together with the even plainer and less expensive monochrome
atlās fabrics, were used in the majority of silk garments, and even these garments, less
expensive than other silk clothing in a relative sense, could be afforded only by the wealthiest
sections of society. And we should not be misled by our conventional notions about
Islamic art to assume that the more complex designs and the brighter and more colourful
textiles were necessarily preeminent either in price or in status. Certainly no more majestic
Ottoman textile has come down to us than the simple, indeed austere *kemhā* from Lyons
with its great crescent forms (plate 115). And various sources attest to the Ottoman taste
for fortuitous or quasi-fortuitous patterning. This frequently results in art of an almost
abstract simplicity, such as the bizarre imitation-marble designs on Ottoman tiles, or the
Ottoman love of cut veined stones of various sorts. *Ebrū* or marbled paper was a high

art form in Ottoman times, and abstract calligraphic patterns were much cultivated (plates 165, 174 to 183); we should therefore not be surprised to find *moiré* patterning frequently employed in textiles. The very word itself derives from *mohair* (itself derivative of the Arabic *mukhayyar* or 'by choice') used to describe cloth woven from the hair of the Angora (Ankara) goat, which was given a pattern by the deliberate application of 'waves' of water to the surface of the textile. Various sources speak of 'watered camlet' or mohair cloth in Turkey, but the technique was also applied to monochrome silks, the most impressive being the black silk kaftan woven for Sultan Süleyman the Magnificent around 1555. Melchior Lorichs of Flensburg, the north European artist who accompanied the Habsburg ambassador Busbecq to İstanbul, depicted the awesome ruler in this garment (plate 126), which has survived in excellent condition in the Topkapı collection.[14]

Embroideries

We have so far discussed what is probably the best-known aspect of Ottoman textile production, the woven silks—velvets, brocaded figured textiles, and satins—produced mainly by the guilds of Bursa and İstanbul, and to a lesser extent in some provincial centres in the Ottoman Empire from Chios to Damascus. There is, however, another category of Ottoman Turkish textiles, less understood in an historical sense, which although less well known in the West until the nineteenth century, represents an equally fascinating group of artistic creations. These are embroideries—textiles consisting of a one-colour or undyed, unornamented basic woven ground, on which the design is then added by means of a needle and threads of many colours. Whereas in brocaded textiles the design is woven into the fabric on the loom, requiring complex technology in the form of heddles manipulating the warps and wefts, the technique of embroidery can create designs of equal or greater complexity with the simplest of technologies: a piece of plain-woven cloth of silk, cotton, linen or wool stretched on a frame; a basket of coloured yarns; a simple bone, ivory, or metal needle; plus a repertoire of basic decorative stitches and a great deal of imagination. Embroidery as an art form in Ottoman times does not appear to have been organized extensively on a commercial basis until the seventeenth century, and remained throughout Ottoman history a largely domestic activity, and hence not subject to guild control, *ihtisāb* regulations, or an organized system of marketing. The earliest and in some senses the most impressive examples of Ottoman imperial embroidery, such as two magnificent kaftans from the first half of the sixteenth century in the Topkapı collections (plate 135), follow strictly the traditions of book illumination and textile design then current at the court, interpreting the *chintamani* and cloud-band motifs in an entirely orthodox way in line with the classical precepts governing Ottoman art at the time. By contrast, other branches of this intriguing art form represent the alter ego of the classical Ottoman style: a sixteenth-century *bohça* in the Topkapı collections (plate 149) impresses one by its gay colours and literally free-wheeling design.

Ottoman embroidery follows a basic repertoire of stitches, which vary in fineness according to the ground material and the function of the particular object, as well as to the whim of the artist. The very heavy embroidery in silk and metal thread found on the early kaftans mentioned above is despite the large size of the garments themselves done in very fine stitches dictated by the curvilinear nature of the designs, and executed with no reference at all to the weave of the ground cloth, which in any event is completely covered by the embroidery. The more commonly-encountered Turkish embroideries of the late sixteenth century and beyond, by contrast, employ a group of standard stitches, such as the rectangular *atma* stitch, the diagonally-twilled 'Turkish' stitch, and the *ince* or 'narrow' stitch, all of which use the weave of the ground cloth as a basis of fineness, and which can be termed 'counted' stitches.[15]

Extrapolating from the number of surviving examples in the Topkapı collections, embroidered kaftan robes and other embroidered forms of ceremonial dress were made in earlier Ottoman times in far smaller numbers than the ubiquitous brocaded, satin and velvet robes. Indeed, there appears to be a sort of implied hierarchy for the use of various techniques in textiles, in which embroideries play a restricted role. Brocaded figured silks were used primarily for ceremonial robes; velvets were the preferred technique for draperies, curtains, pillows, and the like; silk embroidery was a preferred technique for clothing accessories, smaller and more intimate furnishings, and for the squares—kerchiefs, napkins, and wrappers or *bohça*—which formed a part of house etiquette and ceremony. Embroidery in heavy metal thread, a restricted form, seems to have been practised, on the basis of surviving examples, largely on military attire, being found on saddles, quivers, cuirasses, and the like (plate 136).

The freedom from strict control is evident in their great freshness of design, but it makes their dating problematic, and one is again forced to rely on the more or less unreliable dates associated by tradition with much of the Topkapı material. The two kaftans mentioned above can be easily dated by comparing them with book illumination and ceramic building decoration. But how does one date the red-ground *bohça* from the Topkapı on plate 149 with its design of multicoloured rotating pinwheels? There is a compelling magic to the design, and the simplicity of conception together with the high quality of execution tempt one to assign a desirable sixteenth-century date, but one looks in vain for a dateable parallel. Closely similar in its bold use of a simple design is the *bohça* with *chintamani* design in plate 148, each threesome of crescent-like 'pearls' flanked by two curved leaves, embroidered on a yellow *atlās* ground. Here there is more evidence for a secure seventeenth-century dating, especially in the simplified form of the serrated lancet leaves, with their parallel in other seventeenth-century decoration. Generally speaking, the use of brightly-coloured satin as a ground for embroidery appears to be characteristic of many of the earlier examples, giving way by the second half of the seventeenth century to a predominance of cotton, linen, or even silk gauze as a ground material.

The two largest groups of Turkish embroideries to come down to us are those on plain white or off-white fabric: the large panels using classical floral designs and frequently showing ogival layouts; and the smaller 'Turkish towels' and Ottoman domestic embroideries of the eighteenth to the twentieth centuries[16] which were created in great variety in most urban areas in the Ottoman Empire from Belgrade to Baghdad.

The larger white-ground panels with designs related to the Ottoman classical tradition form an enigmatic chapter in the history of Turkish art. There is no question that their designs are in keeping with the broader range of court art of the sixteenth and seventeenth centuries, but the dates of the panels themselves are still open to question. Scholars such as Macide Gönül have assigned certain examples to the magical sixteenth century,[17] but as more and more examples have come to light, we are able to see in their chronology a steady evolution from the sixteenth to the nineteenth century.

The designs of these textiles are generally not unique but of a repetitive nature with the exception of the smaller *bohça* and kerchief squares. The techniques are likewise limited to a few basic types of counted stitches.[18] These factors suggest that the large white-ground panels of Ottoman embroidery may have been produced under stricter control than the familiar domestic embroideries of the nineteenth century, and that many if not all of the white-ground panels were destined to be sold on the market rather than used by their makers as furnishings or gifts. The question of their intended function is also intriguing; like most of the velvets and brocaded silks, most of these panels have a definite top and bottom. Since these embroideries were not obviously intended for cutting and tailoring into costumes (few such costumes survive, and embroidery on costume was normally done after the tailoring process), they present some analogies with later Ottoman velvets in terms of their probable function. The smaller squares or *bohça* were almost certainly used as storage wrappers or kerchiefs, but the larger panels were probably intended to be curtains or simply flat decorative panels hung on interior walls of dwellings, a common form of interior decoration in all traditional cultures and one especially favoured in the Middle East. The white ground in these panels, and the particular choice of designs, also suggest they were used as wall decoration, for in both colouring and design the bulk of these panels imitate the white-ground brilliantly coloured İznik ceramic tile revetments gracing secular and religious buildings of the sixteenth and seventeenth centuries.[19]

127. İznik tile panels from the mosque of Rüstem Paşa, Istanbul, mid-16th century

A well-known example in the Art Institute of Chicago illustrated in plate 147 amply demonstrates this relationship: the design shows a diapered pattern of tulips flanked by the serrated *saz* style leaves. The first dateable appearance of this sort of design is in 1561, in the tile revetments of the Rüstem Paşa mosque in İstanbul (plate 127), but the setting of the basic motif in the ogival lattice in the Chicago piece suggests a date around 1600, still placing this example among the earliest known on the basis of its careful execution and relative closeness to the ceramic prototypes.

By contrast, two more examples show a development away from the original theme. On one, illustrated in plate 152, the diapered lattice has disappeared, and small floral forms without direct parallel in classical Ottoman art have made their appearance in the interstices among the tulips. In accordance with later Ottoman decoration, the tulips themselves are plump and almost fruit-like, with their three petals and the calyx separated from each other by the white ground, in exactly the same fashion as tulips were portrayed in the famous sealing wax red pigment on the surface of İznik tiles and table wares. The border, with its alternating leaves and tulips, still bears a relationship to the field. A striking development of the design is seen in another example (plate 153), where the sense of a diapered pattern has been preserved in a wiry lattice decorated with tiny red tulips and white carnations. Here the large red tulips are even plumper and juicier, and their petals themselves bear decorations of still smaller tulips. The border is a complex ornamental reciprocal stripe, and the infinite arabesque-like nature of the field design, as in a field of repeating modular tiles, is cut by the narrow border stripe at each edge of the panel.

Another favourite design used in Ottoman white-ground embroideries with an overall

128. İznik tile panel, second half of the 16th century. MMA 17.190.2083

diapered or ogival pattern is the floral escutcheon (plate 128), a device which first appears in Ottoman art at the end of the sixteenth century in the Takyeci İbrahim Ağa mosque in İstanbul, and which enjoyed a brief vogue in the early seventeenth century in tile-work of both Istanbul and Kütahya.[20] The escutcheon itself is probably derived from a serrated palmette found frequently in sixteenth-century brocaded textiles and velvets as that illustrated on plates 116 and 132. It represents a design which moves from textiles to ceramics, and then back again to textiles. In some examples, closely related to brocaded prototypes, the embroidered escutcheon is set in an ogival lattice formed by curved leaves (plate 138) while in others there is a much heavier emphasis on the framing of the constituent elements (plate 139). In each case there are prototypes in wall tiles which again strongly suggest both the origins of the designs of the embroideries and their probable function.

A third motif, found less frequently in embroideries but with a much deeper lineage in Islamic art, is the lotus palmette. First appearing in Islamic art in the fourteenth century, undoubtedly having found its way into the Near East through lines of communication with China established under the Il-Khanid Mongols, the lotus flower, with its crab-like petals around a complex central calyx, is again one of the basic elements of the *hatāyī* or 'Cathayan' repertoire of Ottoman Turkish art, but was well-established in Egypt, Anatolia, and Iran as early as 1350. In one of its relatively rare appearances in embroidery the lotus flower is used again in an upright, repetitive design, on a lobed bright red surround, in the company of multicoloured tulips and serrated leaves (plate 143). The composition is of extraordinary impact and shows the capacity of Ottoman artists to create fresh and original compositions using the familiar classical vocabulary in new combinations.

The eighteenth century began in Ottoman Turkish art with a period known retrospectively as the 'Epoch of Tulips'. During the reign of Ahmed III (1703-30), there was a self-conscious attempt in the Ottoman Empire to recreate the glories of the past, not so much through military conquest as through cultural eclecticism and the revival of older types of artistic expression, thus emphasizing a continuity in the arts with what Ottoman historians nostalgically recognized as the great days of the Empire in the sixteenth century. All of the arts of this period show that conscious attempts were made to emulate the classical style. At enormous expense the Grand Vezir re-opened a ceramic factory in a site on the city walls of İstanbul so that buildings of the period might have their interiors decorated with the appropriate white-ground tile panels. When we look at embroideries of that period we see continuity with earlier traditions, but also a perceptible distance from the sixteenth-century canons filtered as they were through the prism of the seventeenth. This is accompanied in some cases by a coarsening in the stitches, and even by a restricted range of colours employed. The familiar patterns continued in use: the floral escutcheon remained a favourite device (plate 141), but the floral forms themselves became progressively more stylized, simplified, and formulaic in nature, exchanging their naturalism for a more abstract beauty (plate 142). The context in which flowers appeared still frequently recalled much earlier prototypes: the fat and extremely stylized tulips nodding to left and right along vines on plate 155 have lost the stencil-like form they had in the seventeenth century, but the overall disposition of forms is derived directly from tile panels created in 1560 for the Rüstem Paşa mosque shown on plate 127. The glorious *chintamani* forms which ushered

Russian chasubles made with 16th-century Ottoman silk brocade, Armoury museum, Kremlin:
129a. *Sakkos* of the Metropolitan Anthony of Moscow (1572–1581)
129b. *Sakkos* of the Metropolitan Dionyssi of Moscow (1581–1587)

in the great age of Ottoman velvets in the fifteenth century also appear in later embroideries as on plate 156 having taken on new decorative serrations in the crescent forms, with no sign of the waves which originally surged under the pearls of Buddhist origin.

Ottoman Turkish textiles were embedded in social custom in a variety of ways which affected their artistic nature. Embroidery was an activity closely linked with the upbringing of young women, being an appropriate way for girls, confined by social custom to their urban dwellings, to pass the time in useful activity.[21] Unlike the impersonality of the weaving process, where the weaver labouring on a bolt of cloth had no idea whether the final product would emerge as a kaftan robe, a pair of *şalvar* or baggy pants, or even as a European ecclesiastical cope gracing the shoulders of a clergyman celebrating Mass in some far-away cathedral (plate 129), the embroidery artist knew that she was working on a final product. The works of art she created were connected with social customs of Ottoman life; the popular folklore of the Sultan's harem, for example, told of a custom whereby the ruler selected his bedmate from among a group of eligible young women by bestowing upon the favoured one an embroidered *çevre* or kerchief. Ogier Ghiselin de Busbecq, in his mid-sixteenth-century commentary on Turkish customs, mentions the award of an embroidered kerchief as a prize in archery competitions held outside the walls of Galata above the Golden Horn.

The larger *bohça* was a square embroidered textile used as a wrapper or carrying bag, and is mentioned in the scholarly literature as used for the wrapping and storage of other textiles. Be this as it may, it is often difficult to imagine that any textiles so wrapped could have been of higher quality or greater beauty than the *bohça* itself, as two examples decorated with carnations strongly attest (plates 144 and 145).

Panels or even entire bolts of cloth found various uses in Ottoman society. Bolts of cloth were frequently employed by civil authorities as barriers to hold back crowds during royal processions, as testified by a well-known painting from the reign of Mehmed III, in the Topkapı Palace Library, which shows recognizable and familiar patterns on the textiles themselves.[22] The custom of laying bolts of cloth on the ground before the mounted sovereign on festive occasions is also documented in miniature painting, with an example in the *Sūrnāme* or 'Book of Festivals' of Murad III, painted in 1584, showing what appear to be bolts of silver and gold cloth being employed in this fashion.[23] Another ceremonial use of textiles was in the form of banners. Flags, pennants, and banners of all sorts made in brocaded, *appliqué*, and embroidery techniques were in common use in Ottoman society. They accompanied army detachments, they were used in religious processions, and they appeared in abundance on festival days.[24]

The giving of a kaftan or robe of honour was an established custom in many royal courts, and its importance in Islamic society can be documented from early times, when *ṭirāz* or royal factories were established specifically for the production of such royal gifts. The ceremonial robe also formed a contractual part of the remuneration of salaried government officials and kaftans were also given as gifts to foreign ambassadors, thus finding their way to the West. Although Tahsin Öz surmised that a certain type of very coarse off-white silk robe brocaded with large-scale dull-yellow designs could be identified with fourteenth-century Ottoman production (plate 120), an identical example preserved in the Berlin collections was given as a ceremonial gift to an ambassador of Frederick the Great of Prussia in the eighteenth century.[25]

Furnishings in the middle and upper-class urban dwellings in Ottoman times provided another market for textiles. The formal living quarters (*selāmlık*) in a Turkish house were generally furnished around the periphery with low built-in benches, which were covered with carpets, heavy textiles, and cushions known as *yastık*. In village society such cushions were made of small carpets, but in the urban setting they were made of velvet, often brocaded with metal thread.

The official audiences and meetings of royal and court officials were held amidst lavish furnishings of textiles of all kinds. Carpets were spread on the ground before the Padishah or Sultan when he held a royal audience, and the expression 'called on the carpet' richly suggests the abject state in which a courtier prostrated himself before his all-powerful sovereign. Miniature paintings of the early eighteenth century, illustrating a 'Book of Festivals' of Ahmet III and painted by the famous court painter Levni, show elaborate forms of textile architecture, with a multitude of tents, walls, canopies, barriers and ground coverings of all sorts creating miniature cities. Woven, embroidered and *appliqué* buildings such as arenas, amphitheatres, dining and audience halls were made expressly for the complex royal ceremonies associated with the circumcision of the Sultan's sons.[26]

For such occasions, although the gorgeous robes of honour worn by the various officials must have attracted considerable attention, there were other articles of clothing which also called forth examples of the textile arts. Among the most beautiful were leather and cloth boots, often elaborately worked in embroidery and *appliqué*, of brilliant colours and rich arabesque designs as those in plate 137.

The position of textiles in the religious context of Islamic society is much more ambig-uous than the secular opulence we have just discussed might indicate. There are strong traditions (*Ḥadīth*) ascribed to the Prophet Muhammad which argue against the wearing of silk and other luxurious materials, especially by men, and there is a popular saying that 'he who wears silk in this world will forego it in the next.'[27] The coexistence of Islamic fundamental beliefs with the opulence of the Ottoman royal court was in many ways an uneasy one, but the lack of an independent power base for religious authorities in the Ottoman state, and the role of the Sultan as propagator of the Holy War against the infidel, meant in practical terms that the religious authority had to find a *modus vivendi* with the court and the powerful guilds involved in the production of such luxury goods. Miniature paintings depicting the high religious dignitaries attending court functions invariably show them wearing coloured robes without any brocaded designs, although it is open to speculation whether the material used was silk.

The silk industry in particular adapted its techniques to serve religious ends. A well-established genre of Ottoman weaving was the so-called 'tomb cover', actually a textile meant to decorate cenotaphs in the shape of sarcophagi or *sandūka* found in the commem-orative structures or *türbe* erected over the burial sites of sultans, important secular officials and holy men. These textiles exhibit a design of zig-zag stripes ornamented with various sorts of inscriptions brocaded on either a green or a red satin ground in ivory-coloured undyed silk. The inscriptions on the red-ground pieces like the one illustrated on plate 160 tend to be the same, including the Profession of Faith ('There is no God but God; Muham-mad is the Messenger of God'), various invocations of the attributes of God ('Oh all-Merciful!') and short Qur'ānic passages.[28] The inscriptions found on the green-ground pieces such as plate 158 are much more varied, but again are drawn from the Qur'ān or from prayers (*duʿā*) appropriate to the commemorative function. Many of these textiles have found their way to the West, and only a very few are still to be found in Turkey, among which are those in the *türbe* of Sultan Süleyman.

In the world of Ottoman Turkish textiles, rugs obviously occupy a most important place. Abundant literature exists on knotted-pile and flat-woven rugs of Ottoman court-related ateliers, Turkish commercial factories, and the countless village and tribal rug weaving traditions which even today live on in vestigial form in Anatolia.[29] There is a marked interplay in design between certain genres of village rugs and silk textiles, es-pecially the velvets, in small-format pieces such as the *yastık* pillow-covers, and through the centuries one can see silk patterns having a profound influence on many types of knotted pile carpets, such influence moving in the other direction much more infrequently.

For reasons of scope carpets cannot be treated in detail here. There are however some carpets which reflect a particular stylistic concept of Ottoman art referred to elsewhere in this book as 'the plain tradition'. It is more commonly associated with the decoration of architectural exteriors, metalwork and some textiles and shows through its simplicity a remarkable elegance and grandeur. An early *saf* or multi-niched prayer rug from the Berlin collections illustrated on plate 157 is one example of how the austerity and simplicity of the arched design, in combination with the brilliant colouring which is the hallmark of Anato-lian weaving, produce an effect of great richness without abundant detail. This combination of simplicity and richness may also be seen on plate 159, a fragmentary carpet of the sixteenth or seventeenth century, where a small medallion, incorporating a form of split leaf arabesque in a quatrefoil disposition, long part of the Turkic carpet tradition, sits in the middle of an unornamented red field in a stark but powerful composition. The elegant cloud band pattern in the border should also be compared with those on metalwork (plate 24), ceramics (plate 103), textiles (plate 136) and painting (plate 204).

The so-called Ottoman court carpets were executed in the same technique as the 'Mamluk' Cairene carpets, from designs made in the *nakkāshāne* or court design ateliers in İstanbul. They utilized the *hatāyī* designs and the stylized flowers commonly found on silk textiles but their range of colours was more restricted, akin to that found on the 'Mamluk' Cairene carpets.

On very rare occasions one medium affected another; such is the case of an unusual embroidered carpet, illustrated on plate 130, which was probably made in İstanbul around the year 1600. Here, the colours and forms of a knotted pile carpet from the court ateliers have been quite literally translated into a large and impressive embroidery. Executed in polychrome silks on a multicoloured ground, its range of colours includes maroon, blue, green and ivory, recalling the palette of the court carpets.

One last technique of Ottoman carpets is that of the tapestry woven rug or *kilim*, which until fairly recently was assumed to be confined to a village or nomadic production in Anatolia, with little if any relationship to the tradition of court textiles. Here again, our point of view has been modified by recent discoveries of *kilims* in curvilinear designs such as the prayer rug illustrated on plate 154, which can be dated as early as the seventeenth century, and which partake of the full vocabulary of decorative forms seen in other genres of textile production[30] and Ottoman art in general.

It is clear that the production of textiles was an artistic endeavour which in Ottoman times was of great economic, social, and cultural importance. In an empire where many races and social groups lived in relative tranquillity side by side, sumptuary conventions and laws defined one's presentation in public very largely in great detail. In a highly structured society which stipulated complex systems of rank, costume and the textiles used in costume were the chief determinants of the manner in which one moved through society on an everyday basis. And in an economy where textile weaving was a prime area of manufacture and therefore taxation, one should not be surprised to see a great deal of attention being paid to velvets, brocaded silks, satins, embroideries, *appliqué* work, rugs and other fabrics. What makes this situation more important than simple historical curiosity is that it involved artistry, human creativity of a very high order.

The combination of creative processes which produced Ottoman decorative textiles was successful in its own time, but the artistic voice with which the best Ottoman textiles not only speak but sing has lasted for many centuries. Its clarity and pitch have not altered and the charm and fascination intensify as we turn from the lonely cacophony of the age of mass production to the visual music of another time.

THE PLATES

1 (frontispiece)
Velvet

First half of 16th century

Large carnations in repeat are common ornaments on Bursa *kadīfe* or velvet, but rarely appear in this disposition on brocaded silks. Unlike most such velvets, however, the carnations here are interrelated, the lines separating the petals forming elegant parabolic curves. The elegance of the drawing may suggest an early date within the internal chronology of these carnation velvets.

115 (detail)
Brocaded Silk; 'kemhā'

First half of 16th century

Few Ottoman brocaded silks can match the stark simplicity and power of this piece whose diagonally offset rows of crescents are adapted from the *chintamani* motif (see plate 54).

Published: *Etoffes Merveilleuses*, vol. III, Tokyo 1976, plate 61

Musée Historique des Tissus, Lyons, no. 35488 (972.IV.1)

Width (of whole): 66 cm; Length: 124 cm

130 (detail)
Needlework Carpet

Probably 16th century

With few stylistic ties to the mainstream of Turkish embroidery over the centuries, this virtually unique piece represents an attempt to create a large needlework carpet with the general patterning of the so-called 'court carpets'. As with many of the Ottoman court rugs, the major design elements (the medallion and quarter-medallions) are not well adapted to the overall shape. The stereotyped quality of the paired cloud-bands suggests that the artist or artists responsible for this lavish piece did not have complete familiarity with either the enormous scale of the work or the carpet designs used in it.

Published: M. Gönül, *Turkish Embroideries*, İstanbul, plate 30

Topkapı Sarayı Müzesi, İstanbul, no. 10
Width (of whole): 212 cm; length: 548 cm

131
Velvet

Second half of 16th century

Of the same basic design as plate 1, this piece is unusual for its length. The ivory-coloured areas of the pattern are brocaded with silver threads.

Width: 60 cm; length: 279 cm

132
Velvet

c. 1600

The two leaves sprouting from the calyx at the base of each palmette give an intimation of a diapered or ogival pattern in this typically patterned Bursa velvet. Small tulips and carnations punctuate the larger elements of the design both within and without the palmette forms.

The Freer Gallery of Art, Smithsonian Institution, Washington D.C.

Width: 63 cm; length: 85 cm

133
Brocaded Silk; 'kemhā'

Late 16th century

This richly designed brocade shows a complex development of the *chintamani* motif into double crescents, one within another, far removed from the austerity of plate 114, as sprays and garlands of small flowers add texture to the design. Another piece with this pattern is in the Musée des Arts Décoratifs in Paris.

Published: *La Collection Kelekian*, Paris 1908, plate 41

Width: 69 cm; length: 142 cm

134 (detail)
Velvet; 'çatma'

Second half of 15th century

The unusually fine weave and lustrous nap of this fragment of a garment help to identify it as Bursa *çatma* of the later fifteenth century. Most of the surviving fragments in this weave have variants of the *chintamani* design of stripes and dots.

Published: L. Mackie, *The Splendour of Turkish Weaving*, Washington DC 1973, plate 1

The Textile Museum, Washington D.C., no. 1.77

Width (of whole): 62 cm; length: 76 cm

135 (detail)
Embroidered Kaftan

First half of 16th century

Of the many ceremonial robes surviving in the İstanbul collections, few early examples are decorated with embroidery. This one made of red silk *atlās* or satin with a border heavily embroidered in yellow and blue silk, gold and silver wire, utilizes the *chintamani* motif, which various sources attest to be a favoured ornament for early Ottoman textiles, with its powerful associations as a talisman. The outline of the border should be compared with that of the central medallion in plate 150.

Published: E. Atil (ed), *Turkish Art*, New York 1980, p. 335, plate 64

Topkapı Sarayı Müzesi, İstanbul, no. 47

136
Embroidered Envelope

16th century

Historical sources mention the containers used for royal gifts, messages, diplomas and the like in Ottoman times. Here we have a relatively rare survivor of this genre, a velvet envelope lavishly embroidered in silk, gold and silver wire with curved *saz* leaves and sinuous Chinese cloud-bands (compare with a tile in plate 103 and an illuminated border in plate 204).

Published: M. Gönül, *Turkish Embroideries*, İstanbul, plate 24

Topkapı Sarayı Müzesi, İstanbul, no. 168

Length: 41 cm; height: 19 cm

137
Pair of Boots

16th century

Leather *appliqué*, gilt, and silk embroidery combine in these exquisite boots attributed to Selim II. The overall design of *rūmī* split-leaf arabesques is one of the most conservative and effective patterns in the Ottoman decorative vocabulary.

Published: *Splendeur de l'Art Turc*, Paris 1953, no. 488, plate 22

Topkapı Sarayı Müzesi, İstanbul, no. 2/1117

Length: 54 cm

138
Embroidered Panel

17th century

The artist of this panel owed considerable inspiration to tile designs and to earlier multicoloured *kemhā* brocaded silks, but by using a light blue for the almost wispy decorated *saz* leaves which form the diapering of the pattern, she allowed the red of the 'escutcheon' palmettes to dominate the design. A similar piece is published in *Imperial Ottoman Textiles*, London 1980, plate 28.

Width: 148 cm; length: 242 cm

139
Embroidered Panel

Mid-17th century

In contrast with plate 138 this panel emphasizes the diapering elements of the design as much as the powerful 'escutcheon' palmettes. The tulips, carnations, hyacinths and rosebuds within these palmettes are easily decipherable and should be compared to the tile panel in plate 128.

Width: 176 cm; length: 176 cm

140 (detail)
Embroidered Bed-Cover

17th century

This piece clearly demonstrates the spread of the Ottoman decorative repertoire to the provinces of the Empire. In the same stitch and basic colours as the preceding example, this Greek bedspread has a plain centre and is decorated along the four sides with a wide band containing the familiar tulips, rosebuds, hyacinths, serrated *saz* leaves and *chintamani*.

Private collection, Cologne

141
Embroidered Panel

Late 17th or 18th century

A powerful, if rather late, example of the use of the 'escutcheon' design, this example presents the familiar stylized flowers in heavily simplified and sometimes almost unidentifiable form, but the overall impression, due to the large scale of the repeating design units, is unusually strong.

A peculiar compositional feature common to

most white-ground embroideries is the manner in which the borders frame the field pattern. The latter is parallel to the side borders in the vertical direction; in the horizontal, however—at either top or bottom—the border cuts the pattern at an angle, often halfway through the motifs. This feature, far from being an imperfection as has often been suggested, adds a subtle dynamism to the composition and enhances the effect of the border forming a window into an endless repeat pattern.

H. Bartels collection, Bonn

Width: 160 cm; length: 230 cm

142
Embroidered Panel

18th century

The distance between the ascending vine-like forms is sufficiently great on this example for the sense of ogival design units to be almost entirely lost. Stylization and simplification of forms, a restricted palette of colours, and a very large scale of design add to the strength of the design, while blurring its historical heritage.

Wher Collection

143
Embroidered Panel

Early 17th century

The major repeating motif on this lovely example is the crab-like lotus palmette, a part of Ottoman decorative vocabulary from the fourteenth century onward. All of the forms are clear and easily readable, and the artist has borrowed from ceramic tile prototypes the device of showing elements of floral petals as if stencilled on the white ground. An intriguing aspect of this and other similar embroideries is the tendency to cast the major forms, such as the lotus blossoms here, against a red surround. While the result is to strengthen the sense of staggered rows of major motifs, the motifs themselves become more difficult to read.

A *bohça* with a very similar pattern is in the Topkapı Sarayı Collection, no. 159.

Wher Collection

Width: 142 cm; length: 239 cm

144
Embroidered Kerchief

Early 17th century

Almost small enough to be an *uçkur* or kerchief, this lovely example uses the *karanfil* or carnation as the major motif. It is most unusual among these white-ground embroideries in having no top and bottom. The rotation of the carnations and the use of the field motif for the border add subtlety and movement to the composition.

Antaki Collection

Width: 71.5 cm; length: 74.5 cm

145
Embroidered 'Bohça'

17th century

Much larger than on the preceding example, the carnations here are disposed in staggered rows as on the velvets (plate 131). The artist, working from bottom to top, has made each row of carnations marginally smaller than the preceding one and has created the impression of an endless repeat pattern by terminating the pattern halfway through the upper row of blossoms, a feature common to most of these white-ground panels. (For a related design in metalwork decoration see plate 34.)

Published: M. Gönül, *Turkish Embroideries*, İstanbul, plate 11

Topkapı Sarayı Müzesi, İstanbul, no. 16

Width: 100 cm; length: 100 cm

146 (detail)
Embroidered Panel

Late 17th or 18th century

One of the few examples in embroidery to derive from the brocaded silks with ogival cartouches (plates 118–21), the small-scale floral elements of this delicate example are given a focus through the red ogival outline. The interstices are decorated with floriated cloudbands and the small blossoms of the ogival medallions appear in a different arrangement in the borders.

Width (of whole): 151 cm; length: 252 cm

147 (detail)
Embroidered Panel

Late 16th–early 17th century

Closest in design to the ceramic wall-tile prototypes found in the sixties and seventies of the sixteenth century (plate 128), this magnificent embroidery also echoes the diapered design of sixteenth-century *kemhā* brocaded silks (plate 115). The tulips are attenuated, the embracing leaves are decorated with lovely five-petalled blossoms, and the ascending bands give the design a flowing quality not found in later examples.

Published: M. Gentles, *Turkish and Greek Island*

Embroideries, Chicago 1964, plate 6

Art Institute of Chicago, Burton Yost Berry Collection, no. 49.299

148
Embroidered 'Bohça'

17th century

The well drawn *chintamani* motifs are unusually enclosed within pairs of serrated leaves in this embroidery. The embroidery is executed in a counted stitch with a twill-like surface and all of the forms have been crisply outlined with contrasting colours. As in the carnation kerchief illustrated in plate 144 the border is decorated with the same design as the field.

Published: M. Gönül, *Turkish Embroideries*, İstanbul, plate 12

Topkapı Sarayı Müzesi, İstanbul, no. 7

Width: 137 cm; length: 137 cm

149
Embroidered 'Bohça'

Late 16th or early 17th century

On display in the Embroidery Galleries of the Topkapı Sarayı Müzesi for several years, this lovely *bohça* square is probably one of the best-known and certainly one of the most beautiful of classical Ottoman embroideries. The pinwheel design is roughly echoed in late-sixteenth-century tile patterns and is more frequently seen in incised metalwork (plate 5) and in Ottoman door fixtures, but the alternation of green and white on these motifs gives a strength here which is not encountered in other media. The smaller pinwheels used on the yellow ground border, and the exquisite corner articulation, all accomplished by varying the three basic colours between ground and two-colour motifs, add to the paradoxical impression of great subtlety within extreme simplicity.

Published: M. Gönül, *Turkish Embroideries*, İstanbul, plate 14

Topkapı Sarayı Müzesi, İstanbul, no. 6

Width: 124 cm; length: 130 cm

150
Embroidered Satin Kerchief

16th century

The curved *saz* leaves with their cockade leaflets on this very finely embroidered square argue for its Ottoman provenance; otherwise, its design vocabulary is common to both Iranian and Ottoman art of the sixteenth and early seventeenth centuries. Such squares are probably those referred to by Busbecq and others as being used for prizes in archery contests and other sports; this example is of unusual, royal beauty and richness, and one must suppose that many other examples from this period may have perished in the late-sixteenth-century fires in the Topkapı Sarayı living-quarters.

Width: 85 cm; length: 87 cm

151
Embroidered Panel

Late 17th or 18th century

Later panels of this type frequently trade clarity for visual texture; such is the case in this example, where the small floral forms within red cartouches, embraced by large serrated leaves, are not easily readable. Tiny dots stipple the red-ground areas, and the calyxes and cockades at the top and bottom of each basic unit in the design are free and loose in their drawing.

A similar example is in the Victoria and Albert Museum in London (published *The Old Textiles of Turkey*, Tokyo, plate 78), and another in the Arts Institute of Chicago (published M. Gentles, *Turkish and Greek Island Embroideries*, Chicago 1964, plate 15).

Width: 160 cm; length: 230 cm

152
Embroidered Panel

Late 17th or 18th century

A descendant of the embroidery in plate 147, this example has a pattern of ascending rows of tulips flanked by leaves. Comparable in stitch and colours to plate 151, the stippling of light-coloured dots on the petals of the tulips and the serrated leaves adds rich texture to the design.

Wher Collection: ex col. Prince S. A. Radziwill

Width: 155 cm; length: 253 cm

153
Embroidered Panel

Mid-17th century

Earlier than the similar panel illustrated in plate 152, this panel shows greater clarity in the disposition of rows of fat tulips, their petals decorated by rosebuds, in an orderly lattice of vines. The design is crisp and there are no departures from the discipline of the pattern; the narrow reciprocal border echoes the sense of orderliness of the field.

A. Ramsay Collection, London

Width: 175 cm; length: 266 cm

154
Tapestry Woven Prayer-Rug

17th or 18th century

One of a group of recently identified Turkish *kilim* rugs with affinities to classical court designs, this example incorporates floral motifs familiar from white-ground embroideries. The two inscriptions, both good wishes, read 'let there be blessings' and 'let there be prosperity'. The same inscription appears on a gilt copper jug with related floral decoration in plate 13d.

Published: Y. Petsopoulos, *Kilims*, London 1979, plate 61

Yanni Petsopoulos Collection

Width: 99 cm; length: 173 cm

155
Embroidered Panel

18th century

In comparing this example to the sixteenth-century prototype from the mosque of Rüstem Paşa (plate 127), we can see how simplified and schematized the design has become without, however, losing any of its charm.

Yanni Petsopoulos Collection

Width: 131 cm; length: 245 cm

156
Embroidered Panel

18th century

Appearing in the earliest datable Ottoman textiles (see plates 114 and 134), the power of this motif both in artistic tradition and as a popular talisman (*nazarlık*) is nowhere better witnessed than in its continual popularity in all media of Turkish art over the centuries. Here the 'crescent pearls' are grouped in the traditional threesomes, without the accompanying 'wave stripes'. The eye-like aspect of these forms has been emphasized by the artist, to the point of adding what appear to be 'lashes' in each pearl form.

Width: 112 cm; length: 206 cm

157
Knotted Pile 'Saf' Carpet

16th–17th century

Probably woven near Uşak in western Anatolia, this fragmentary rug with multiple prayer-niches was originally intended for a Turkish mosque. The arches, strongly evocative of the 'plain tradition' in the decoration of architectural exteriors, together with the reciprocal border and trefoil guard-stripe, blend with the simple colouring to give it a grandeur and an impact seldom rivalled. It exemplifies that peculiar tendency arising again and again in Ottoman art (plates 30, 33, 88 and 114) of reasserting a sense of elementary structure and clarity almost as a counterpoint to the complex and elaborate decorative repertoire.

Published: K. Erdmann, *700 Years of Oriental Carpets*, London 1970, plate XI

Museum für Islamische Kunst, Berlin-Dahlem, no. 25/61

Width: 329 cm; length: 128 cm (fragmentary)

158
Brocaded Green Silk Tomb-Cover

18th century

An examination of the available examples of green calligraphic tomb-covers shows that, unlike their red counterparts, they were made in a much larger variety of calligraphic patterns. The present example contains the Profession of Faith and verses from the Qur'ān (Sūra XXXIII, verses 40 and 56) concerning the Prophet. Another piece with an identical pattern is in the Musée Historique des Tissus, Lyons, published in A. Welch, *Calligraphy in the Arts of the Muslim World*, Austin 1979, no. 34.

159
Small Medallion Carpet

16th or 17th century

At one time west Anatolian carpets such as this were clearly thought to date from the seventeenth century, due to the simplification of the spandrel forms and border designs when compared to more sinuous and flowing prototype forms in bookbinding and manuscript illumination. However, evidence from European paintings of similar carpets existing in the West from the early sixteenth century onwards has broadened the possibilities for dating such carpets. Like the *saf* in plate 157, this carpet relies on the basic strength of simple colours and strong forms for its visual impact. Although this basic design of spandrels and medallion is common to countless examples of Anatolian carpet weaving, in few examples is the underlying structure of the design and especially the cloudband border allowed to speak more eloquently by the weaver than this example.

Published: Spuhler, König, Volkmann, *Old Eastern Carpets*, Munich 1978, no. 12

Private Collection, Bonn

Width: 81 cm; length: 149 cm (fragmentary)

130

131·132
133

13

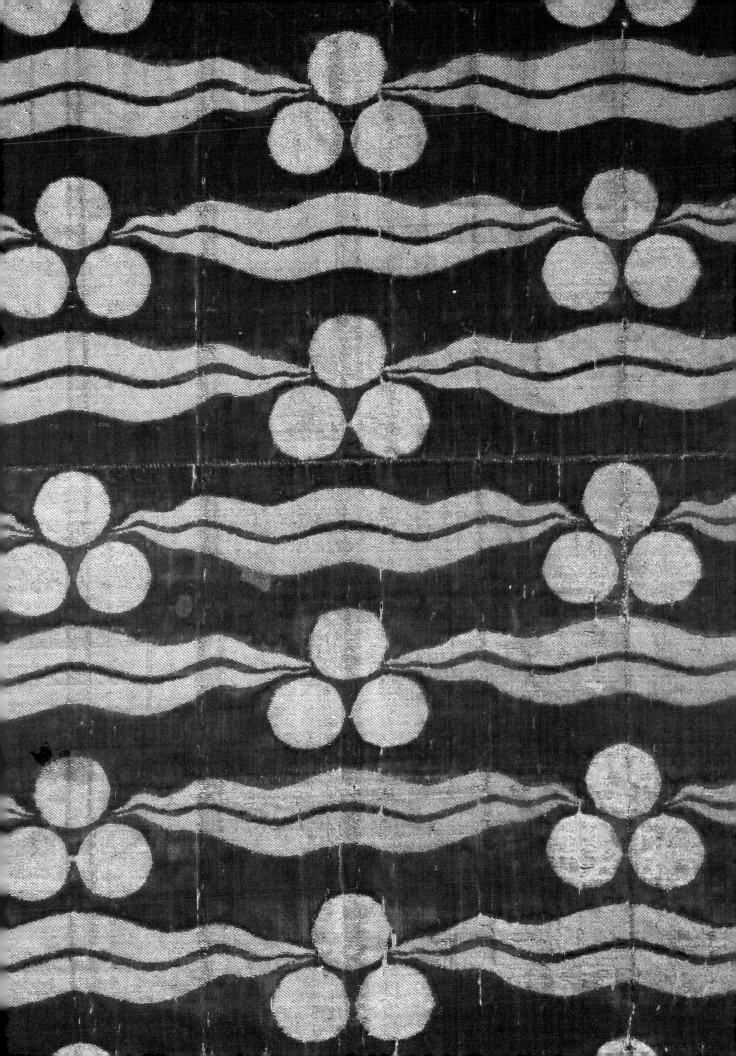

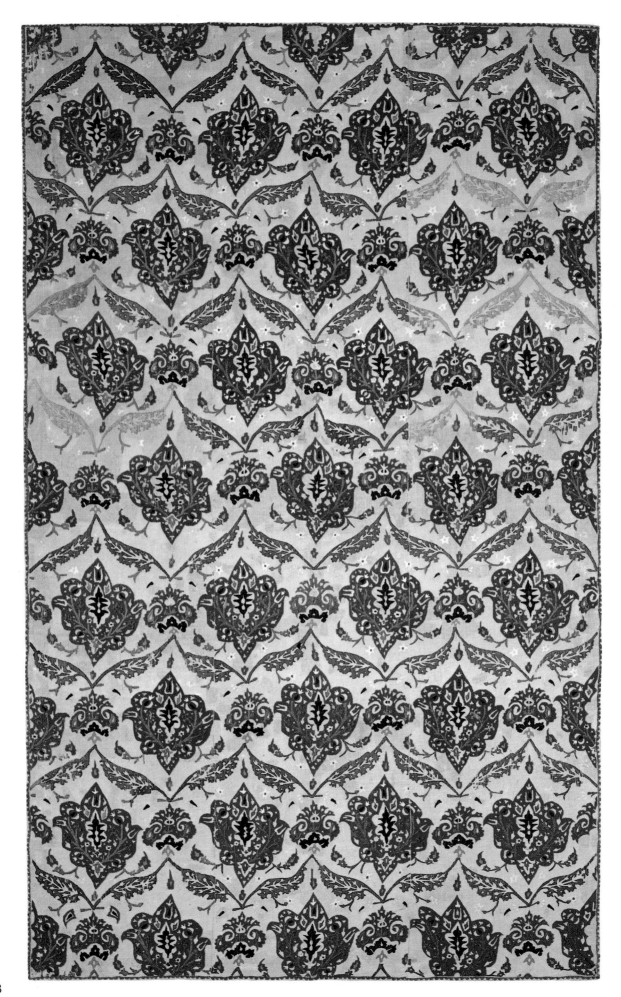

138

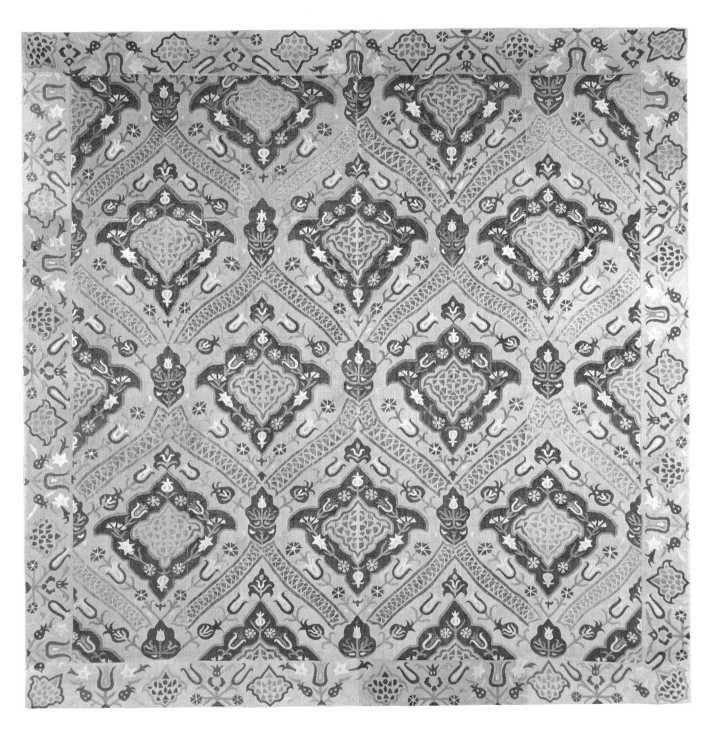

139
140

141

142

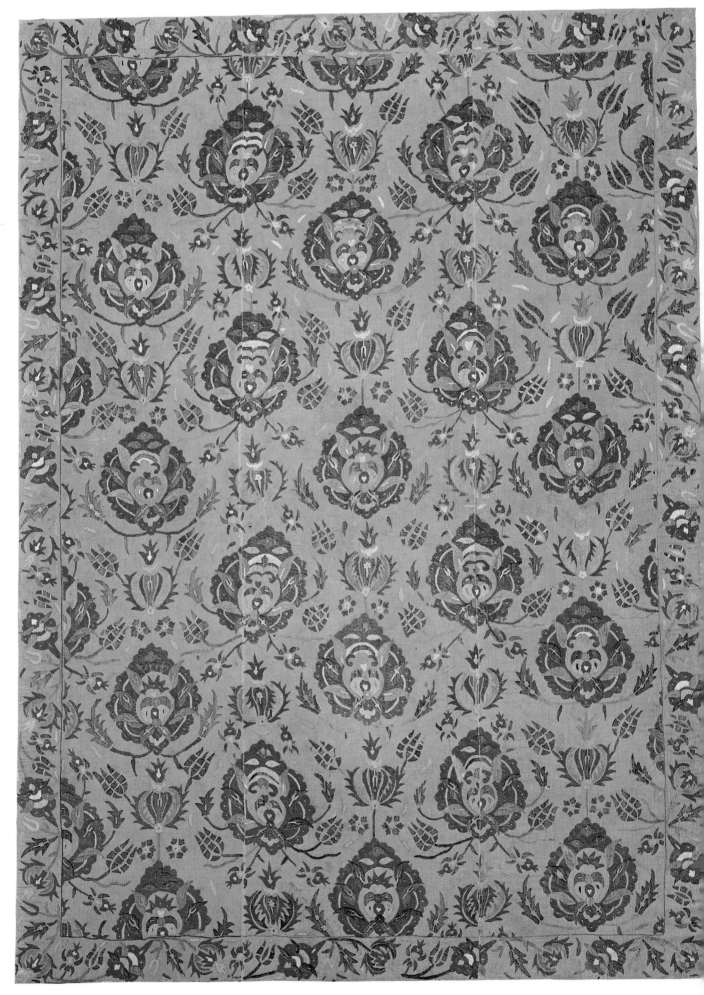

143

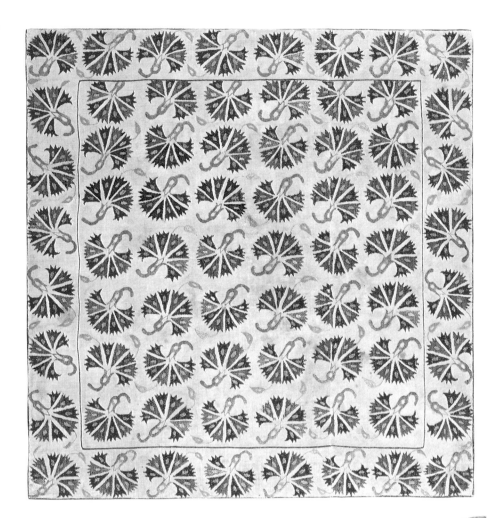

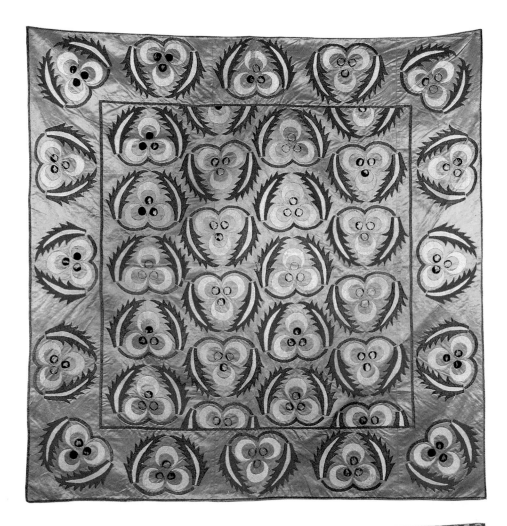

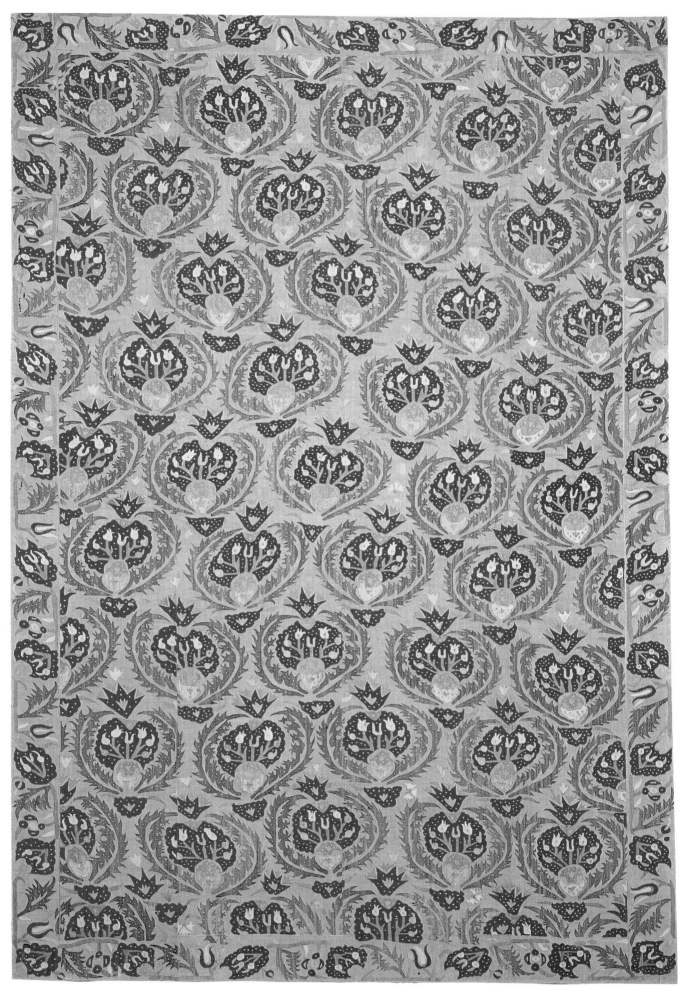

151

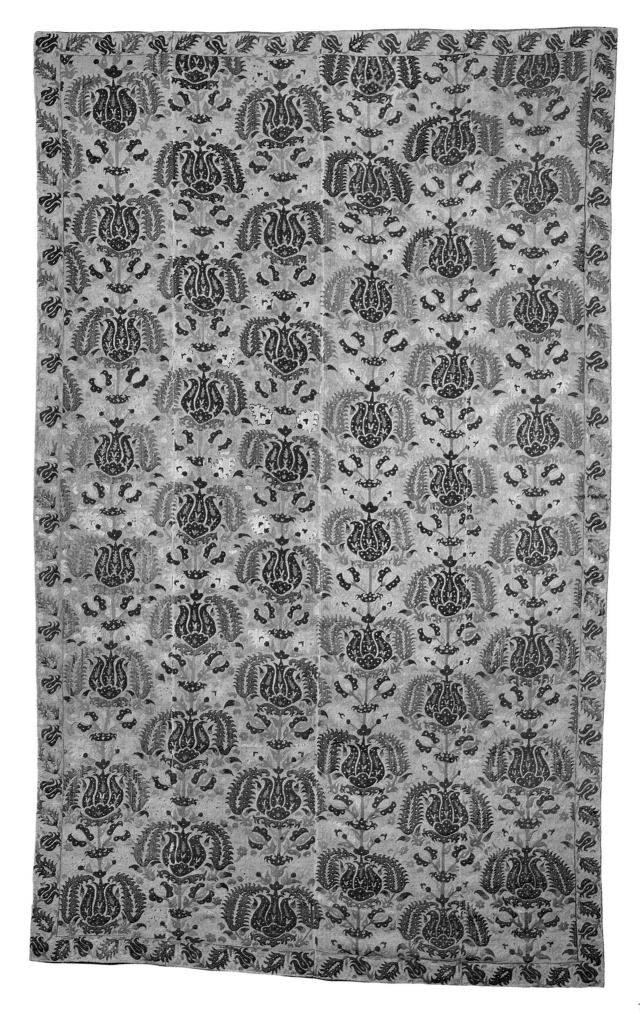

152

153

154

155

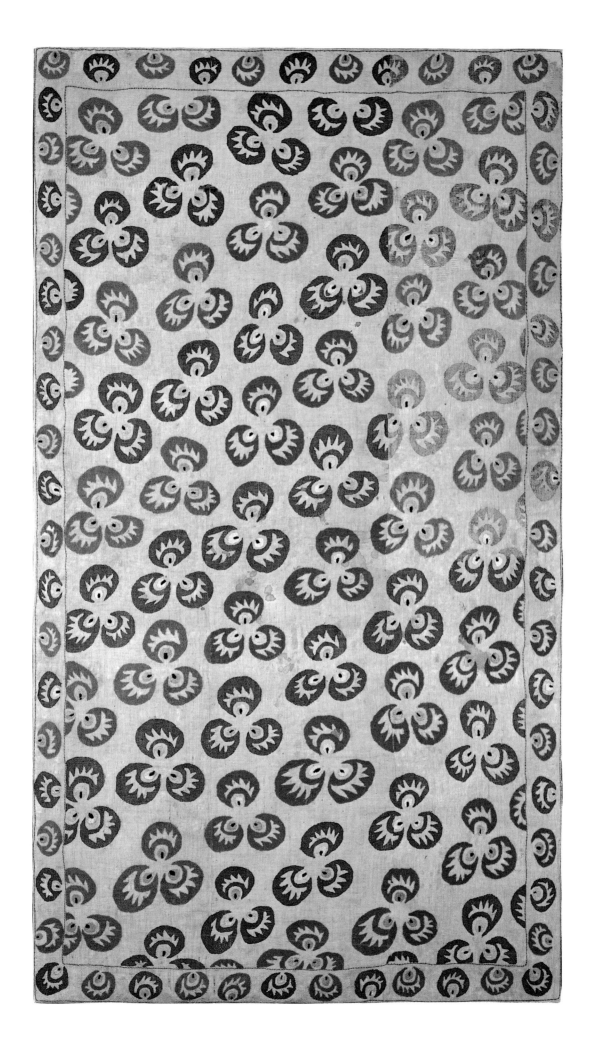

156

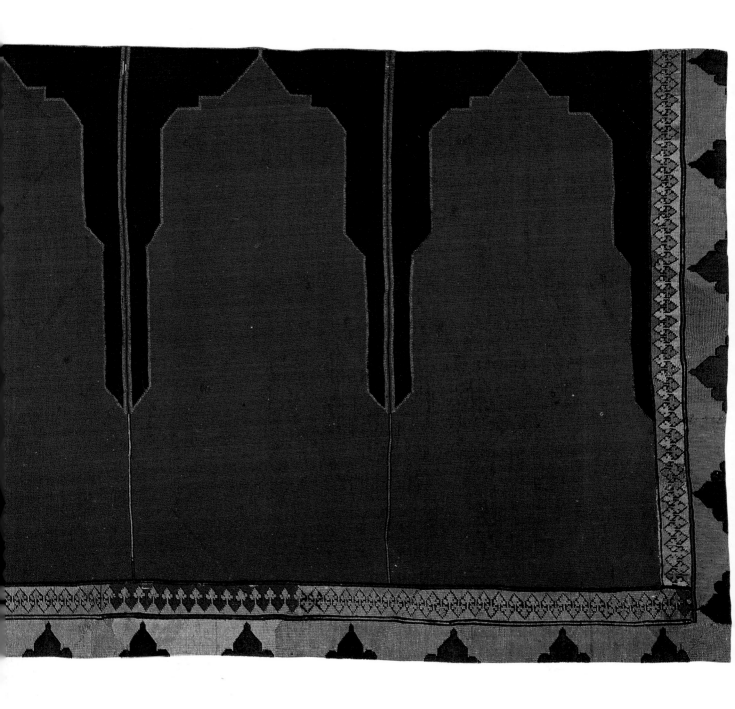

Calligraphy—Hüsn-i Hat

Heath Lowry

'*Yazı üstādın öğretişinde gizlidir,*
kıvamı çok yazmakladır, devamı
İslam dini üzere olmakladır.'[1]

'The art of calligraphy is hidden
in the teaching of the master,
its essence is achieved through
repetition, and it exists to serve
the religion of Islam.'
    (Saying attributed to the Caliph Ali)

To comprehend the role of calligraphy in Ottoman art one must begin by understanding the relationship of the three components introduced in the above quotation: the role of the master, the importance of repetition, and the almost mystical attachment which serves to bind the art of writing and the religion of Islam. Looking at this another way, we may trace the development of this art form via an unbroken chain of masters, each of whom built on the foundation of his predecessors with countless hours of practice in copying and repeating earlier models. Only when a student had achieved perfection in emulation was he issued an *icāzet* (diploma)[2] which allowed him to practise his art and in time train pupils of his own. If there was an underlying motivation tying the successive generations of calligraphers together it was their shared dedication to the glorification of Allah through the medium of the 'Beautiful Writing' of his words. For throughout Islamic history the primary subject matter of the calligraphers was the Holy Qur'ān, the word of God as revealed to his Prophet Muhammad. Each practitioner of the art proudly traced his *şecere* (pedigree)[3] back through generations of his predecessors to the Caliph Ali, honoured throughout the world of Islam as the first calligrapher.

In no period or place did the art of Islamic calligraphy rise to the heights that it achieved in the city of İstanbul between the fifteenth and nineteenth centuries. The Ottomans, as the last in the long line of great medieval Islamic dynasties, inherited the calligraphic traditions of Islam, preserved them, and raised them to a pinnacle never attained before. The frequently quoted Arabic saying: 'The Qur'ān was revealed in the Hicaz, recited in Egypt, and written in İstanbul',[4] reflects this reality which has long been accepted in the

Islamic east. In an art form whose greatness stems from repetition, this should not be surprising; in western eyes trained to appreciate individual styles, Ottoman calligraphy has yet to receive the recognition which is its due.

How may we explain this apprent discrepancy between the esteem granted to the art of *Hüsn-i hat* in the Islamic world and its failure to generate a similar interest in the west? First and foremost is the fact that to the Muslim, calligraphy is an integral part of the 'mystery' attached to his religion. Passed from generation to generation by an unbroken chain of masters it serves to unify a religious body divided by distance and culture but bound by its reverence for the word of God as revealed to his Prophet Muhammad and recorded in the Arabic language. It is the calligrapher's art which has preserved and transmitted this message throughout the past 1,400 years of Islamic history.

Implicit in this art is a 'timelessness' which is disturbing to the modern western eye, trained as it is to recognize the styles of individual artists in a given period of their work. For in Islamic calligraphy greatness must be judged first by the success of the practitioner in mastering the inherited past. Individual contributions to this heritage often take the form of subtle embellishments, appreciable only to the trained observer.

. Further, we bring to our appreciation of art a tendency to focus our attention upon the work of a few individual great masters of their crafts. When this approach is applied to Islamic calligraphy it forces a shift from the essential emphasis which must be placed upon the unbroken chain of fourteen centuries of development, to the highpoints or major links within it.

Finally, our training predisposes us to search for influences upon the art and artists we examine. While this approach may well be justified in the analysis of such Ottoman forms as architecture and miniature painting, it is unrewarding when applied to a cumulative art such as Islamic calligraphy, marked as it is by a gradual and steady development. For Ottoman calligraphy reached its zenith not in the glorious sixteenth century, but rather in the late nineteenth at a time when the empire was in collapse and most other art forms had succumbed to western influences.

Only by overcoming our own cultural predilections and prejudices, and by attempting to approach the study of Ottoman calligraphy from the perspective of its own practitioners, may we begin to appreciate its greatness.

The Calligraphers

It is to the ever-popular Islamic genre of 'Biographical Dictionaries' that we owe our ability to trace the unbroken *silsile* (chain) of Ottoman calligraphers. A whole series of such works, beginning with the *Menākıb-ı Hünerverān* of Mustafa Ali (1541–1600)[5] and continuing without a break through İbnülemin Mahmud Kemal's *Son Hattatlar*[6] (which covers calligraphers working between 1787 and 1955), provides us with the basic biographies of each and every Ottoman calligrapher. While often the biographical detail provided is scanty, it never fails to mention the names of the teachers from whom each calligrapher received his *icāzets* (diplomas), signifying his mastery of a particular script.

An analysis of the literally hundreds of calligraphers who flourished in the Ottoman Empire from the mid-fifteenth through to the end of the nineteenth century allows us to place them in one of three general categories in accordance with their primary activities. The first group consists of salaried teachers of penmanship; those calligraphers who instructed the young in the empire's religious primary schools. While on occasion we see a first-rate calligrapher in this category, this was the exception rather than the rule. In general their contribution consisted of encouraging students with obvious talent to follow up their interest in *Hüsn-i hat*.

The second group were the professional copyists or scribes who in a society bereft of printing earned their livelihoods by copying manuscripts on commission. Generally, though not always, the rigours of their occupations denied them the time necessary to train students of their own.

Finally, there were the professional teachers and artists: those calligraphers who spent their lives training the next generation of students. They were supported through stipends provided in return for their services in either the palace schools or the higher religious schools. In addition they undertook commissions for wealthy clients.

It was this latter group which supplied the overwhelming majority of calligraphers whose reputations have survived until the present. Consequently it is through a few selected members of this category that we must begin our examination of the role of calligraphy in the Ottoman Empire.

The 'chain' of every Ottoman calligrapher led back to Yakut al-Musta'simi (d. 1299), a Turk from Amasya who served as a secretary to the last 'Abbasid Caliph in Baghdad, al-Musta'sim (1242–58). Yakut was the first calligrapher to master completely the so-called *Aklām-i sitte* (Six Scripts, plate 161) with all their variations. By his formulation of the characteristics and rules for the writing of the 'Six Scripts' (Turkish: *Sülüs, Nesih, Muhakkak, Reyhānī, Tevkī'* and *Rık'a*), Yakut established the basis for calligraphy as it was to develop in the Ottoman period.[7]

During the next two hundred years, as the Ottomans began to spread their control throughout Anatolia and the Balkans, each succeeding generation of calligraphers faithfully copied the models laid down by Yakut. In the few scattered examples which have survived from the individual schools of calligraphy which flourished in the cities of Bursa, Amasya and Edirne, the most striking feature is the degree of faithfulness with which each preserved and transmitted the *Aklām-i sitte* of Yakut al-Musta'simi.

The first major step in the development of Ottoman calligraphy occurred following the conquest of Constantinople in 1453. Under the guidance of Sultan Mehmed II (1451–81) and his successors, the ruined shell of Byzantine Constantinople was transformed into İstanbul, the thriving capital of the Islamic world. A massive building programme which encompassed mosques, palaces, schools and public buildings (the decoration of each of which called for the special talents of the calligrapher) was begun. From all corners of the empire and the Islamic world artists and scholars found their way to the new centre of Islam.[8] Prominent among the 'Islamic Sciences' which developed as a result of this influx

161. A page setting from the *Aklām-i sitte* and their variations written by Kamil Akdik (1862–1941).

a. *Kūfī*
b. *Sülüs*
c. *Nesih*
d. *Reyhānī*
e. *Mukakkak*
f. *Tevkī'*
g & h. *İnce Tevkī'*
i. *Ta'līk*
j & k. *İnce Ta'līk*
l. *Dīvānī*
m. *Celī Dīvānī*
n. *Rık'a*
o. *İcāze*

was that of *Hüsn-i hat*. Given such a fertile atmosphere it was only a matter of time before the Ottoman love of and interest in calligraphy began to bear results.

It was during the reign of Mehmed's son and successor, Sultan Bayezid II (1481–1512), that the first great genius of Ottoman calligraphy was to manifest itself. As a prince ruling in the provincial capital of Amasya, Bayezid had begun the study of calligraphy under the tutelage of a local teacher, one Şeyh Hamdullah (1429–1520).[9] Upon assuming the Sultanate, Bayezid invited his former teacher to İstanbul and gave him a workroom in the palace. Legend has it that the Sultan frequently sat for hours holding Hamdullah's inkstand as he wrote. In the course of one such visit, while discussing the work of Yakut al-Musta'simi, Bayezid inquired of the Şeyh as to whether it was possible to improve upon the *Aklām-i sitte* as set down by Yakut? Hamdullah's response was to secrete himself away for forty days, after which he emerged with a completely new style of writing the 'Six Scripts'. Known as the *Şeyh Hamdullāh üslūbu* (style), the forms he created not only brought an end to the dominance of Yakut's influence, but set the pattern which Ottoman calligraphy was to follow until the eighteenth century. So closely was his style copied by successive generations that the highest compliment later calligraphers could aspire to was to be called a *Şeyh-i sāni*, 'the Second Şeyh' (plate 173).

The only major figure in the sixteenth century who was able to withstand the influence of Şeyh Hamdullah was Ahmed Karahisari (1469–1566).[10] He took Yakut as his model and succeeded in advancing his own *üslūb*. His work, much of which is particularly appealing to the western eye, is marked by its innovation and boldness (plate 183). While responsible for many major works during the reign of Süleyman the Magnificent (1520–66), he failed to establish a school of his own or to dislodge the *Şeyh Hamdullāh üslūbu*. Later calligraphers frequently copied his work as an exercise, but it was the 'style' of the Şeyh to which they devoted their efforts.

The influence of Hamdullah remained paramount until the second half of the seventeenth century when it was broken by the man who was to emerge as perhaps the greatest of the Ottoman practitioners of the art, Hafiz Osman (1642–98).[11] Based on a synthesis of the styles of Yakut and Hamdullah, to which he added the refinements of simplicity and purity, he evolved an *üslūb* of his own which for succeeding generations was to replace that created by Şeyh Hamdullah (plate 174). His reputation and widespread popularity throughout the Islamic world, even today, stems in part from the fact that it was the Qur'āns which he had written that were printed and reproduced in the nineteenth century. The real measure of his greatness, however, is attested to by the devotion with which later generations of calligraphers imitated and emulated his 'style'.

He became the prototype of the calligrapher in later centuries and the stories of his life and activities make up an essential part of the 'lore' which each master passed on to his students. One such story, frequently repeated to stress the fame he enjoyed in his own lifetime, concerns his crossing by boat from Beşiktaş to Üsküdar. Halfway across the Bosphorus Hafiz Osman realized that he did not possess even the small copper coin necessary to pay his fare. Accordingly he took out a piece of paper and pen and wrote a single word which he handed to his boatman. Unable to read, but silenced by the age and bearing of his passenger, the boatman, barely concealing his displeasure, accepted the paper. At the end of the day he retired to his neighbourhood coffee-house where he related the story to his fellow customers, one of whom asked to see the paper. No sooner was it produced than a crowd formed and a lively bidding began. The amazed boatman ended up receiving more than a week's salary for his single word. As fate would have it, the very next morning upon his return to the city Hafiz Osman happened to choose the same boatman. As he proffered the necessary coin the boatman shook his head in refusal and handed Hafiz Osman a scrap of paper. 'Efendim', he said, 'just write one letter, that will do.' Clearly he had no wish to cheat his passenger!

Renowned as much for his piety as his poverty, Hafiz Osman initiated the practice, followed by several later calligraphers, of setting aside one day a week for the instruction of students of promise who had no money to pay for his services. Among his better known 'paying students' were Mustafa II and Prince Ahmed, later to become Ahmed III.

For the next hundred years the *Hāfiz 'Osmān üslūbu* remained the model for the calligraphers of İstanbul; often copied, it was never matched until the appearance of two brothers in the second half of the eighteenth century, İsmail Zuhdi (d. 1806)[12] and his

162. *Levha* in *Celī Sülüs* by Sami Efendi AH 1289/1872 AD (*Allāh yu'āwinukum fi kull al-umūr*, may God help you in all matters)

sibling and student Mustafa Rakım (1757–1826).[13] Basing themselves upon the *üslüb* of Hafız Osman, which they had mastered to perfection, these two brothers, and in particular the younger Mustafa Rakım, introduced a new development to Ottoman calligraphy, that of aesthetic composition. Aided no doubt by his early training as a painter, Rakım became a master of *istif*, the composite arrangement on a given surface of letters, words and lines.

Rakım's sense of aesthetic proportion is nowhere more apparent than in the changes he introduced in the design of the Sultan's Imperial *Tuğras* (monograms). A comparison of plates 185 and 184 illustrates this point, as the *Tuğra* of Süleyman (1520–66) with its elaborate decoration is more a result of the painter's art, while that of Mustafa IV (1807–8), executed by Rakım, is a masterwork of calligraphic composition. Among Mustafa Rakım's many talented students was Sultan Mahmud II who is accepted by consensus as the finest in the long line of calligraphers provided by the Imperial dynasty of Osman.

It was the combination of Mustafa Rakım's sense of composition (*istif*) and the Ottoman style (*üslüb*), with its gradual evolution from Yakut through Şeyh Hamdullah to Hafız Osman, that produced a whole line of great nineteenth-century calligraphers. Such masters of the art as Kadıasker Mustafa İzzet Efendi (1801–76),[14] Mehmed Şefik Bey (1819–80),[15] and Sami Efendi (1838–1912)[16] (plates 164 and 162) added elements of technique and refinement which resulted in some of the finest works ever to come from the reed pen and ink.

Yet throughout the six-hundred-year history of Ottoman calligraphy, marked as it was by the periodic appearance of masters such as those described above, the most important element was that of continuity. An unbroken chain of approximately twenty generations of artists faithfully preserved and transmitted the work of their predecessors. Viewed against

163. *Kıt'a* by Şeyh Hamdullah (1429–1520). (The top line written in *Sülüs*, the bottom in *Nesih*)

164. *Kıt'a* by Kadıasker Mustafa İzzet Efendi (1801–1876)

this background, the periodic innovations in form and style appear as logical developments rather than as individual achievements.

Plates 163 and 164 provide a fitting climax to our discussion of the most important individual practitioners of the art of Ottoman calligraphy. Identical examples of the popular form known as *kıt'a* ('piece'), they are separated in date of composition by four hundred years. Plate 163 was written in the fifteenth century by the great Şeyh Hamdullah, while its exact copy was produced in 1846 by the nineteenth-century master, Kadıasker Mustafa İzzet Efendi. The latter piece is inscribed as follows by its artist: 'A copy by el-Hac Mustafa İzzet modelled upon the Şeyh'. The work of a student in his formative years? No, rather the work of an artist of 45 years of age, acknowledged by his peers as the greatest calligrapher of his century. Mustafa İzzet was paying homage to an artist whose work not only inspired but made possible and indeed shaped his own lifework.

'The art of calligraphy is hidden
in the teaching of the master,
its essence is achieved through
repetition, and it exists
to serve the religion of Islam.'

Types and Uses of Calligraphy

Hüsn-i hat literally permeated every facet of cultural life in the Ottoman Empire. Through an in-depth examination of its usage we may trace not only the various forms it employed, but also the means by which its practitioners, the *Hattāts* (calligraphers), earned their livelihoods. Such a discussion must focus upon five general categories into which we may group the products of the calligraphers.

YAZMALAR (MANUSCRIPTS)

A visitor to the city of İstanbul today is immediately struck by the large number of libraries which have survived from the Ottoman period. More than a hundred such libraries, containing several hundred thousand manuscripts, have been preserved. Initially endowed by wealthy individuals who left their private manuscript collections for future generations, these libraries attest to the love of the written word which was such a characteristic feature of Ottoman society. Printing, while introduced in the early eighteenth century, failed to take hold, primarily because of the opposition of the calligraphers who feared its effect on their livelihood, much of which stemmed from the copying of manuscripts. Only in the second half of the nineteenth century was printing to make significant inroads on the traditional preserve of the calligraphers.

Quantitatively, the Holy Qur'ān was far and away the most frequently copied work. Indeed the reputation of a calligrapher was to a large part based upon his copies of the holy book of Islam, and the Biographical Dictionaries of Calligraphers frequently provide us with the total number of Qur'āns penned by each entry. Up to the end of the sixteenth century the scripts generally employed in copies of the Qur'ān were *Sülüs*, *Reyhānī*, and *Muhakkak* (plate 171), while from that time forward *Nesih* emerged as the popular favourite.

One unusual aspect of the *Kur'an-i kerīms* (Holy Qur'āns) penned by the Ottoman calligraphers is that they usually contain the name of their copier, thus signifying both the willingness of the artists to be judged by the effort they put into this form, and the desire of the owner to have the copier acknowledged. It was the effort expended by Ottoman calligraphers in this particular genre which gave rise to the Arabic saying quoted earlier: 'The Qur'ān was revealed in the Hicaz, recited in Egypt, and written in İstanbul.'

In addition to the Qur'āns the most frequently copied manuscripts were those dealing with the religious sciences, poetry and history (plate 172). In works commissioned for the

Palace artists were sometimes employed to illustrate the texts penned by the imperial calligraphers.

KIT'A ('SINGLE PIECE')

This form was by far the most frequent employed by the Ottoman calligraphers (plates 163 and 164). By definition a *kıt'a* was simply any normal-sized paper (generally 4″ × 8″) covered with calligraphy. Usually, though not always, it consisted of one line in a large hand across the top, followed by three or four lines in a smaller hand underneath. While any and all variations of the 'Six Scripts' could be used, Ottoman calligraphers favoured the *Sülüs-Nesih* script in their *kıt'as*. The overwhelming popularity of this form stems from the fact that it was the *kıt'as* composed by earlier calligraphers which were most frequently copied by their successors (plates 163 and 164). When a number of *kıt'as* by a particular calligrapher was collected and bound into an album, the result was known as a *murakka'*.

LEVHA (FRAMED INSCRIPTIONS)

Compositions on paper of larger dimensions than those used in the *kıt'a* form are collectively known as *levhas*. Generally intended to be viewed from a distance, they were hung in mosques, homes and businesses. *Levhas* were frequently decorated with *tezhīb* (gilding) or *ebrū* (marbled paper), and sometimes, as in the case represented in plate 174, a combination of the two was employed. The subject matter represented in this form was generally religious in nature, either a passage from the Qur'ān, a saying of the Prophet, or a moral platitude. As *levhas* were intended for hanging and therefore viewing from a distance, a great deal of attention was paid to the composition and arrangement of their texts (plates 162 and 165).

As the demand for such works increased in the nineteenth century, stencils were often made of popular pieces which were then reproduced by lesser artists. Such 'copies'

165. *Levha* by Hamid Aytaç in *Ta'līk* script dated AH 1378/1958 AD

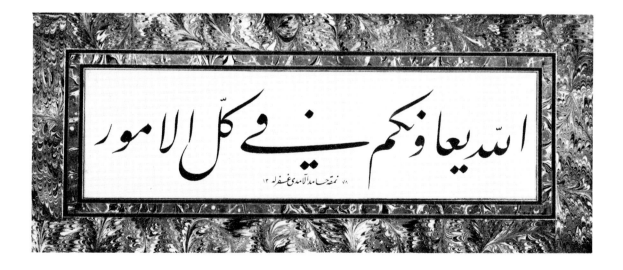

were generally produced on backgrounds of dark blue, green or black paper.

While any and all variations of the 'Six Scripts' were employed in this form, *Sülüs* and its variants seem to have been the favourite of the Ottoman calligraphers, probably because it was one of the more easily decipherable of the scripts.

MOSQUE DECORATION

It was in the mosques of the Ottoman Empire that the talents of the calligraphers were given full vent. While any calligrapher could and did try his hand at the forms discussed above (*yazma*, *kıt'a* and *levha*), only the recognized masters of each generation were given the opportunity to decorate the places of worship built during their lifetimes. In Islam, with its emphasis on the five daily ritual prayers, the mosque was the centre of life for the Muslim community. Marked as it was by its graceful domes and sweeping expanses of open wall space, Ottoman mosque architecture provided the perfect setting for the talents of the calligrapher.[17] Typically three sections of the interior of each mosque were filled with calligraphic inscriptions: the *kubbe* (dome), the *kuşak* (sash or girdle, i.e. a line running around the point at which the walls and ceiling meet), and the corners and ends of the sanctuary where were hung the six roundels bearing the names of Allah, his Prophet Muhammed, and the first four Caliphs of Islam.

The *kubbe* (dome), together with the lintels and tympani over the windows, were generally covered in painted or gold-leaf inscriptions executed in the *Celī Sülüs* script. Among the best examples of such a *kubbe* inscription is that of the Ayasofya Camii (formerly the Church of St Sophia) in İstanbul.

Until the end of the seventeenth century the *kuşak* (girdle) was generally covered by inscriptions on ceramic tiles (plate 179) executed in *Celī Sülüs*, though on occasion, as attested to by the sixteenth-century Çoban Mustafa Paşa Camii in the town of Gebze, the Kufic script was used in this area. From the beginning of the eighteenth century onwards the *kuşaks* of newly built mosques were either left undecorated or covered with calligraphic inscriptions in paint.

The roundels employed in the Ottoman mosques were usually made of wood covered by paint or gilding (plates 175 to 178).

In addition to the calligraphic decoration found in the above areas, *levhas* (framed inscriptions on paper) donated by the members of the congregation were often hung at random on the whitewashed walls of mosques. The archetype of this practice is found in the Ulu Camii in the first Ottoman capital of Bursa, where literally every bit of available wall space is covered with the calligrapher's art.[18]

KITĀBELER (INSCRIPTIONS)

This is a term used to cover calligraphy carved on stone. Inscriptions used to decorate a whole range of architectural exteriors including mosques, *Medreses* (schools), *Tekkes* (dervish lodges), *Kütübhānes* (libraries), *Hammāms* (public baths), and *Çeşmes* (fountains) are collectively referred to as *kitābes*. Any public building or monument erected in the

Ottoman period normally included a *kitābe* upon which was recorded the name of its endower, the date of construction and sometimes a verse from the Qur'ān or a line of poetry. Usually carved on marble, these *kitābes* provided a major source of livelihood for the calligraphers. Also falling into this category were the ornamental *mezār taşları* (tomb stones) covered with religious verses and the basic biographical data of the deceased.

MISCELLANEOUS USES OF CALLIGRAPHY

While the basic activities of the Ottoman calligraphers may be categorized in one or another of the five 'forms' discussed above, *Hüsn-i hat* was also utilized as a decorative device on numerous other items as well. Among these miscellaneous uses of calligraphy we may mention the textile covering for tombs (plates 158 and 160), the highly stylized figurative representations which became extremely popular in the nineteenth century (plate 166 in the shape of a 'pear' and plate 167 in the form of a 'vase' are typical examples of this form), and the always popular use of calligraphy as a motif on ceramic tile panels (plates 179 to 182).

166. Stylized calligraphy in the shape of a pear. 19th century

167. Inscription in gold *Sülüs* applied on a gold-painted leaf. 12.5 × 16.5 cm

The Calligrapher's Tools

The basic 'tools' of the calligrapher's art consisted of the reed-pen (*kamış kalem*), ink (*mürekkeb*), and paper (*kāğıd*). In addition, each of these had various other 'implements' utilized in their construction, as well as several crafts employed in their preparation.

KAMIŞ KALEM (REED PEN)[19].

Essential to the calligrapher was a steady supply of uncut reeds (*kamış*) which were imported to İstanbul from countries as far away as India. Ottoman calligraphers preferred the *kamış* which grew along the shores of the Caspian Sea in Iran and those from along the banks of the Tigris and Euphrates rivers in Iraq. The literature includes frequent warnings against the 'brittleness' of reeds from areas such as India with their 'hot climates'.

The nibbing of the pen, or 'opening of the reed', called for a special type of knife (the making of which was an art in itself), known as the *kalemtrāş*. In the nineteenth century there were scores of *kalemtrāş ustas* (master craftsmen) and *çıraks* (apprentices), located in a special İstanbul street, who were employed in this craft. The knives themselves consisted of a tempered steel blade which was attached by a band to the *sap* or handle. The *saps* were variously constructed from bone, ivory, wood or stone. Well known *ustas* (masters) stamped their names into the steel of the blade, both as a sign of the pride they took in their craftsmanship and as an advertisement to the knowing calligrapher.

Prior to its 'opening' the *kamış* (reed) was placed on a flat piece of carved bone or ivory known as the *makta'*, the design and making of which was the prerogative of yet another

168. Scribe's table inlaid with mother-of-pearl and tortoise-shell, 17th–18th century. H: 26 cm; W: 30.5 cm; l: 62 cm

169. *Karalama* (calligraphic exercise) signed 'al-sayyid Ahmad' and 'executed in the style of Cerrahzade'

calligraphy-associated craft. Carved into the face of the *makta'* was a narrow channel designed to keep the *kamış* from slipping under the pressure of the *kalemtraş*. Once the *kamış* was cut to the desired shape and angle, in accordance with the requirements of the script it was to be employed in, its transformation into a *kamış kalem* (reed-pen) was completed.

MÜREKKEB (INK)[20].

The basic ingredient of the inks used by the Ottoman calligraphers was soot or lampblack (*is* or *dūde*), and the Biographical Dictionaries contain numerous examples of the 'types' favoured by the great masters of the past. Particularly prized was the soot which collected in the *is menfezleri* (soot-vents) high in the gallery of the Süleymaniye Mosque in İstanbul. Once the desired *is* was obtained it was mixed with a type of paste or glue, known as *cellābī*, which was imported from the Sudan in Africa. Then, depending on the preference of the ink-maker (*mürekkeb ustası*), any number of other items such as rose-water, saffron, pomegranate rinds, vinegar and so on might be added. The exact amounts and types of additives were a closely guarded secret passed from master to student. Finally, iron sulphate, known by the ink-makers as *zāc-ı kıbrısī*, was added and the result was ink.

When purchased by the calligrapher or scribe the *mürekkeb* was transferred to a container known as a *hokka* (ink-pot) which had previously been filled with raw silk (*lika*). The *lika* had a sponge-like effect on the ink and prevented the nib of the pen from over-filling when it was dipped into the *hokka*. A specially designed pen-case known as the *divit*, with a container for a selection of pens and a *hokka*, was carried in the girdle of calligraphers. Each and every step described above was the preserve of a separate group of craftsmen.

KĀǦID (PAPER)[21].

The Ottomans imported 'raw paper' from China, India, Samarkand and Europe. However, before it could be used by the calligrapher it underwent a transformation which consisted of dyeing, varnishing and polishing. Only when this process was completed was it cut to size and delivered to the calligrapher. Here again, every step involved with the preparation of *kāǧıd* was carried out by its own group of craftsmen.

By the time the Ottoman calligrapher dipped his reed-pen into the ink-pot and stretched forth his hand to begin writing, the combined skills of scores of craftsmen spread throughout the borders of the Islamic world had been employed to make possible the 'Beautiful Writing' which was to result.

170. Calligraphy in the shape of a vase, 18th-19th century. H: 68.5 cm

As indicated by even this cursory discussion of the major trends in Ottoman calligraphy and the uses to which the products of the calligrapher's art were put, *Hüsn-i hat* was the Ottoman art form *par excellence*. In a society where the public depiction of the human form was discouraged, 'Beautiful Writing' served in its stead. Society's artists were its calligraphers. To be a patron of the arts meant being a patron of the calligrapher's art. Guided by the tastes of the Ottoman dynasty, members of the ruling class were constantly commissioning the services of the calligrapher. The books they read, the monuments they erected and ultimately the tombstones they were buried under, all bore the stamp of the calligrapher.

Marked by an unbroken chain of development, with its roots stretching back to the early days of Islam, Ottoman calligraphy stands alone as the one form of expression employed by the Ottomans which was impervious to outside influence. While Ottoman fortunes waxed and waned between the fourteenth and early twentieth centuries, the art of its calligraphers continued to grow until the final years of the Empire. Only the introduction of a Latin script in 1928 and the consequent banning of the use of Arabic scripts managed to slow down, though not completely halt this tradition.

The accumulated heritage and techniques of hundreds of years of experience was passed on from master to student, generation after generation. Without break or interruption the art of calligraphy was learned by succeeding generations of artists, each of whom spent countless hours copying the works of past masters. The occasional appearance of great masters such as Şeyh Hamdullah, Ahmed Karahisari, Hafiz Osman, Mustafa Rakım and Kadıasker Mustafa İzzet Efendi and the reshaping of techniques and embellishments which they added provided the stimulus that set the tone for succeeding generations.

Limited in its subject matter to topics of religious concern, the art of the calligraphers has provided through the ages a vital link to bind together the history and peoples of the Islamic world. When viewed against this background Ottoman calligraphy emerges as a major art form.

'The art of calligraphy is hidden
in the teaching of the master,
its essence is achieved through
repetition, and it exists
to serve the religion of Islam.'

THE PLATES

160 (detail)
Brocaded Red Satin Tomb-Cover

17th–18th century

A typical example of the tomb-covers with a red ground, this well preserved complete piece carries many inscriptions, among them the *şehâdet* or Profession of Faith: 'There is no God but God; Muhammad is God's Messenger', various pious invocations of the attributes of God and an inscription from the Qur'ān, Sūra II, verse 144, referring to the *qibla* or direction of Mecca, towards which Islamic burials were oriented. Fragments of red tomb-covers with the same loom pattern are in the Victoria and Albert Museum, London, the Textile Museum, Washington D.C., and the David Collection, Copenhagen. A complete piece can be seen on one of the sarcophagi in the *türbe* of Sultan Süleyman in İstanbul.

Published: *Calligraphy and the Decorative Arts of Islam*, London 1976, plate 18

Width: (2 panels) 133 cm; length: 189 cm

171
Illuminated 'Sūra' Heading

15th century

Heading of *Sūra* XXV ('*al-Furqān*'), written in *Sülüs* script, from a Qu'rān attributed to Mehmed II.

Height: 2.5 cm; length: 13.8 cm

172
Double Page of Calligraphy

c. 1500

Frontispiece of an anthology from the Mevlana mosque in Konya. The lobed cartouche on the right, written in mirror writing in a *Sülüs* script, bears the name of Bayezid II ('*Sultan Bāyezīd Hān ibn Mehmed*') while the round medallion on the left contains a *du'ā* (prayer) for the same Sultan.

Published: *Art Treasures of Turkey*, Smithsonian

Institution, Washington D.C. 1966, no. 177

Konya Museum, Konya, no. 143

Height: 17.5 cm; width: 22 cm (overall)

173
Page of Calligraphy

15th–16th century

The common Islamic invocation: *bi'smi'llāhi'l-raḥmāni'l-raḥīm* ('In the name of God, the Compassionate, the Merciful'), written in the *Reyhānī* script by Şeyh Hamdullah (1429–1520).

Türk ve İslam Eserleri Müzesi, İstanbul, no. 246

174
Page of Calligraphy

17th century

A *bi'smi'llāhi'l-raḥmāni'l-raḥīm* in the *Reyhānī* script written by the seventeenth-century calligrapher Hafiz Osman (1642–98).

Topkapı Sarayı Müzesi, İstanbul, no. 3655

175–178
Four Wooden Roundels

17th–18th century

Four carved and painted mosque roundels from a standard set of eight, bearing the names of Allah, Abu-Bakr, Uthman and Hasan (the Prophet's grandson) respectively. Missing are those with the names of the Prophet Muhammad, Husayn and the Caliphs Umar and Ali. The letters stand out in relief against a recessed ground. The paint is applied over a thin layer of gesso.

Published: Hayward 1976, No. 466a–d; A. Welch, *Calligraphy in the Arts of the Muslim World*, Austin 1979, no. 35

Diam: 63 cm

179
Ceramic Tile Panel

Dated AH 1011/1602

A calligraphic tile panel decorated with a central roundel containing repetitions of the letter *vāv*. Along the sides are the names of Allah, Muhammad, Hasan, Husayn, Abu Bakr, Umar, Uthman and Ali.

Topkapı Sarayı Müzesi, İstanbul (Harem)

Height: 107.5 cm; width: 107.5 cm

180–182
Ceramic Tile Panels

Dated AH 1017/1608–9 AD

Three ceramic tile panels with abstract calligraphic decoration based on the letter *vāv*. They are signed by Kemānkeş Mustafa and dated 1017.

Topkapı Sarayı, İstanbul (New Library)

180: height: 42 cm; width: 36 cm

181: height: 97.5 cm; width: 67 cm

182: height: 68 cm; width 58 cm

183
Double Page of Calligraphy

16th century

Four examples of the work of Ahmed Karahisari (1469–1566). On the left-hand page, written in a joined *Sülüs* script, is the phrase 'Praise be to the praiseworthy', while on the right-hand page from top to bottom are the inscriptions: *al-ḥamdu li'llāh* ('Praise be to God') in a squared Kufic script, *bi'smi'llāhi-raḥmāni'l-raḥīm* ('In the name of God, the Compassionate, the Merciful') in a stylized variant of the *Sülüs* script and also in a squared Kufic script is yet another *bi'smi'llāhi-raḥmāni'l-raḥīm* followed by the Sūra of the Qu'rān on Unity (CXII 1–4).

Published: *Art Treasures of Turkey*, Smithsonian Institution, Washington D.C. 1966, no. 179

184
Firman

Early 19th century

A Firman (Imperial Edict) bearing the *Tuğra* of Sultan Mustafa IV (1807–8). This ruler's *Tuğra* was designed by the calligrapher Mustafa Rakım (1757–1826). The *Tuğra* is executed in the *Celī Sülüs* script, while the text of the Firman is written in *Dīvānī*.

Length: 129.5 cm; width: 50 cm

185
Tuğra of Süleyman the Magnificent

First half of 16th century

A *Tuğra* (Imperial Monogram) of the Ottoman Sultan Süleyman the Magnificent (1520–66). The *Tuğrakeş* (calligrapher) who drew it is unknown. The scrolling background illumination is of the same type as is found on 'Golden Horn' ceramics (plates 73 and 74).

Türk ve İslam Eserleri Müzesi, İstanbul

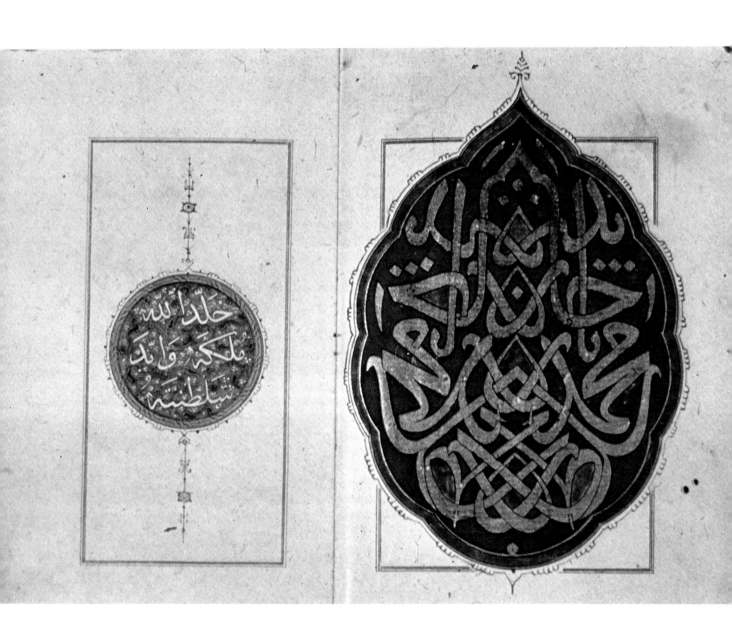

180
179·181
182

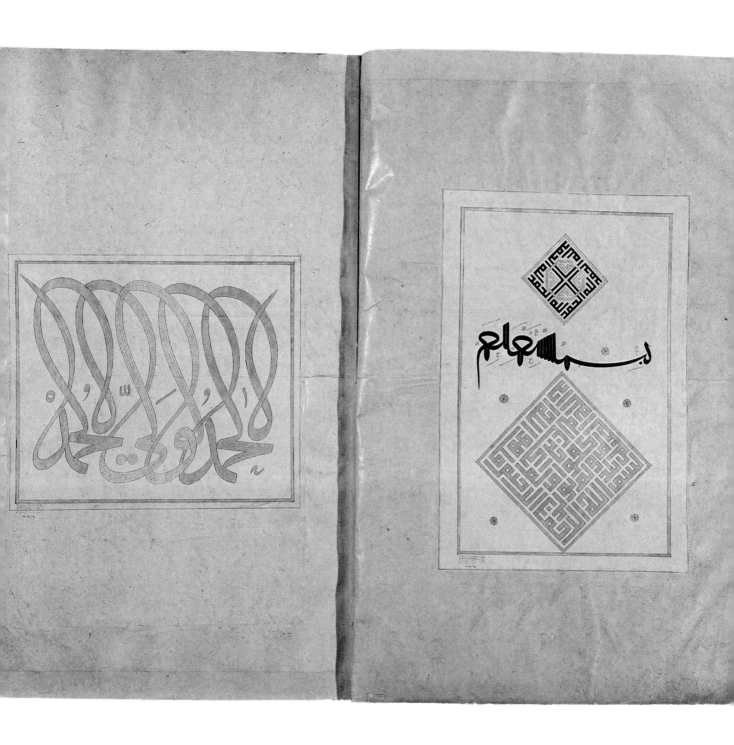

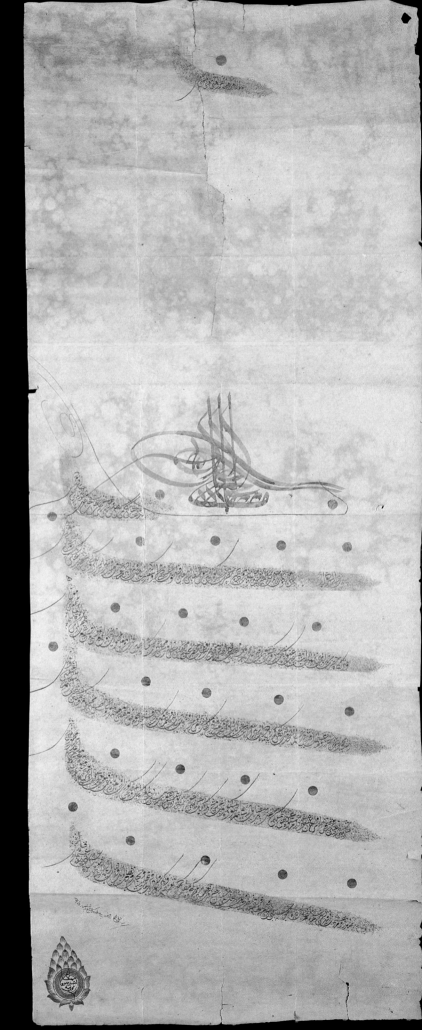

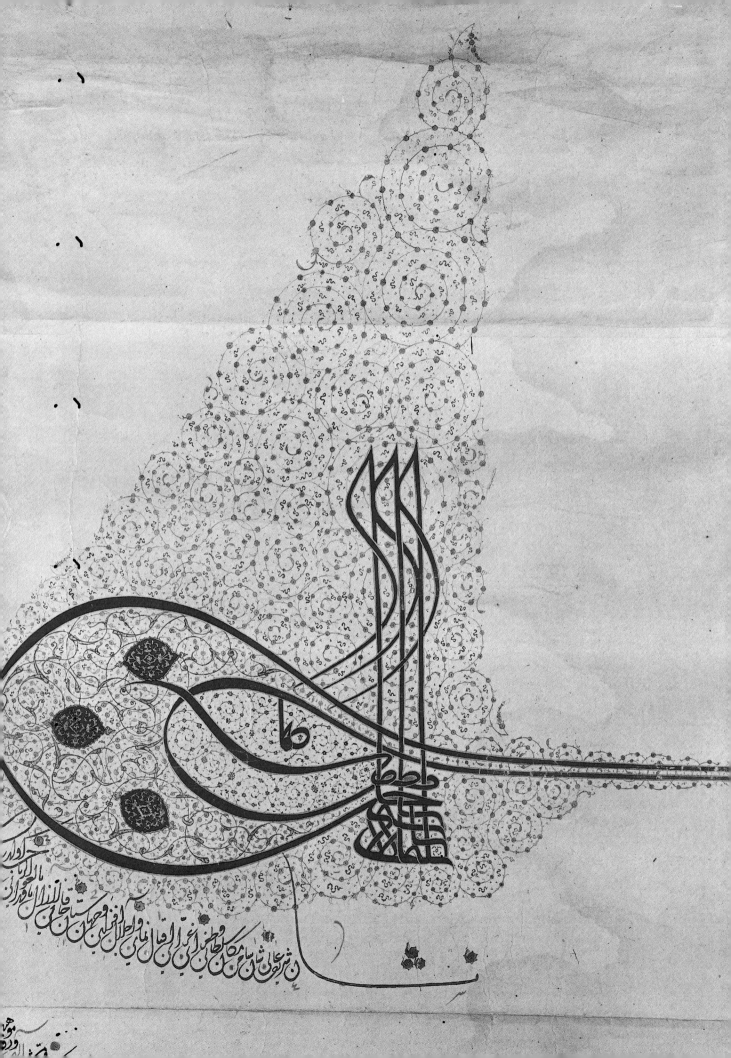

Painting

Ernst Grube

Present evidence suggests that Ottoman painting came to flower only after the beginning of the sixteenth century. But it would be quite wrong to assume that its roots do not reach much further back. How far, in fact, is still a difficult question to answer as nothing has survived from the first century of Ottoman rule, but recent documentation of painting executed for Ottoman Sultans of the late fifteenth century and an analysis of its peculiar quality has at least pointed to the necessity of recognizing a much more complex cultural and historical background for Ottoman painting than had hitherto been considered.[1]

Turkish painting has a distinctive quality of its own. As with all other aspects of Ottoman art, it is the result of a successful synthesis of disparate and heterogeneous elements which, once adopted, are changed and adapted to create a cohesive vocabulary with a life and development of its own. It can never be confused, even by the totally uninitiated, for more than a brief moment with anything that the Muslim world has produced elsewhere. It is with this peculiar quality that we shall concern ourselves here rather than attempt to write a comprehensive history of Ottoman painting.

The first quality that must strike anyone confronted with a work of Ottoman pictorial art is its unmistakable individuality. Even though it may at first be difficult to define in so many words what constitutes this particular quality, there cannot be any question that Ottoman painting is definitely different from anything else done in the Muslim world at any time. There are in Ottoman painting reflections of models of various kinds, among them those of early fifteenth-century provincial painting in Iran. So often thought to have been not only the main but practically the only source of inspiration, Persian painting plays quite a minor part in the formation of the Ottoman style. There are elements of a realism that must be traced back to the inspiration of Byzantine and western European models, which were amply accessible to Ottoman artists both in Anatolia and in Constantinople/İstanbul through Byzantine frescoes, mosaics and panel icons on the one hand, and European prints, paintings and, eventually, through direct contact with European artists working at the Ottoman court in the late fifteenth century on the other. It evolves, therefore, as much as a reaction to western as to eastern traditions.

Nevertheless, Ottoman painting datable to the late fifteenth and early sixteenth century is in its ultimate analysis totally different from any of the sources just mentioned.

Even paintings as close to Persian models of the early fifteenth century as that of a scene

187. Adam and Eve in Paradise. *Zubdat al-Tawārīkh* copied in
1583. Chester Beatty Library, Turk. Ms. 414. Fol. 531.
395 × 250 mm

188. Bahram Gur in the Sandalwood Pavilion.
Amir Khusrow Dihlavi's *Khamse* AH 903/1498
AD. TKS H. 799 fol. 186v

of battle between Alexander's soldiers and an army of monsters in the Venice *Iskandarnāme* of about 1460 (plate 194)[2] are of such unselfconscious liveliness and vitality that they
are immediately set apart from paintings in manuscripts produced in the Fars region
during this period. There is in this *Iskandarnāme* almost nothing of the stiff, mannered,
impersonal and abstract quality that characterizes Persian painting. And if one looks at
the illustrations of the story of Bahram Gur and his seven princesses in Amir Khusrow's
Khamse of 1498 (plate 188),[3] or those of the copy of Hatifi's *Khusrow and Shirin* of 1498-9
(plate 195),[4] one must recognize that the painters of these late fifteenth-century pictures
produced for Mehmed the conqueror and Bayezid II a new concept of pictorial presentation, entirely different from that of their Iranian contemporaries.

Ottoman painters quite clearly strive, at first perhaps not altogether successfully,
towards a representation of the real world, even though, at the beginning, they still deal
with the imaginary heroes of times long past. They put their figures in landscapes that are
full of observation of the detail of this real world. They place people into architectural
settings which have the real quality of tectonic three-dimensional volume, with slanting
roofs, round towers, shaded tile-work, bulbous cupolas set squarely on the ground and
which, unprecedented in painting in the Muslim world, cast real shadows and draw real
receding lines into a space that is conceived in a form of perspective. We have here, of

course, the non-classical form of perspective prevalent in Byzantine and medieval art, a concept which takes the beholder as the principal point of reference, as the vanishing point in fact, in which all lines converge, rather than placing the vanishing point in the distance behind the picture plane. The result is, of course, that all objects so drawn narrow down in front and widen towards the back in clear and logical contrast to western perspective design, but a form of perspective it is all the same and the reality of volume in space is equally clearly conceived and portrayed.

These elements of reality of the world and its objects (human beings at this early stage appear to be exempt from such scrutiny and are allowed to hide behind the mask of abstract traditionalism), become an integral part of Ottoman painting, ultimately determining its very character. This realism has few, if any, true parallels in Muslim painting. There is, of course, the painting of Mughal India, but there realism is carried to a point that goes far beyond anything Ottoman art has ever attempted, at least until the later eighteenth century when it follows a similar, basically western, and in the ultimate sense non-Islamic manner of pictorial representation. In its classical form Ottoman court painting never truly breaks with Muslim tradition and even in its most extreme cases of depicting actual landscapes and cities, and of course portraits of the Sultans and the nobles of the realm, there is never a true and total realism in the sense of recognizable naturalism. But this early form of realism in Ottoman painting is sometimes abandoned in favour of a more traditional Islamic, especially Persian idiom (plate 196), due mainly to the fact that Persian artists who had gravitated towards Istanbul worked for the Ottoman scriptoria and imposed what must, even at the time, have been recognized as a basically alien style. In fact, whenever it appears, it does so almost completely intact in the form of paintings in the Turkman or the Safavid styles of Qazvin and Shiraz.[5]

The final proof of the 'difference' of Ottoman pictorial art comes with the fundamental turning away from the traditional subject of Islamic and again especially Persian painting, the fantasy world of the classical poetic texts. The Ottomans make the fundamental choice for contemporary history, and with that choice an entirely new world is opened for the Muslim painter. Even the 'realistic' paintings of the thirteenth-century ateliers of Baghdad and Damascus have nothing of the immediacy of Ottoman painting because both their literary and their pictorial models are fanciful and traditional, the texts being based on an ancient tradition of satire and political parabola, the pictorial idiom harking back to Hellenistic models still alive in local provincial Byzantine painting in Syria and Iraq at the time. The much remarked new awareness of everyday life is nothing but a revival of classical tradition as formal and unreal as anything within Muslim pictorial tradition of the time.[6]

Ottoman painting is totally different both in intent and, ultimately, in quality. It even produces portraits, a fact unparalleled in Islamic art save in Mughal India, and it includes in its revolutionary vision of the world all of history including that of the Prophet and his predecessors, from both the New and the Old Testaments. It finally concentrates almost obsessively on the life of the Sultans. There are genealogies (plates 197 and 198), individual portraits (plates 199 and 200), and a never-ending succession of renderings of the Sultans' exploits, showing the ruler and his generals, the princes of the realm, ambassadors from foreign countries, friends and enemies, and all kinds of 'real persons' in all kinds of 'real situations' that had never before been the subject of Islamic painting.

The very subject-matter of Ottoman painting indicates that the art of the painter was almost exclusively commanded by the court; and Ottoman painting is indeed a highly controlled court art. From the sixteenth century onwards it becomes not only an instrument for the glorification of the ruling dynasty, it at the same time serves as a visual record of contemporary events.[7]

As a visual record-keeper the Ottoman painter must, of course, give a recognizable rendering of the real world and its distinguishing features, including the physical appearance of specific human beings. As an artist called upon to celebrate the glories of the ruling house he must find a manner that elevates the ordinary into the realm of the extraordinary, that gives the somewhat pedestrian individuality of things and events an aura of grandeur that demonstrates the superb quality and absolute power of the ruler and his world.

The genius of these court painters lies in the creation of a style and a manner that accommodate both of these often contrasting and at times mutually exclusive qualities. Ottoman painting has in fact succeeded magnificently in incorporating the minutiae of the real world into a symbolic form that shows the real image of the individual Sultan and his court in an infinite variety of real settings in a manner that elevates each event into the realm of the absolute.

The Ottoman painter achieves this feat through the creation of a highly formalized style in which complex, rigidly observed compositional formulae, large planes of strong, unbroken colour, and the depiction of all details act together in such a manner as to create a fully balanced final image in which each detail appears as if in its immutable, 'perfect' place, becoming part of a greater, supranatural order imposed from beyond the reality of the world depicted in any given painting. In this manner the individual acts of devotion such as Sultan Süleyman's Pilgrimage to Eyüp (plate 207),[8] become symbolic absolute images of such events while at the same time, because of their accurate individual detail, losing nothing of their specific, historical 'record' quality. The supranatural or the historic moment of times long past can be depicted without danger of sacrilege or absurdity. The Prophet can be shown in heaven among angels encountering Moses standing in front of his heavenly throne (plate 209),[9] or a Vision of Paradise with Adam and Eve flanking the Tree of Life (plate 208)[10] can be presented that has all the quality of an actual historical event, while at the same time in its extraordinarily powerful rendering of the main figures in lapidary monumental forms it has all the quality of a true religious image of transcendental value and significance.

In the best pictures of this fully developed, classical court style, the Ottoman painter of the sixteenth century has created forms that stand on an awesome level of perfection rarely achieved by any other school of Muslim painting.

But Ottoman painting is hardly as one-sided as this particular emphasis on the great images of the official court style would make us believe. There is a great variety of form and manner, from the lyrical to the downright humorous and the almost wickedly satirical.

But perhaps the most important 'other' aspect of Ottoman pictorial art is that developed with close reference to the exceptionally highly developed Ottoman calligraphic sense. Ottoman calligraphy counts among the most powerful and accomplished in the

189. Angel, mid-16th century, from album 261, Musée Jaquemart-André

190. Angel, mid-16th century, from an album attributed to Shah Quli, Freer 33.6

Muslim world, and it is not astonishing, in fact, that in present-day Turkey calligraphy is still being practised by masters who have no equals.

Out of the intense pre-occupation with calligraphy as an art form Ottoman artists developed a form of calligraphic design that would appear to have its principal roots in a long tradition of arabesque and floral patterns, first perhaps developed to a high art form in the centres of Timurid culture. Some of the finest of these designs were collected and partly created for an album produced for Sultan Murad III[11] (plates 186, 202 to 206).

The principal feature of these designs, which are of superb quality and are works of art in their own right, is generally a central calligraphic bold black line—the rib of a leaf, the stem of a flower or palmette blossom, the wing-feather of a bird, the undulating backbone of a dragon or the wing contour of an angel—around which the other elements of the pattern are arranged in an often breathtaking exuberance of highly energetic, perpetual movement. Some of these designs, such as that of a dragon moving through a continually twisting and intertwining lancette leaf scroll (plate 191), facing a bird-like creature whose head quite literally grows from a swirling mass of serrated *saz* leaves, were undoubtedly created by the *nakkāshāne* artists who specialized in this form of decorative drawing for the royal albums prepared for the Ottoman princes and Sultans. Others may well have been study exercises on a larger scale for designs that decorate the margins of manuscripts and album leaves containing examples of the court calligraphers' art.

The work of these court artists lies at the heart of the Ottoman decorative style. The royal kaftans (plate 123), the glorious tiles (plate 96)[12] and the precious metalwork (plate 23) all bear witness to this stylistic unity, the recurring theme of this book. The same artists working in different branches of the royal ateliers created drawings, cartoons or stencils which were then sent out to the four corners of the empire for execution in a variety of media.

The perfect fusion between purely decorative and figurative elements makes these drawings both extremely pleasing to the eye and highly exciting to the mind of the beholder who, contemplating the infinite variations on basically one and the same theme, finds in them a spirit fundamentally different from that of the illustrations of the manuscripts decorated by the official court painters. And yet these designs are clearly made for the same court, as their appearance in the royal albums demonstrates.

The two styles, in fact, never mix; there is no painting which is executed in this manner, nor are there manuscripts illustrated with drawings of this type. One must accept, at least until evidence to the contrary is produced, that there exist two fundamentally different Ottoman court styles that would appear to appeal to two basically different tastes. But if one sees these drawings in the greater context of Ottoman decorative art, it becomes quite clear that if anything it is in these drawings that the true dynamic spirit of Ottoman art

191. A dragon among foliage, drawing from an album circa 1550-1570. The Cleveland museum of Art 44.492.

expresses itself. These drawings do, in fact, as already indicated before, find ample parallels in almost all other forms of Ottoman decorative art.[13] It is really the style of Ottoman court painting that stands by itself and forms a curious if obviously consciously developed contrast to this general decorative Ottoman style. The explanation offered above for this development of that Ottoman court style may also lead us to understand why it was limited to court painting. It made that painting a special, separate, symbolic entity that communicated the power and hierarchy of the Ottoman state. And by including the history of the Muslim religion and its background it relates the dynasty to Islam as a political-historical phenomenon. It may well be recollected here that the Ottoman Sultans claimed the caliphate,[14] and that their genealogies, so richly illustrated with portraits of all the persons included, frequently reach back to the founder of Islam and beyond to the divine beginning of the human race.

THE PLATES

186, 202–206
Illuminated Pages

Second half of 16th century

From an album of Murad III (1574–93). These exquisite illuminations show the fundamental role of the court painters in the establishment of a style for use throughout the Ottoman decorative arts.

Österreichische Nationalbibliothek, Vienna, Codex Mixtus 313, folios: 26r, 46r, 17v, 30r, 31v and 3v respectively.

Height: 33.4 cm; width: 22.2 cm

193
Miniature Painting

c. 1500

Painted in strong colours, this painting, which represents a rider fighting a chimera (wyvern), is from an album in İstanbul. The subject bears strong thematic affinities with St George slaying the dragon.

İstanbul University Library, no. F 145, folio 27

Height: 11 cm; width: 17.5 cm

194
Miniature Painting

c. 1460

Iskandar's army fighting an army of monsters.

This painting is in a copy of Ahmedi's *Iskandarnāme* probably executed in Edirne in about 1460.

Biblioteca Marciana, Venice, Cod. Or. XC

195
Miniature Painting

Dated AH 904/1498–9 AD

Shirin, looking from the window in her house, sees Khusrow's painting hanging from a tree in the garden. Painting in a manuscript of Hatifi's *Khusrow and Shirin* copied and illustrated in AH 904, probably in İstanbul.

Metropolitan Museum of Art, New York, no. 69.27, folio 22r

Height: 12 cm; width: 7.5 cm

196
Miniature Painting

First half of 16th century

This painting from an unidentified album represents a seated Peri. It is probably painted in İstanbul in the manner of Qazvin.

Formerly in the coll. of Vera Amherst Hale Pratt

Height: 13.8 cm; width: 11 cm (painting only)

197-198
Genealogical Miniatures

Early and late 17th century

A set of twenty-one miniature paintings tracing the Ottoman genealogy back to Adam and Eve via the Prophet Muhammad. Until Osman II (1618-22) all the paintings appear to be the work of one artist, while those from his successor Mustafa I (1622-3) to Mustafa II (1695-1703) seem to have been done subsequently by another painter in an attempt to bring this genealogy up to date.

Height: 21 cm; width: 11.3 cm (painting only)

199-200
Portraits of Sultans

c. 1600

These portraits of Sultans Mehmed II and Süleyman I are from a copy of Lokman's *Physiognomy of the Ottomans*. The first page of this manuscript has an inscription written by a later owner which states that it was painted by the court painter Ustad Osman. It contains the portraits of all the Ottoman sultans from Osman to Mehmed III, which would probably date this copy to the latter's reign (1595-1603). Sixty-seven folios with an illuminated frontispiece and thirteen portraits, bound in brown morocco, stamped and tooled.

Private collection, England

Height: 25.6 cm; width: 18 cm

201
Miniature Painting

c. 1550

The subject taken from the Old Testament represents Jacob with his father in a cave surrounded by his eleven brothers.

Height: 11.5 cm; width: 10.8 cm

207
Miniature Painting

Dated AH 987/1579 AD

From a manuscript of the *History of Sultan Süleyman* copied by Qasim al-Husayni al Aridi of Qazvin in AH 987, this painting represents the pilgrimage of Sultan Süleyman to the shrine of Ebu Eyyub.

Chester Beatty Library, Dublin, Turk. MS. no. 413, folio 38r

Height: 37.8 cm; width: 26 cm

208
Miniature Painting

Dated AH 991/1583 AD

Representing Adam and Eve in Paradise flanking the tree of Life, this painting is in a manuscript of Lokman Ashuri's *Zubdat al-Tawārīkh* ('The Cream of History'), copied in AH 991.

Chester Beatty Library, Dublin, Turk. MS. no. 414, folio 53r

Height: 39.5 cm; width: 25 cm

209
Miniature Painting

Late 16th century

The Prophet Muhammad with the archangel Gabriel meeting Moses in Heaven. This painting is from a copy of Mustafa Zarir's *Kitāb-i Siyar-i Nabī* ('The Book of the Life of the Prophet'), probably from the edition made for Murad III in AH 1003/1594 AD.

Museum für Islamische Kunst, Berlin-Dahlem, no. I.26/76

Height: 31 cm; width: 20.5 cm

210
Miniature Painting

Dated AH 965/1558 AD

This scene from courtly life is from a manuscript of Arifi's *Süleymānnāme*, copied by Ali ibn Amir Baykh Shirvani in Ramadan 965/June 1558.

Topkapı Sarayı Müzesi, İstanbul, Hazine 1517, folio 18A

Height: 25.8 cm; width: 20 cm

211
Map

Middle of 16th century

Representing İstolni Belgrad (Székesfehérvár) in connection with Süleyman's campaign of 1543, this painting is from a manuscript of the *Süleymānnāme* by Matrakçı Nasuh.

Topkapı Sarayı Müzesi, İstanbul, Hazine 1608, folios 114B-115A

Height: 23 cm; width: 28 cm (overall)

212
Painting of Hoca Nasreddin
on his Donkey

Topkapı Sarayı Müzesi, İstanbul, Hazine 2142, folio 24a

Height: 12 cm; width: 20.5 cm

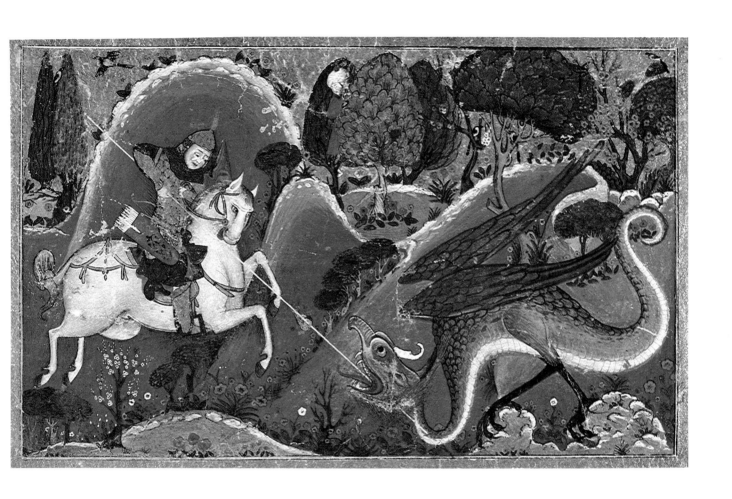

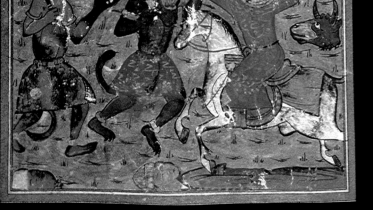

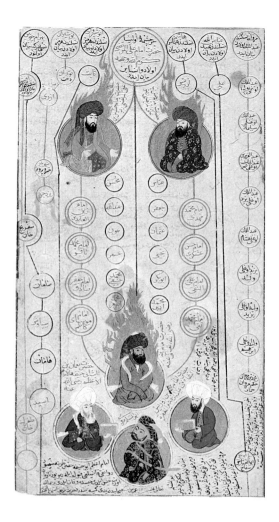

202

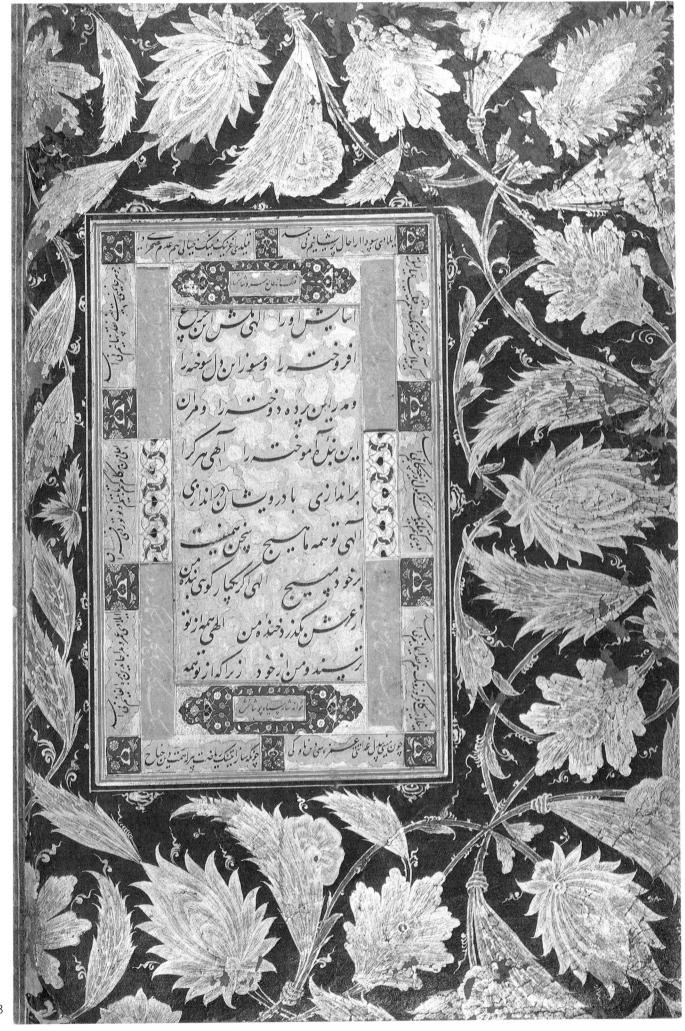

صلوة في اليوم والليلة وصام ثلث شهرنى كل سنة فقا

لى موسى ان امتك ضعيف لايطيقون ذلك فارجع الى رب

انت وجبريل و سأله التخفيف لامتك قال النبى عليه السلام

فرجعت الى ربى عزوجل فقلت يا سيدى و مولاى ان امتى لايطيقو

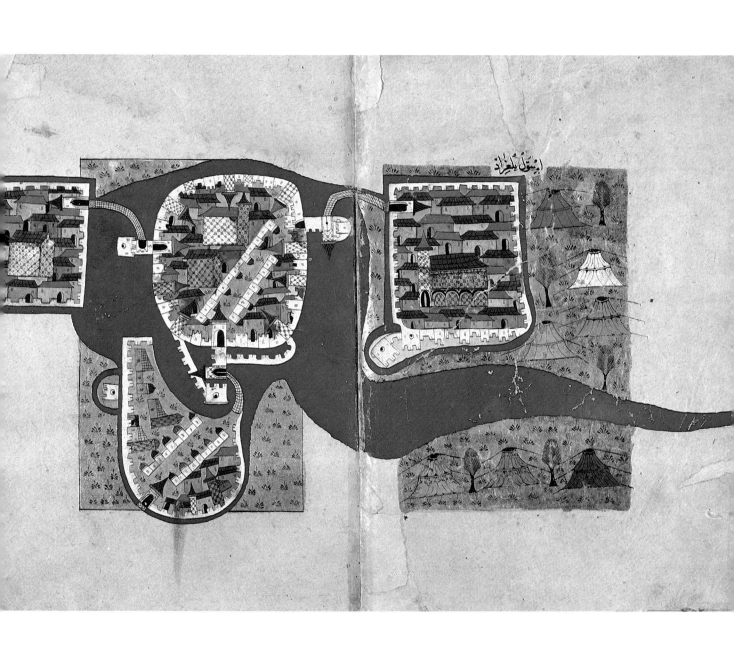

211

Analysis of Ottoman Metalwork

A. M. Pollard

For analytical purposes, the material was divided into five groups, i.e.
Gold—sample 27
Silver—samples 9, 21, 23, 30
Copper—samples 19, 32, 33, 34, 36, 37
Brass—the rest
The last will be labelled copper alloys.

1. Gold Objects
Eight standards used, covering the ranges
Au   50.2–99.5%
Ag   2.5–39.8%
Cu   0.5–10%
Results were calculated using the Ag/Au and Cu/Au ratios.

Six areas were analysed, twice each. The alloy was found to be relatively homogeneous over the whole object, with the exception of the loop connecting the chain. The compositions were:
Body   90.0% Au, 5.8% Ag, 3.2% Cu
Loop   85.2% Au, 9.1% Ag, 5.6% Cu

The accuracy is expected to be ±0.2% (wt. %) Cu, ±0.5% (wt. %) Au, Ag.

2. Silver Objects
Eight standards used, covering the ranges
Ag   59.3–99.5%
Cu   2.5–28.0%
Au   0.5–23.0%
Pb   copper calibration used—see later
Bi was looked for but not found (i.e. less than 0.1%).

The Cu/Ag and Au/Ag ratios were used in calculations, but Pb was obtained directly.

Each object was analysed at least twice in two separate areas. In all cases the objects were found to be uniform to within the accuracy of the measurements.

The accuracies are expected to be:
Ag ± 0.5% (metal)   Au ± 0.1%
Cu ± 0.5%   Pb ± 0.2%*
The results on the silver objects were:

Illus. no.	% Ag	% Au	% Cu	% Pb
21.	95.7	0.6	3.7	0.1
9.	91.8	0.4	9.3	not determined
23.	94.3	1.1	3.7	0.9
30.	93.8	0.3	5.8	0.1

*Note: In the absence of suitable lead standards in silver alloy, the calibration for lead in copper was used. At the levels found, this is unlikely to introduce errors in excess of those quoted (i.e. ±0.2% Pb).

3. Copper Objects
Nine standards used, covering the following ranges:

Cu	84.5–99.5%	Au	0.5–2.5%
Sn	0.5– 8.0%	Ag	0.1–3.0%
Zn	0.4– 4.5%	Ni	0.3–1.0%
Pb	0.1– 5.0%	As	3.3% (single
Sb	0.1– 3.6%		standard)

The following metals were not detected above the levels noted:
Ni   <0.1%   Ag   <0.2%
Zn   <0.5%   Sb   <0.2%
Au   <0.5%

The results were calculated from direct calibration curves in the case of Sn, Pb and As (one value only); Cu was then calculated by difference from 100%. Each of the objects in this section were found to be homogeneous to the accuracy of the measurements, which for Cu is approximately ±0.5%, and for As, Pb and Sn ±0.2%.
The results on the copper objects were:

Illus. no.	% Cu	% Sn	% Pb	% As
19.	99.5	0.1	0.3	0.2
32.	99.9	<0.1	<0.1	0.1
33.	99.4	<0.1	<0.1	0.6
34.	99.4	<0.1	0.6	nd
36.	100	<0.1	<0.1	<0.1
37.	98.9	0.5	0.3	0.4

Of the gilded objects (34, 19, 32, 33), only the large candlestick (33) shows definite traces of Hg, but mercury gilding cannot be ruled out for the other objects.

The two 'bronze' candlesticks (36 and 37) show definite surface tinning, possibly with some traces of lead. There is no sign of silver.

4. Copper Alloys
This section deals with both brasses and bronzes. A total of twelve standards were used, covering the ranges:
Cu   61.0–96.6%   Fe   0.02–0.42%
Sn   0.5– 9.0%   Ni   0.1–1.1%
Zn   0.4 –38.0%   As   0.05–3.30%
Pb   0.1 –11.0%   Sb   0.04–3.59%
Mn   0.01– 0.96%

The ratios Sn/Cu, Zn/Cu, Pb/Cu were used to calculate the major elements, and the trace elements were determined directly.

The following metals were not found in excess of the levels quoted:
Mn   <0.2%   Au   <0.3%
Ni   <0.25%   Ag   <0.2%

Each object was analysed repeatedly in at least two areas. Where the object is thought to have been fabricated from more than one alloy, this is shown.

Results

Illus. nos.	% Cu	% Sn	% Zn	% Pb	% Fe	Others
35.	70.0	1.3	26.4	1.9	0.2	As 0.2%
38. Top,	75.7	6.4	16.7	0.9	<0.1	
Base	80.3	<0.1	16.8	2.7	0.1	
40. Top,						
Base	83.7	3.5	9.2	3.3	0.2	
41. Top,						
Base	81.9	2.0	11.5	4.4	0.3	Ni 0.1%
*patch	82.5	2.6	0.8	13.6	0.2	
42.	80.8	2.0	14.3	2.7	0.1	
43.	80.1	0.1	19.0	0.2	0.1	As 0.4%
46. Body,						
Lid	72.0	0.4	21.0	6.0	0.3	Ni 0.2%
47. Top,						
Tray	78.5	2.4	14.2	4.4	0.4	
48. Lid,	65.9	0.2	32.6	0.9	0.1	
Base,						
Handle,						
Spout	77.8	7.0	11.3	3.7	0.3	

*Denotes single measurement

The expected errors in the above measurements are:
Cu ± 1.5% (metal)   Pb ± 1.0%
Sn ± 0.5%   Fe, Ni, As ± 0.1%
Zn ± 1.0%
Unless otherwise stated, the Fe, Ni and As results are less than 0.1%.

Footnotes

The numbers referred to in the footnotes apply
to the bibliography.

INTRODUCTION

1. Lane, (1957), p. 254.
2. Migeon, G., Sakissian, A., *La Céramique d'Asie Mineure et de Constantinople* (Paris, 1923), p. 45.
3. Lane, (1957), p. 262; Denny, (1977), p. 8.
4. Medley, M., *The Chinese Potter* (Oxford, 1976), p. 218.
5. Lane, (1957), p. 262; Denny, (1977), p. 8.
6. *Turkish Art*, ed. Atil, E., 1980, p. 280; Denny, (1977), p. 10.
7. Soustiel, J. 'La décoration aux quatre fleurs des céramiques Turques', *Faenza* XXXIX, 1953.
8. du Sommerard, E., *Catalogue et description des objets d'art*, Musée des Thermes et de l'Hotel de Cluny, (Paris, 1883), pp. 178-93.

METALWORK

1. *Topkapı Sarayı Müzesi Arşivi Kılavuzu* II (Istanbul, 1940), facs. 21.
2. Hammer-Purgstall (1827-35) II, p. 366.
3. J. von Karabacek, *Abendländische Künstler zu Konstantinopel im XV. und XVI. Jahrhundert* (Vienna, 1918), pp. 18-21.
4. Aşıkpaşazade 51: Ç. N. Atsız, *Osmanlı Tarihleri* I (Istanbul, 1949), p. 130; trans. R. F. Kreutel, *Von Hirtenzelt zur hohen Pforte* (Graz, 1959), pp. 88-9. Cf. Hammer-Purgstall (1827-35) I, pp. 419, 445, on Ottoman embassies to Emperor Sigismund in 1424 and 1433. The Ottoman ambassador to Venice in 1479 also took a great gold cup: *Diarium Parmense*, apud L. A. Muratori, *Rerum Italicarum Scriptores* XXII (Milan, 1733), col. 309A.
5. De la Broquière (1892), pp. 191-2.
6. E. J. Grube, 'Notes on the arts of the Timurid period', *Gururājmañjarika: Studi in onore di Giuseppe Tucci* I (Naples, 1974) p. 252.
7. See below, fn.13.
8. J. Ebersolt, *Les Arts somptuaires de Byzance* (Paris, 1923), 108f.
9. G.-M. Angiolello: I. Ursu, *Donado da Lezze, Historia Turchesca (1300-1514)* (Bucharest, 1909), pp. 56-7. F. Babinger, *Dizionario Biografico Italiano* (Rome, 1961) ad vocem.
10. F. Babinger, *Die Aufzeichnung des Genuesen Jacopo de Promontorio-De Campis über den Osmanenstaat um 1475*, Bayerische Akademie der Wiss., phil.-hist. Klasse, Sitzungsberichte 8 Heft (1956), pp. 38, 42. The 'other Italian' is Angiolello: ed. A. Capparozzo, *Di Gio. Maria Angiolello e di un suo inedito manoscritto* (Nozze Lampertico-Balbi) (Vicenza, 1881), p. 37. Cf. K. Dilger, *Untersuchungen zur Geschichte des osmanischen Hofzeremoniells im 15. und 16. Jahrhunderts* (Munich, 1967), 107f.
11. Al-Bukhari, 74 n.28: O. Houdas. *El-Bokhâri, Les Traditions Islamiques* IV (Paris, 1914), 47.
12. Dilger, *Hofzeremoniells*, pp. 106-8, esp. 107 fn.896. Ali in İ. H. Uzunçarşılı, *Osmanlı devletinin Saray teşkilatı* (Ankara, 1945), p. 69, fn.2.
13. N. Jorga, *Geschichte des osmanischen Reiches* II (Gotha, 1909), p. 440. According to Feridun, Selim put his chief goldsmith in charge of the Safavid booty: quoted Ünal (1969), p. 101. Three goldsmiths are recorded among the thirty-eight craftsmen taken by Selim from Tabriz: O. Aslanapa, 'Täbriser Künstler am

Hofe der osmanischen Sultane in Istanbul', *Anatolia* 3 (1958), p. 15.
14. G. A. Menavino, *I costumi, et la vita de Turchi* etc. (Florence, 1551), pp. 132-3; cf. the 17th-century traveller Tavernier, quoted B. Miller, *Beyond the Sublime Porte, the Grand Seraglio of Stambul* (New Haven, 1931), p. 217.
15. M. Spallanzani, Gebrauch und Ausbreitung chinesischen Porzellans am ottomanischen Hof im 17. Jahrhundert, *Kunst des Orients* (forthcoming). I am grateful to Dr Spallanzani for sending me a typescript of his article.
16. Tavernier, quoted B. Miller, *The Palace School of Muhammad the Conqueror* (Cambridge, Mass. 1941), pp. 138-9; cf. Dilger, *Hofzeremoniells*, pp. 111, 120-1.
17. A. Refik, *Onaltinci asırda İstanbul hayatı*, 2nd ed. (İstanbul, 1935) 2, doc. n.3; Dilger, *Hofzeremoniells* 110, esp. fn.927; Miller, *Sublime Porte* 180. For the candlesticks, Babinger, *Promonorio* 41; Menavino, *Costumi* 134.
18. Hammer-Purgstall (1827-35) VI, 707-13. On Erzerum, Evliya-Hammer (1834-50) II, 113.
19. R. M. Meriç, Bayramlarda padişahlara hediye edilen san'at eserleri ve karşılıkları, *Türk Sanatı Tarihi, Araştırma ve İncelemeleri* 1 (1963), pp. 764-78. İ. H. Uzunçarşılı, *Belleten* 24 (1960), pp. 103-110. In 1573 the Sultan gave a present of silver, including two ewers, to the French 'agent', Ph. Du Fresne-Canaye, *Le Voyage du Levant*, ed. M. H. Hauser (Paris 1892) 58. Vice versa, the so-called *Türckenverehrung* often consisted of silver plate, which the Sultan promptly consigned to the Imperial Treasury: Kurz (1975), pp. 23, 28, 32, 35, 42, 44; Dilger *Hofzeremoniells*, p. 103.
20. İ. H. Uzunçarşılı, Sancağa çıkarılan Osmanlı şehzadeleri, *Belleten* 39 (1975), pp. 659-96.
21. For the *müteferrika*, Angiolello: Ursu, *Historia Turchesca*, p. 134. Ö. L. Barkan, H.933-4 (M. 1527-8) Mali yılına ait bütçe örneği, *İ.Ü. İktisat Fakültesi Mecmuası* 15 (1953-54), pp. 316, 326.
22. Menavino, *Costumi*, p. 121, ch. xix, fn.13.
23. British Library MS Harleian 3408, fol. 108r. On Domenico, Jacobs (1919) 32f. For a description of the metalworkers' guild, Evliya-Hammer (1834-50) I/ii, 187f.
24. Evliya-Hammer (1834-50) I/i, 52; I/ii, 188. Evliya (1314/1896) I, 570; II, 91.
25. Jacobs (1919) 81, fn.1.
26. İ. Baykal, Selim III devrinde 'İmdad-i Sefer' için para basılmak üzere saraydan verilen altın ve gümüş avani hakkında, *Tarih Vesikaları* 3 (1944), 36-50.
27. Evliya-Hammer (1834-50) I/i, 120. We cannot ignore accidental destruction, by fire for example: Miller, *Sublime Porte*, 106.
28. Z. Zygulski Jr., 'Turkish trophies in Poland and the Imperial Ottoman Style', *Armi Antiche* (Turin 1972), 25-81. Yücel (1970), p. 48.
29. R. Skelton, Characteristics of Later Turkish Jade Carving, *Fifth International Congress of Turkish Arts*, ed. G. Fehér (Budapest, 1978). *Türk Sanatı Tarihi, Araştırma ve İncelemeleri* 1 (1963), pp.677-714.
30. E. Akurgal, C. Mango, R. Ettinghausen, *Treasures of Turkey* (Geneva 1966), p. 236. It seems more likely that this flask is tarnished silver rather than 'zinc' as is usually claimed.
31. H. Fillitz, *Die Schatzkammer in Wien* (Vienna, 1964), p. 133, p. 17; O. Kurz, 'A gold helmet made in Venice for Sultan Sulayman the Magnificent', *Gazette des Beaux-Arts* 6e ser. 74 (1969), pp. 249-58, *Helmet*, 254. Kurz discusses a four-tiered crown Venetian craftsmen made to sell to Sultan Süleyman.
32. F. Çağman, paper read to the Sixth Int. Congress of Turkish Arts, Munich 1980. The information about boiled water (*acqua cotta*) is

given by Domenico Hierosolimitano, British Library MS. Harleian 3408 f.112r.
33. Evliya-Hammer (1834-50) II, p. 108.
34. J. Szablowski, *Zbiory zamku Królewskiego na Wawelu* (Warsaw, 1969), cat. n.250.
35. Ed. Fr. Sarre & F. R. Martin, *Die Ausstellungen von Meisterwerken muhammedanischer Kunst in München, 1910* (Munich, 1912), II, pls. 160-1. For Evliya on enamellers, see below, fn. 69.
36. For a jewelled penbox described as having an enamel ground, *Art Treasures of Turkey* (1966), cat. n. 222. For two Ottoman daggers with opaque enamelling, H. Stöcklein, *Münchener Jahrbuch der bildenden Kunst* 9 (1914-15), p. 141, & fn.109.
37. Melikian-Chirvani (1975), pp. 151-52.
38. T. Esnaf, Turkish metalwork of the Ottoman period, University of London, SOAS Thesis n. 817, p. 47.
39. Lane *Ars orientalis* esp. figs. 6, 16-19.
40. Yu. Miller, Turetski serebryani kuvschinchik XVI.v (Petite cruche turque en argent du XVIe siècle), *Soobscheniya Gosudarstvennogo Ermitazha* 15 (1959), pp. 52-4. Miller reads the assay stamp as Selim b. Süleyman, that is, Selim II (1566-74). The stamp might better be read Süleyman b. Selim, referring to Süleyman I (1520-66).
41. 1537 bowl: Fehér-Koşay (1964-5), p. 27; Fehér (1964), p. 119; Fehér (1975), p. 17. Daggers: *Meisterwerke München 1910* III, pl. 242; Fehér (1964), p. 122, fn.50. B. Radojković, 'Plaques de reliure des évangeliaires des XVI et XVII siècles', *Muzej Primenjene Utmenosti* 3-4 (1958), pp. 5-84, French res. pp, 85-7, fig. 9.
42. R. Anhegger, *Beiträge zur Geschichte des Bergbaus im osmanischen Reich. I. Europäische Türkei* (İstanbul, 1943), esp. ch. 4; N. Beldiceanu, *Südost-Forschungen* 21 (1962), pp. 144-67, 26 (1967), pp. 1-21; both articles are reprinted in N. Beldiceanu, *Le monde Ottoman des Balkans (1402-1566)* (London, 1976); F. W. Carter, *Dubrovnik (Ragusa). A Classic City-State* (London & New York, 1972), pp. 223-7, fig. 31 is a useful map of the principal Balkan mining sites; Sp. Vryonis, 'The question of Byzantine mines', *Speculum* 37 (1962), 1-17.
43. V. Han, 'Une coupe d'argent de la Serbie médiévale', *Actes du XIIe Congrès d'Etudes Byzantines* III (1964), pp. 111-19. Radojković & Milovanović (1981).
44. Carter, *Ragusa*, pp. 313-315.
45. Bach & Radojković (1956), I, p. 9.
46. 1458: B. Krekić, *Dubrovnik (Raguse) et le Levant au Moyen Age* (Paris, 1961), p. 398. 1582: Jean Palerne, *Peregrinations* etc. (Lyons, 1606), p. 450.
47. H. Kovač, 'Nikolaus Ragusinus und seine Zeit', *Jahrbuch des Kunst-historischen Instituts der K.K. Zentralkommission für Denkmalpflege* 11 (1917), col. 81, fn.290.
48. D. G. Giurescu, 'Maîtres orfèvres de Chiprovać en Valachie au XVIIe siècle', *Revue des études sud-est européennes* 2 (1964), pp. 467-510; Nicolescu (1968), p. 339; Fehér (1964), p. 113, fn.2.
49. Fehér (1964), esp. p. 114 fn.6: in Buda itself there is said to have been a flourishing metal-working industry under Turkish rule. The well-known Eger mug is a possible product of this industry: Fehér-Koşay (1964-5), 22f.
50. Radojković & Milovanović (1981).
51. Fehér-Koşay (1966), esp. p. 30 fn. 116, p. 31, p. 32 fn.136, p. 33 fns.141, 144; Fehér (1964); Fehér (1965); Fehér- (1975) p. 14; Nicolescu (1968) p. 94, cat. nos. 65-6; Bach & Radojković (1956) I, figs. 47 & 44 (latter dated 1596). One bowl came from the church of Saške in Novo Brdo: Fehér (1964), p. 120 fn.35, p. 121 fn.43. A fine bowl in the Benaki Museum, Athens, has a Greek inscription in the name of

a 16th-century Metropolitan of Euripos. This and other early Ottoman silver in the Benaki museum are the subject of a current study by Anna Balian. For a reference to a goldsmith, Petar Smederevac, active in 1540? Polish Koşay (1964-5), p. 26 fn.62.

52. A solitary Persian example is to be found in the Demotte Shahname, ed. J. V. S. Wilkinson, *The Chester Beatty Library: A catalogue of the Persian Manuscripts and Miniatures* I (Dublin, 1959), pl. 21; one can cite two Ottoman examples, in the *Süleymānnāme* of the 1490s, idem, *A catalogue of the Turkish Manuscripts and Miniatures* (Dublin, 1958), pl. 2, in the western-influenced miniature illustrated here, pl. 193. The wyvern is, however, a common denizen of Eastern Christian iconography.

53. *Persian art, an illustrated souvenir of the exhibition of Persian Art* (London, 1931), pl. 22. K. Erdmann, 'Eine seldschukische Silberschale', *Jahrbuch der Hamburger Kunstsammlungen* I (1948), pp. 35-43. J. Raby & M. Wenzel, 'Mediaeval Persia or the Ottoman Balkans? A misattributed group of silver bowls' (in preparation).

54. Grube, see above fn.6.

55. Apart from the Victoria and Albert Museum and Hermitage examples illustrated (and see above fn.40), comparable jugs are known from the monastery of Bistriţa in Rumania and the old orthodox church in Sarajevo: resp. Nicolescu (1968), p. 87, cat. n. 56, pl. 41; Bach and Radojković (1956), fig. 49. In general, B. Radojković, Tursko-persijski uticaj na srpske utmeničke zanate XVI i XVII veka (Les influences turco-persanes sur les métiers d'art serbes au XVIe et XVIIe siècles Fr. res.) *Zbornik za Likovne Umetnosti* I (Novi Sad, 1965). A further five jugs in the Benaki museum are at present unpublished.

56. Bach & Radojković (1956), fig. 48; Radojković, *Influences*, fig. 13.

57. B. Narkiss (ed.), *Armenian Art Treasures of Jerusalem* (Jerusalem, 1979), fig. 182.

58. E. Vattai, Budapesti Erzüstlelet a XV-XVI Századból (Budapester Schatzfunde aus dem XV. und XVI. Jahrhundert), *Budapest Régiségei* 16 (1955) 207-17, German res. 218. For examples of other Ottoman fountain ladles, S. Çetintaş, Türklerde su-çeşme, sebil, *Güzel Sanatlar* 5 (1944), esp. 138-9; E. Vattai, A. Körmendi lelet (XVI-XV. szd.) (La trouvaille de Körmend), *Archaeologiai Értesito* 83 (1956), pp. 67-75, French res. 75. The hoard is believed to have been buried by the Franciscans in 1524, two years before the battle of Mohács.

59. The second cited piece is also in the same collection, cf. B. Y. Berry, 'Old Turkish silver', *The Connoisseur*, 101 (1938), p. 132 fig. 7c, which he dates c. 1750.

60. A. S. Melikian-Chirvani, *Le Bronze Iranien. Musée des Arts Décoratifs* (Paris 1973), 92-3.

61. Ünal (1969), p. 100.

62. Bosch, G., Carswell, C., Petherbridge, G., *Islamic bookbindings and bookmaking*. A catalogue of an exhibition. The Oriental Institute, The University of Chicago (Chicago, 1981), pp. 68-70. K. Çiğ, *Türk Kitap Kapları* (Istanbul, 1971), pp. 10, 13. One should not forget the related art of coin-die cutting. According to Evliya Çelebi, Selim I was a goldsmith, coin-die cutter and assay-stamper in his 'idle' moments!

63. Cf. V. Han, 'Les courants des styles dans les métiers d'art des artisans chrétiens', *Balcanica* 1 (1970), p. 247.

64. Evliya-Hammer (1834-50), I/ii, p. 190. A. Refik, *On altıncı asırda İstanbul hayatı, 1553-1591*, 2nd. ed. (İstanbul, 1935), p. 136: firman dated Jumada I AH 1000/1592 AD.

65. E. C. Dodd, *Byzantine silver stamps* (Dumbarton Oaks, Washington D.C., 1961).

66. For the *damga resmi*, which was applied also to textiles, R. Mantran, *Istanbul dans la seconde moitié du XVIIᵉ siècle* (Paris, 1962), pp. 315-16.

67. *Aleppo*: Teixeira (1902), p. 116. *Baghdad*: Teixeira ( ), p. 60. Cairo: Andreasyan (1964), p. 109, according to the Polish-Armenian traveller, Simeon, the Cairo goldsmiths at the beginning of the seventeenth century included craftsmen from Aleppo, Diyarbakır and İstanbul. *Diyarbakır*: Andreasyan (1964), p. 98; *Erzerum*: Evliya-Hammer (1834-50), II, p. 113, Evliya Çelebi (AH 1314/1896 AD), II, p. 91; *Gümüşhane*: Evliya-Hammer (1834-50), II, pp. 187-8. *Trabzon*: Evliya-Hammer (1834-50) II, p. 48; Evliya Çelebi II, p. 91. In Rumelia, Evliya mentions a goldsmiths' quarter in Edirne, K. Kreiser, *Edirne im 17. Jahrhundert nach Evliyā Çelebi* (Freiburg, 1975), p. 177.

68. S. Gerlach, *Dess Aelteren Tage-buch* (Frankfurt, 1674), p. 204, May 1576.

69. Andreasyan (1964), pp. 108-9, 112, 118; Evliya-Hammer (1834-50), I/ii, p. 193; Evliya Çelebi (AH 1314/1896 AD), I, p. 576.

70. A. K. Sanjian, *A catalogue of medieval Armenian manuscripts in the United States* (University of California Publications, Near Eastern Studies 16) (1976), 16-22; C. Dowsett, 'An Armenian Gold Pyx (Kayseri AD 1687)', *Revue des études Arméniennes* 7 (1970), 171-86. I am grateful to Professor Dowsett and Kevork Hintlian for help with Armenian references. Armenian metalworkers promoted an 'Oriental style' in Poland in the 16th and 17th centuries: Dowsett 184-6.

71. A. Sakisian, 'L'orfèvrerie arménienne à influence occidentale de Constantinople aux XVIIIᵉ et XIXᵉ siècles', *Pages d'Art Arménien* (Paris, 1940), 86f.

72. Little has been written on post-1453 Greek metalwork. R. Byron, 'Byzantine metalwork before and after the Fall of Constantinople', *Burlington Magazine* 52 (1928), pp. 189-91 is no more than a note on three items from Athos.

73. Evliya-Hammer (1834-50), I/i, 27; see above, fn.80. A Greek goldsmith is mentioned in Tripoli, Syria, in the 1570s: Kurz (1975), 46.

74. N. Jorga, *Geschichte des osmanischen Reiches* III (Gotha, 1910), pp. 195-6.

75. Aleppo: Teixeira (1902), p. 116. Cairo: G. Bremond, *Voyage en Egypte de G.B. 1643-45*, ed. G. Sanguin (Institut Français d'Archéologie Or. du Caire) (1974), p. 47. In general, *The Jewish Encyclopedia* (New York/London 1904), Goldsmiths and Silversmiths, s.v.; *Encyclopedia Judaica* (Jerusalem, 1971), Goldsmiths and Silversmiths, s.v.

76. For a Venetian goldsmith in Istanbul in the 1560s, trans. E. S. Forster, *Busbecq* (1927), pp. 115-16; Letter III, Constantinople, 1 June 1560.

77. De Jesus (1980), maps 7, 21.

78. Allan (1969), Dish A, contrary to my published description is gilded not tinned.

79. Melikian-Chirvani (1975), p. 148 fn.6.

80. Uluçay (1970), fig. 9.

81. Ors (1970), fig. 9.

82. A. Banck, *Byzantine Art in the collections of the USSR* (Leningrad, 1966), pl. 83.

83. Goodwin (1977), pl. 78.

84. Melikian-Chirvani (1975), p. 151.

85. Miller (1965), pl. 10.

86. Melikian-Chirvani (1974), figs. 21-25.

87. Scerrato (1967), fig. 16.

88. Rice (1953), pl. VII p. 497.

89. Bodleian mss. Pococke 80 fol. 29v, Bruce 35 fol. 32 quoted by Kahle, (1940), p. 42.

90. See Maqrizi/Quatremère, *Histoire des Sultans Mamlouks* (Paris, 1837-45), p. 114.

91. Allan (1977), pp. 160-1 and (1978).

92. Wiet (1932), pls. XXIX-XXXIV.

93. Wiet (1932), pls. XV-XVII.

94. Wiet (1932), pls. XV-XVII.

95. Wiet (1932), pl. XXXV, nos. 4395-6; Melikian-Chirvani (1975), pp. 152-3.

96. Raby (1977/8), pl. 157.2.

97. Cf. Fehér (1976) p. 78 bottom: examples from the Esztergom Museum in Hungary.

98. To be published by Carswell and Hintlian.

99. Smithsonian (1966), no. 232.

100. Migeon (1922), pl. 53.

101. Kalus (1975), pp. 23-8.

102. Etem (1936), no. 1; Survey, pl. 1407.

103. Stöcklein (1934), fig. 13 left.

104. *The life of Benvenuto Cellini, written by himself* (London, 1949), pp. 54-5.

105. K. Çiğ, *Türk Kitap Kapları* (Istanbul, 1971), pl. 34; F. Preyger, 'The Imperial treasury', *Apollo* 101 (1970), pl. IV, p. 42. For the throne, L. A. Mayer, *Islamic woodcarvers* (Geneva, 1958), p. 43. The Throne's traditional ascription has been called into question by F. Preyger, Bayram Tahtı, *Türk Etnografya Dergisi* 13 (1973), pp. 71-8. For a few base metal objects attributed to named artists, L. A. Mayer, *Islamic metalworkers* (Geneva, 1959), pp. 49-51.

106. One item with inscriptions, which are, however, standard abbreviations crudely executed, is the incense burner in the Hopp Museum in Hungary: Ju. A. Miller, 'A Hopp Ferenc Keletársiai Müvészeti Muzeum "török" fustölöjenek meghatározása', *Az Ipar müvészeti muzeum Évkönyvei* 3-4 (1959), pp. 363-5.

CERAMICS

1. Lane (1971), Lane (1960).

2. Lane (1957), pp. 247-82.

3. Aslanapa (1965), Aslanapa (1970).

4. This analysis was carried out by the research laboratory for Archaeology and History of Art at Oxford, thanks to the kind permission of the Director and with the help of Mrs Anne Millet. The results are included in Carswell (11).

5. Riefstahl (1937), pp. 244-81.

6. Raby (1976), pp. 149-88, especially pp. 160 and 182.

7. loc. cit. p. 159.

8. Lane (1971), p. 44.

9. (trans.) 'first red herring'.

10. My views on this were first expounded in Carswell (1972) (5) I, pp. 78-9, II, 4-6. My interpretation is that this and the 1529 Godman water bottle are both Kütahya pieces. This has been further reinforced by the recent (1979) excavations of kiln sites in the centre of Kütahya, which has produced sherds of an early Miletus-type ware and quantities of both 'Abraham of Kütahya' and 'Golden Horn' ware, see F. Şahin 'Kütahya Çini keramik sanatı ve tarihinin yeni buluntular açısından değerlendirilmesi', *Sanat Tarihi Yıllığı*, Vol. IX-X 1979-80, Istanbul, 1981, pp. 259-86.

11. (trans.) 'second red herring'.

12. Carswell (1972) (5), II, pp. 5-6, pl. 3a.

13. *op. cit.*, I, pp. 79-80, pl. 21b.

14. Pope (1972), pp. 125-40.

15. Lane (1971), p. 59.

16. Raby (1976).

17. Carswell (1966), pp. 77-90.

18. Carswell (1972) (5).

19. Carswell (1979).

20. Carswell (1978), pp. 269-92.

21. Julian Raby, Venetia Porter and myself spent three weeks in January 1981 carrying out a survey of the dismantled tiles, with the support of grants from the British Academy and the American Philosophical Society. This was part of the larger survey of all tiled monuments in Syria, now in its final stages.

22. Raby (1977/8), pp. 429-59.

TEXTILES

1. The basic sources on the economics of Bursa silk production are to be found in Dalsar (1960) and İnalcık (no. 17), pp. 209-18.
2. See the article 'Hisb' in the *Encyclopedia of Islam*, New Edition; also Mantran (1962) for a detailed discussion of the role of the *muhtesib*.
3. See Dalsar, *op. cit.*, Chapter IX.
4. See İnalcık, *op. cit.*, pp. 217-18.
5. For an account of legal proceedings, see the 1502 financial code of Bursa, Öz, (1950), pp. 48-9.
6. A striped textile is discussed by Ettinghausen (1969), pp. 134-40.
7. See the review of Öz's work, Denny (1971), pp. 38-41.
8. The design discussed by Mackie (1976), pp. 4-20. For the Chinese interpretation of the design, I am indebted to Professor Schuyler Cammann of the University of Pennsylvania.
9. See Denny (1973), pp. 13-14.
10. For example, see the ogival silk in West Berlin, illustrated in *Museum für Islamische Kunst Berlin* (Berlin, 1971), catalogue 527, plate 73.
11. A method outlined in Denny (1977).
12. See Denny (1981).
13. *Ibid.*
14. The engraving is reproduced in W. S. Maxwell, *The Turks in MDXXXIII* Vol. II (London, 1873), pp. 53-4.
15. See Gönül (1969).
16. For the latter group, see Gentles (1964) and Black and Loveless (1978).
17. See Gönül No. 16 plates 1, 4, 6, 27.
18. See 'Embroidered Flowers from Thrace to Tartary' Black and Loveless (London 1981).
19. Denny (1977), pp. 180-4.
20. Tiles using this design were employed in the decorations of the mosque of Sultan Ahmed (c. 1616), in the additions of this period made to the Imperial palace in Edirne; and Kütahya copies are today found in considerable numbers on the tomb of Ebu Eyyub near İstanbul.
21. See Denny (1978), pp. 22-3.
22. See Topkapı Palace Library, *Hazine* 1609, *History of Mehmed III and the conquest of Eger* for the best-known miniature paintings depicting the use of textiles as parade barriers (also illustrated Öz (1950) plate XVII).
23. Topkapı Palace Library, Hazine 1344, folios 11B-12R (illustrated in Öz (1950), plate XII).
24. See Denny (1974), pp. 67-81.
25. See Kuhnel (1952), pp. 72-81.
26. See colour plates 22 and 32 and E. Atil, 'The Art of the Book' in E. Atil, ed. *Turkish Art* (New York, 1980).
27. Religious attitudes towards silk are discussed in İnalcık (No. 17), pp. 209-10.
28. Examples illustrated by Mackie (1980), fig. 215, and in Denny (1979), p. 190.
29. See Petsopoulos (1979), pp. 53-4.
30. *Ibid.*

CALLIGRAPHY

1. This phrase and its meaning is discussed by U. Derman (No. 53: p. 49). Mr Derman, an excellent calligrapher, is Turkey's leading expert on Ottoman Calligraphy and this author readily acknowledges his debt to his published works (See Nos. 38-65 and 129-30).
2. The only work devoted to this extremely important aspect of the calligrapher's training is No. 61. For a general discussion see No. 53.
3. For the *seceres* of Ottoman Calligraphers the 'Biographical Dictionaries of Calligraphers' are the standard source. Works of this genre include the *Bibliography* entries: Nos. 13; 41; 68; 70; 82; 83; 84; 91; and 94. Via comparisons

of the 'masters' who taught each succeeding generation of calligraphers it is possible to establish the individual pedigree (*secere*) of each calligrapher (See also No. 5).
4. For this expression and its usage see No. 46: p. 62.
5. See No. 82.
6. See No. 70.
7. For a discussion of the 'Six-Scripts' and their development see No. 129—pp. 86-105.
8. The most comprehensive discussion of the rebuilding of İstanbul is found in the works of İnalcık. In particular see: 'İstanbul', *The Encyclopaedia of Islam* (New Edition), Vol. IV (1973), pp. 224-48; and 'The policy of Mehmed II toward the Greek population of İstanbul and the Byzantine buildings of the city', *Dumbarton Oaks Papers* 23-4 (1969-70), pp. 229-49.
9. The most comprehensive works dealing with the life of this calligrapher are Nos. 23, 103, and No. 13.
10. Karahisari's life is undoubtedly the best detailed of any Ottoman calligrapher. Nos. 29, 55, 99 and 106.
11. For Hafiz Osman see Nos. 28, 25, 45, and 123.
12. For İsmail Zudhi see No. 105.
13. For Mustafa Rakım see No. 109.
14. For Kadıasker Mustafa İzzet Efendi see Nos. 3, 54, 76, and 107.
15. For Mehmed Şefik Bey see Nos. 117 and 20. The latter detailed his contributions to the calligraphy which decorated the *Ulu Cami* in Bursa.
16. Biographical data and anecdotes concerning the life of Sami Efendi are found in a series of articles by U. Derman, Nos. 50, 38 and 51.
17. A standard introduction to Ottoman Architecture is provided by A. Kuran's *The Mosque In Early Ottoman Architecture* (Chicago, 1968).
18. Baykal's study (No. 20) of this important Ottoman mosque provides a detailed analysis of the 191 '*levhas*' which decorate its walls.
19. See Nos. 47 and 130.
20. For a detailed discussion of the inks and the formulas whereby they were made in the Ottoman Empire, see Nos. 44 and 130.
21. Paper and its preparation for the calligrapher is detailed by U. Derman. See Nos. 49 and 130.

PAINTING

1. Very little has so far been published on Ottoman painting before 1500. Several communications given to date by the author have not yet appeared in print. However, those of the dated or datable 15th-century manuscripts and paintings belonging to this early phase of the arts of the book that have been published or referred to in the literature are the following:
   (1). Paris. Bibiothèque Nationale, Suppl. Turc 309. Ahmedi *Iskandarnāme* copied in Amasya in AH 819/1416 AD. See Stchoukine (1966), pp. 45-6 ms. 1. Only three of the illustrations belong to the period of the manuscript and they are in a style that follows entirely Byzantine models. They are badly damaged.
   (2) Oxford. Bodleian Ouseley 133 *Dilsūznāme* copied in Edirne in AH 860/1455-6 AD. See Stchoukine, Ars Asiatiques, 15, 1967, pp. 47-50; Atil (1973), pl. 2, figs. 3-4; Atil (1980), fig. 64. This manuscript is of crucial importance as it is dated. The style of the miniatures gives a possible date for two undated manuscripts in Istanbul and Venice (Nos. 3 & 4 of this list).
   (3) Revan 989. *Dīwān* of Mawlana Katibi Tab'allah (Tabib-Allah). See F. Çağman in *Sanat Tarihi Yıllığı*, VI (İstanbul, 1974-5), pp. 333-45; Atil (1980) col. pl. 16.
   (4) Venice. Marciana, Cod. Straniero XC (=57). See *Mostre d'arte Iranica*, Rome, 1956, p. 289, no. 561 and pl. CIII (called Persian 16th-century); F. Gabrieli and U. Scerrato,

Gli Arabi in Italia (Milan, 1979), fig. 731 (called Turkish, mid-16th-century). The style of the paintings is so close to the double page painting of the İstanbul *Diwan* (No. 3), which in turn has a single-page painting in a style identical to the dated Oxford manuscript (No. 2), that it is possible to date these manuscripts to the middle of the 15th century.
   (5) Paris. Bibliothèque Nationale. Suppl. Turc 693. Sharaf al-Din, *Jarrāhiye-i Ilkhāniye*, copied in AH 870/1465 AD. See P. Huard and M. D. Grmek, Le premier manuscript chirurgical turc redigé par Charaf-al-Din (1465) (Paris, 1960); Atil (1973), pl. 3, fig. 5-6. The illustrations of this manuscript are a curiosity. They do not follow the general 15th-century style, but seem to adhere to either Byzantine or Ilkhanid models.
   (6) Bombay. Prince of Wales museum MS. 5134. *Kalila wa Dimna*, copied in AH 990/1495 AD. See G. M. Meredith-Owens in *Bulletin of the Prince of Wales Museum of Western India*, No. 10, 1967, pp. 27-31, pls. 29-35; Stchoukine (1966), pp. 46-7, ms. 2.
   (7) İstanbul. Topkapı Sarayı, H.799. Amir Khusrow *Khamse* copied in AH 903/1498 AD. See Stchoukine (1966), p. 47, ms. 3; Atasoy, Çağman (1974), pl. 2; Grube, Çağman, Atasoy (1978), pl. 83; Atil (1980), fig. 70.
   (8) New York. Metropolitan Museum of Art, 69.27. Hatifi, *Khusrow and Shirin* copied in AH 904/1498-9 AD. See Sotheby Sale Biblioteca Philippica, N.S. Past IV. Nov. 26 1968, Lot 190; Atil (1980), fig. 71.
   (9) Uppsala, University Library Vet. 86. Shakhy, *Khusrow and Shirin*, copied in Edirne in AH 905/1499 AD. See C. J. Lamm in *Orientalia Suecana*, I, 1953, pp. 95-114, pls. i-XVI; Stchoukine (1966), p. 48, ms. 4.
   (10) Edwin Binney 3rd Collection. Hamdi, *Layla and Majnūn* copied in AH 905/1499-1500 AD. See Binney (1979), pp. 6-10, no. 4.
   (11) Cambridge, Mass. Fogg Art Museum 1958.155. *Khusrow and Shirin* or *Khamse*. Unpublished.
   (12) Dublin. Chester Beatty Library. ms. 406. Firdevsi of Bursa, *Sulaymānnāme* probably reign of Bayezid II (1481-1512). See Minorsky (1958), pp. 9-10, ms. 406; Stchoukine (1966), p. 49 ms. 5; Atil (1979), fig. 72.
   (13) Edwin Binney 3rd Collection. Attar, *Mantiq al-Tayr*. See Binney (1973), No. 1, pp. 18-21; Binney (1979), pp. 5-10, No. 3.
   (14) London. Keir collection. Four pages from a manuscript of Shaykhi's *Khusrow and Shirin*. See Wiet, Sabry Pasha Collection, No. 86, pl. XLI; Meredith-Owens (1976), pp. 2254, Nos. IV. 1-4, pls. 96-7.
2. For this manuscript see No. 4
3. For this manuscript see No. 7
4. For this manuscript see No. 8
5. There is a manuscript of Ahmedi's *Iskandarnāme* in the Topkapı Sarayı (H.679, see Stchoukine (1966) ms. 6), which was copied in AH 906/1500-1 AD, the illustrations of which are entirely in the Turkman style of Shiraz of the second half of the 15th century. They may well have been executed by a Turkman painter who worked at the Ottoman court. For a typical 16th-century example, see the magnificent pages from a *Shāhnāme* manuscript in Boston at the Museum of Fine Arts, 14.691-692; Ananda A. Coomaraswamy, *Les miniatures Orientales de la collection Goloubew au Museum of Fine Arts de Boston*, Paris, Bruxelles, 1929, nos. 97 a-d and 98, pp. 60-3, pls. LIV-LVIII and New York MMA No. 52.20.9; E. J. Grube in *Beitrage Zur Kunstgeschichte Asiens, In memoriam Ernst Diez*, Ed. O. Aslanapa (İstanbul, 1963),

pp. 237-55, illustrated in the Safavid style of Shiraz.

6. For the argument see R. Ettinghausen, 'Early realism in Islamic Art', *Scritti in onore di Giorgio Levi della Vida I*, Rome, 1956, pp. 250-73; and E. J. Grube, 'Realism or formalism: Notes on some lustre painted vessels', forthcoming in *Yearbook of the Museum of Islamic Art*, Cairo.

7. See E. G. Sims, 'The Turks and illustrated historical texts', *Fifth International Congress of Turkish Art*, Budapest, 1975, Budapest, 1978, pp. 747-72.

8. For this manuscript see a copy of the History of Sultan Süleyman of AH 987/1579 AD. See Minorsky (1958), pp. 19-21, ms. 413.

9. For these manuscripts see E. J. Grube, 'The Siyar-i Nabi of the Spencer collection in the New York Public Library', *Atti del Secondo Congresso Internazionale di Arte Turca*, Venice, 1963, Naples, 1965, pp. 149-76, pls. LXXVI-LXXXIII.

10. Lokman 'Ashuri, *Zubdat al-Tawārīkh*, completed after AH 991/1583 AD. Dublin, Chester Beatty Library, ms. 414 fol. 53R. See Minorsky (1958), pp. 21-5, ms. 414; Stchoukine (1966), pp. 74-5, ms. 43, pls. LVI-LVII.

11. The decorative drawings in the Murad Album in Vienna, brought to the attention of scholars by Kurt Blauensteiner ('Beispiele Osmanischer Buchkunst aus der Zeit Sultan Selim II and Sultan Murad III', *Wiener Beiträge zur Kunst- und Kulturgeschichte Asiens*, X, 1936, pp. 34-55) were first studied in the larger context of Ottoman art by the writer at the *First International Congress of Turkish Art*, Ankara, 1959, Ankara, 1961, pp. 176-209, pls. CXXI-CLXIII, and in *Pantheon* XX, 1962, pp. 213-26 and 306-13.

12. See K. Erdmann, 'Die Fliesen am Sünnet Odasi des Topkapi Saray in Istanbul', *Festchrift für Ernst Kuhnel*, Berlin 1959, pp. 144-53.

13. See also Johanna Zick, 'Der Osmanische Dekorationsstil', *Bustan*, V, 1964, pp. 35-8.

14. For Ottoman claims to the Caliphate D. Sourdel *Encyclopedia of Islam*, IV², 1977, pp. 945-46.

Bibliography

THE OTTOMAN MILIEU

1. De la Broquière, B., Ed. Schefer, C., *Voyage d'outremer* (Paris, 1892).
2. Busbecq, O. G. de, Trans., Foster E. S., *Turkish Letters . . .* (Oxford, 1927).
3. Chandler, R., *Travels in Asia Minor* (London, 1776).
4. Djevad Bey, A., *État militaire ottoman . . .* (Constantinople and Paris, 1882).
5. Elliott, C. B., *Travels in the three great empires of Austria, Russia and Turkey* (London, 1838).
6. Galland, A., *Journal . . . 1672-3* (Paris, 1881).
7. Grelot, C. J., *Relation nouvelle d'un voyage de Constantinople* (Paris, 1680).
8. Grenville, H., Ed. Ehrenkreutz, *Observations sur l'état actuel de l'Empire Ottoman* (Michigan, 1965).
9. İnalcık, H., *The Ottoman Empire* (London, 1973).
10. Lewis, R., *Everyday life in Ottoman Turkey* (London, 1971).
11. Mantran, R., *La vie quotidienne à Constantinople* (Paris, 1965).
12. Miller, B., *Beyond the Sublime Porte* (New Haven, 1931).
13. Penzer, N. M., *The Harem* (London, 1936).
14. Refik, A., *İstanbul hayatı*, iv vol. (Istanbul, 1930-5).
15. Rycault, Sir P., *The History of the Turkish Empire . . .* (London, 1680).
16. Salignac, J. de G. B., *Ambassade en Turquie* (Paris/Auch, 1888).
17. Sanderson, J., Ed. Foster, E. S., *The travels in the Levant* (London, 1931).
18. Tavernier, J. B., *Nouvelle relation de l'intérieur du Serail du Grand Seigneur* (Cologne, 1675).
19. Thévenot, M. de, *Voyages . . .* (Paris, 1664).
20. Tott, Baron de, *Mémoires*, iv vol. (Amsterdam, 1784).
21. Tournefort, J. P. de, *Relation d'un voyage . . .* (Paris, 1717).
22. Wortley-Montagu, Lady M., Ed. Halsband, R., *Complete letters*, vol. 1, 1708-20 (London, 1965).

METALWORK

1. Allan, J. W., 'Later Mamluk Metalwork. A Series of Dishes', *Oriental Art*, N.S. 15 (1969).
2. — 'Originality in bronze', *Iran*, 15 (1977).
3. — 'From Tabriz to Siirt', *Iran*, 16 (1978).
4. — *Nīshāpūr: metalwork of the early Islamic period* (New York, 1981).
5. Andreasyan, H., *Polonyalı Simeon'un Seyahatnamesi 1608-19* (İstanbul, 1964).
6. Anhegger, R., *Beitraege zur Geschichte des Bergbaus im Osmanischen Reich, I Europaeische Turkei* (İstanbul, 1943).
7. Arseven, C. E., *Les arts décoratifs turcs* (İstanbul).
8. *Arts de l'Islam* (Paris, 1971).
9. *The Arts of Islam*, Arts Council, Hayward Gallery (1976).
10. Bach, İ. and Radojković, B., *Le travail artistique des métaux des peuples yougoslaves au cours des siècles*, 2 vols. (Belgrade, 1956).
11. Barrett, D., *Islamic metalwork in the British Museum* (London, 1949).
12. Beldiceanu, N., *Le monde ottoman des Balkans (1402-1566)* (London, 1976).
13. Davis, F., *The palace of Topkapı in Istanbul* (New York, 1970).
14. Etem, H., 'Madenden üç Türk eseri', *Türk Tarih*, 3 (1936).
15. Evliya Çelebi, *Seyāhatnāme* (İstanbul, 1314/1896). Cf. no. 24.
16. Fehér, G., 'Contribution au problème de l'orfèvrerie turque à l'époque de l'Empire Ottoman', *Acta Orientalia Academiae Scientiarum Hungaricae*, 17 (1964).
17. — 'Quelques problèmes des objets d'art métalliques turcosmanlis mis au jour en Hongrie', *Atti del 2⁰ Congresso Int. di Arte Turca*, Venice 1963 (Naples, 1965).
18. — *Craftsmanship in Turkish-ruled Hungary* (Budapest, 1975).
19. — 'Türk çömlekçilik ve bakırcılığının Macaristan'da kalmış hatıraları,' *Türkiyemiz* (Haziran, 1976).
20. Fehér, G. & Koşay, H. Z. 'Macaristan'daki Türk kuyumculuk yadigarlari ve Balkanlardaki kuyumculuğa Türk tesiri', *Türk Etnoğrafya Dergisi* 7-8, 1966, pp. 19-37.
21. Goodwin, G., *Ottoman Turkey* (London, 1977).
22. Grancsay, S. V., 'The new galleries of oriental arms and armour', *Bulletin of the Metropolitan Museum of Art*, 16, no. 9 (1958).
23. von Hammer-Purgstall, J., *Geschichte des osmanischen Reiches* (Pest, 1827-35).
24. —, trans., *Evliya Efendi. Narrative of travels in Europe, Asia and Africa in the seventeenth century*, 2 vols. (London, 1834, 1850).
25. Ivanov, A. A., *The art of Kubachi* (Leningrad, 1976).
26. Jacobs, E., *Untersuchungen zur Geschichte der Bibliothek im Serai zu Konstantinopel I*. (Sitzungsberichte der Heidelberger Akademie der Wiss., Phil.-Hist. Klasse, 24 Abh.) (Heidelberg, 1919).
27. de Jesus, P. S., *The development of prehistoric mining and metallurgy in Anatolia*, 2 vols., BAR International Series 74 (1980).
28. Kahle, P., 'Chinese porcelain in the lands of Islam', *Transactions of the Oriental Ceramic Society*, 18 (1940-1).
29. Kalus, L., 'Boucliers circulaires de l'Orient musulman', *Gladius*, 12 (1974).
30. — 'Un bouclier mamelouk dans les collections du Musée de l'Homme à Paris', *Armi Antiche* (1975).
31. Kocabaş, H., 'Une collection de cuivres seldjoukides', *Atti del secondo congresso internazionale di arte turca*, Venice 1963 (Naples, 1965).
32. Koşay, H. Z. and Çetin, P., 'Etnoğrafya Müzesindeki Alemler', *Türk Etnoğrafya Dergisi*, III (1958).
33. Kurz, O., *European Clocks and Watches in the Near East* (London/Leiden, 1975).
34. Mayer, L. A., *Islamic armourers and their work* (Geneva, 1962).
35. Melikian-Chirvani, A. S., *Le bronze iranien* (Paris, 1973).
36. — 'Recherches sur l'école du bronze ottoman au XVI siècle', *Turcica*, 6 (1975).
37. Migeon, G., *Musée du Louvre. L'Orient Musulman*, 2 vols. (Paris, 1922).
38. Miller, Yu., 'Turetski serebryani kuvschinchik XVIv.', *Soobscheniya Gosudarstvennogo Ermitazha*, 11-15 (1957-9).
39. — *Iskustvo Turtsii* (n.p. 1965).
40. Nicolescu, C., *Argintăria laică şi religiosă în ţările Române (sec. XIV-XIX)*, Muzeul de Artă al Republicii socialiste România secţia de artă românească (Bucharest, 1968).
41. North, A. R. E., 'Islamic arms and armour', *The Connoisseur*, April (London, 1976).
42. Örs, H., 'The history of the Topkapı Palace', *Apollo* XCII (July, 1970).
43. Öz, T., *Turkish ceramics* (n.p., n.d.).
44. Petrasch, E., *Die Türkenbeute* (Karlsruhe, 1970).
45. Pope, A. U., ed., *A survey of Persian art*, 6 vols. (Oxford, 1938-9).
46. Pyle, N. S., 'Ottoman okka weights', *Belleten*, 161 (1977).
47. Radojković, B. & Milovanović, D. Masterpieces of Serbian Goldsmiths' Work. 13thc.-18thc. Exhibition, VA 1981 (London, 1981).
48. Rice, D. S., 'Studies in Islamic metalwork IV', *Bulletin of the School of Oriental and African Studies*, 15 (1953).
49. Sarre, F. and Martin, F. R., ed., *Die Ausstellung von Meisterwerken muhammedanischer Kunst in München 1910*, 3 vols. (Munich, 1912).
50. Schöbel, J., *Türkenschatz aus dem Historischen Museum der Staatlichen Kunstsammlungen Dresden* (Leipzig, 1974).
51. Smithsonian Institution, *Art Treasures of Turkey* (Washington, 1966).
52. Stöcklein, H., 'Die Waffenschätze im Topkapu Sarayi zu Istanbul', *Ars Islamica*, 1 (1934).
53. Teixeira, P., *The Travels of Pedro Teixeira*, trans. W. F. Sinclair, Hakluyt Society (London, 1902).
54. Uluçay, Ç., 'The Ottoman Harem', *Apollo* XCII (July 1970).
55. Ünal, I., 'Çini cami kandilleri', *Türk Sanatı Tarihi, Araştırma ve İncelemeleri*, 2 (1969).
56. Wiet, G., *Objets en cuivre* (Cairo, 1932).

57. Yücel, Ü., *Türk Etnografya Dergisi*, 7-8 (1964-5).
58. — 'Thirteen centuries of Islamic arms', *Apollo* (July 1970).

CERAMICS

1. *The Arts of Islam*, Arts Council, Hayward Gallery (London, 1976).
2. Aslanapa, O., *Turkische Fliesen und Keramik in Anadolien* (İstanbul, 1965).
3. 'Pottery and Kilns from the Iznik excavations', *Forschungen zur Kunst Asiens in Memoriam Kurt Erdmann* (İstanbul, 1970).
4. Atil, E., *Ceramics from the World of Islam* (Washington, 1973).
5. Carswell, J., *Kütahya Tiles and Pottery from the Armenian Cathedral of St James, Jerusalem*, 2 vols. (Oxford, 1972).
6. — 'Pottery and Tiles on Mount Athos', *Ars Orientalis*, VI (1966).
7. — 'Six Tiles', *Islamic Art in the Metropolitan Museum of Art* (New York, 1972).
8. — 'Some Fifteenth-Century Hexagonal Tiles from the Near East', *Victoria and Albert Museum Yearbook*, III (London, 1972).
9. — 'Syrian Tiles from Sinai and Damascus', *Archaeology in the Levant: Essays for Kathleen Kenyon*, ed. P. Moorey and P. Parr (Warminster, 1978).
10. — 'Two Tiny Turkish Pots—Some Recent Discoveries in Syria', VI International Congress of Turkish Art (Munich, 1979) in press.
11. — 'Edirne, Damascus and Fifteenth-century Turkish Pottery', *Proceedings of III International Congress of Turkish Art* (Cambridge), n.p.
12. Denny, W. B., *The Ceramics of the Mosque of Rüstem Pasha and the Environment of Change* (New York, 1977).
13. *L'Islam dans les collections nationales* (Paris, 1977).
14. *Islamic Art, The David Collection* (Copenhagen, 1975).
15. Grandjean, R., *Céramique Orientale* (Paris).
16. Lane, A., *Later Islamic Pottery* (London, 1957); 2nd ed. (1971).
17. — 'The Ottoman Pottery of Isnik', *Ars Orientalis*, II (1957).
18. — *A Guide to the Collection of Tiles*, Victoria and Albert Museum (London, 1960).
19. Miller, D., *Turkish Ceramics* (Leningrad, 1972).
20. Öz, T., *Turkish Ceramics* (n.p., n.d.).
21. Papadopoulos, A., *L'Islam et l'art musulman* (Paris, 1976).
22. Pope, J. A., 'Chinese Influence on Iznik Pottery: A Re-examination of an Old Problem', *Islamic Art in the Metropolitan Museum of Art*, ed. R. Ettinghausen (New York, 1972).
23. Raby, J., 'A Seventeenth-century Description of Iznik-Nicaea', *Deutsches Archäologisches Institut Abteilung Istanbul, Istanbuler Mitteilungen*, Band 26 (1976).
24. — 'Diyarbakir: A Rival to Iznik', *Deutsches Archäologisches Institut Abteilung Istanbul, Istanbuler Mitteilungen*, Band 27/28 (1977/8).
25. Rackham, B., *Islamic Pottery and Italian Maiolica* (London, 1959).
26. Riefstahl, R. M., 'Early Turkish Tile Revetments in Edirne', *Ars Islamica*, IV (1937).

TEXTILES

1. Black, D. and Loveless C., *İşlemeler: Ottoman Domestic Embroideries* (London, 1978).
2. *Calligraphy and the Decorative Arts of Islam*, Bluett and Sons (London, 1976).
3. Dalsar, Fahri, *Bursa'da İpekçilik* (İstanbul, 1960).
4. Denny, W., Review of T. Öz, in *Textile Museum Journal*, III, 2 (1971).
5. — 'Ottoman Turkish Textiles', *Textile Museum Journal*, III, 3 (1972).
6. — 'Anatolian Rugs, an Essay on Method',

Textile Museum Journal, III, 4 (1973).
7. — 'A Group of Silk Islamic Banners', *Textile Museum Journal*, IV, 1 (1974).
8. — The ceramics of the mosque of Rustem Pasha and the environment of change (New York, 1977).
9. — 'Ottoman Textiles and Urban Life', *Warp and Weft of Islam*, ed. J. Bacharach and I. Bierman (Seattle, 1978).
10. — 'Textiles', *Turkish Treasures from the Collection of E. Binney 3rd* (Portland, Oregon, 1979).
11. — 'Dating Ottoman Turkish Works in the Saz Style', *Muqarnas* 1 (New Haven, 1981), forthcoming.
12. *Etoffes Merveilleuses du Musée Historique des Tissus, Lyon*, tome III, 'Tissus de l'Orient, de l'Italie et de l'Espagne', ed. Takahiko Sano (Japan, 1976).
13. Ettinghausen, R., 'An Early Ottoman Textile', *Communications of the First International Congress of Turkish Art* (Ankara, 1969).
14. Gentles, M., *Turkish and Greek Island Embroideries* (Chicago, 1964).
15. Gönül, M., 'Some Turkish Embroideries in the Collection of the Topkapı Sarayı Museum in İstanbul', *Kunst des Orients*, VI, 1 (1969).
16. — *Turkish Embroideries*, Touring Club of Turkey.
17. İnalcik, H., 'Ḥarīr' *Encyclopedia of Islam*, New Edition, vol. III.
18. Kuehnel, E., 'Erinnerungen an eine Episode in der Türkenpolitik Friedrichs des Grossen', *Oriens*, V, 1 (1952).
19. Mackie, L., *The Splendour of Turkish Weaving* (Washington, 1973).
20. — 'A Turkish Carpet with Spots and Stripes', *Textile Museum Journal*, IV, 3 (1976).
21. — 'Rugs and Textiles', *Turkish Art*, ed. E. Atil (New York, 1980).
22. Mantran, R., *Istanbul dans la seconde moitié du XVIIe siècle* (Paris, 1962).
23. Migeon, G. and Guiffrey, M. J., *La Collection Kelekian, Etoffes et Tapis* (Paris, 1908).
24. Öz, T., *Turkish Textiles and Velvets* (Ankara, 1950).
25. Petsopoulos, Y., *Kilims* (London, 1979).
26. *Splendeur de l'Art Turc* (Paris, 1953).
27. Spuhler, König and Volkmann, *Old Eastern Carpets* (Munich, 1978).

CALLIGRAPHY

1. Aksel, M., 'Yazıdan Resme', *Akademi* 3-4 (İstanbul, 1965) 32-6.
2. — *Türklerde Dinî Resimler* (İstanbul, 1967).
3. Aksüt, S. K., 'Kazasker Mustafa İzzet Efendi', *Hayat Tarih Mecmuasi* 2/8 (1966) 52-3.
4. Alparslan, A., 'Bazı Farsça Kaynaklarda Hattatlıkla Alâkalı Bilgiler I.', *I.Ü. Sanat Tarihi Yıllığı* 5 (1973) 579-85.
5. — 'Ecoles Calligraphiques Turques', *İslâm Tetkikleri Enstitüsü Dergisi* 5/1 (1973) 265-78.
6. — '50 Yıl İçinde Hattatlıkla Alâkalı Kitap ve Mühim Makaleler', Türk Kültürünü Araştırma Enstitüsü Yayınları: 41/I/A3 *Cumhuriyetin 50. yılına Armağan* (Ankara, 1973).
7. — 'Hattat Hâmid Aytaç', *Hayat Tarih Mecmuasi* 8/2/11 (1973) 16-22.
8. — 'Khaṭṭ', *Encyclopaedia of Islam* (2nd. Ed.) Vol. IV, 1125-6.
9. — 'Yazı-Resim', *Boğaziçi Universitesi Dergisi* 1 (1973) 1-27.
10. Arndt, R., 'Ebru: The Cloud Art', *Aramco World* 24/3 (1973) 26-32.
11. Arsel, M., 'Das Schriftbild in der türkischen Kunst', *Anatolica* 1 (1967).
12. Aslanapa, O., *Turkish Art and Architecture* (London, 1971) (see Chapter 29—pp. 323-7).
13. Ayverdi, E. H., *Fâtih Devri Hattatları ve Hat Sanatı* (İstanbul, 1953).

14. Baltacioğlu, I. H., 'İslâm Yazıları', *Tedrisatı İptidaiye Mecmuasi* 1/9 (ND) 111-24.
15. — 'İslâm Yazılarının Tarihçesi: 4—Ta'lik Nevi, *Tedrisati İptidaiye Mecmuasi* 3/19 (ND) 63-75.
16. — *Türklerde Yazı Sanatı* (Ankara, 1958).
17. — *Türk Plâstik Sanatlari* (Ankara, 1971).
18. Barin, E., 'Hattat Halim Özyazıcı', *Akademi* 3 (İstanbul, 1965) 18-19.
19. — 'Emin Barın'ın Kûfi ve Celi Divani Yazı Türklerinde yeni uygulamaları', *Türkiyemiz* 5/13 (1974) 23-30.
20. Baykal, K., *Bursa'da Ulu Câmi* (İstanbul, 1950).
21. Binark, İ., *Eski Kitapçılık Sanatlarımız* (Ankara, 1975).
22. Celâl, M., *Reisülhattatin Kâmil Akdik* (İstanbul, 1938).
23. — *Şeyh Hamdullah* (İstanbul, 1948).
24. Cevdet, M., 'Siyakat Yazısı ve Rakkamları', Taken from: *M. Cevdet, Hayatı, Eserleri ve Kütübhanesi* (İstanbul, 1937).
25. Çiğ, K., *Hattat Hafız Osman Efendi: 1642-1698 (A Famous Turkish Calligrapher Hafız Osman Efendi)* (İstanbul, 1949).
26. — 'On Sekizinci Asır Lâke Tezhibcilerinden Ali Al-Usküdari', *Türk Tarih, Arkeologya ve Etnografya Dergisi* 5 (1949) 192-202.
27. — '1640-1690 Yıllarında Hat San'atkârları', *Tarih Dünyası* 2/14 (Istanbul, 1950) 606-7 & 10.
28. — 'Hafız Osman Efendi', *Tarih Dünyası* 2/16 (1950) 698-700.
29. — 'Hattat Ahmed Karahisari', *Tarih Dünyası* 1/6 (1950) 234-5.
30. — 'Hattat Padişahlar', *Tarih Dünyası* 1/5 (1950) 196-7.
31. — 'Hattat Vezirler', *Tarih Dünyası* 2/10 (1950) 429-31.
32. — 'Kadın Hattatlarımız', *Tarih Dünyası* 2/11 (1950) 459-61.
33. — 'Osmanlı-Türk Hattatları', *Tarih Dünyası* 1/4 (1950) 168-9 & 174.
34. — 'Sultan IV. üncü Murad'in bir Kur'anı Kerimine ve bir sözüne 1000'er altun verdiği hattat', *Tarih Dünyası* 3/23 (1951) 982-3.
35. — 'Türk Oymacıları (Katığları) ve eserleri', *A.I.F. Türk ve Islâm Sanatları Enstitüsü Yıllık* 2 (1957).
36. — *Türk Kitap Kapları* (İstanbul, 1971).
37. Çulpan, C., *Türk-İslâm Tahta Oymacılık San'atından Selçuk Devri Bir Kur'an Rahlesi*. İstanbul, 1960 (50 Sanat Sever Serisi: No. 17).
38. Derman, U., *Hattat Sami Efendi (1838-1912) Hayatı ve Eserleri* (İstanbul, 1962) (50 Sanat Sever Serisi: No. 18).
39. — *Hattat Nazif Bey (1846-1913) Hayatı ve Eserleri* (İstanbul, 1963) (50 Sanat Sever Serisi: 19).
40. — *Hattat Mustafa Halim Özyazıcı (1898-1964) Hayatı ve Eserleri* (İstanbul, 1964) (50 Sanat Sever Serisi: 20).
41. — 'Edirne Hattatları ve Edirne'nin Yazı Sanatımızdaki Yeri', *Edirne'nin 600. Fetih Yıldönümü Armağan Kitabı* (Ankara, 1965). (See: 311-19).
42. — *Hattat Hacıt Arif ler: 1) Çarşambalı Arif Bey (?-1892), 2) Bakkal Arif Efendi (1830-1909)* (İstanbul, 1965) (50 Sanat Sever Serisi: No. 21).
43. — *Kardeş İkı Hattatımız: Ömer Vasfî Efendi (1880-1928), Neyzen Emin Efendi (1883-1945)* (İstanbul, 1966) (50 Sanat Sever Serisi: No. 22).
44. — 'Eski Mürekkebçiliğimiz', *Islâm Düşüncesi* 1/2 (1967) 97-112.
45. — 'Hafiz Osman'in Yazı Sanatımızdaki Yeri', *Hayat Mecmuası* 52 (1967).
46. — 'Hat Sanatında Türklerin Yeri (The Turks and the Art of Calligraphy)', *Islam Sanatında Türkler (The Turkish Contributions to Islamic Arts)* (İstanbul, 1967) (See: 52-83).
47. — 'Kalem', *İslâm Düşüncesi* (Part 1) 1/3 (1967) 161-176; (Part 2) 1/4 (1967), 255-66.
48. — 'Hattat Halim Efendi', *İslâm Düşüncesi* 2/6 (1968) 399-406.
49. — 'Kâğıda Dair', *İslâm Düşüncesi* 2/5 (1968)

338-47.

50. — 'Büyük Bir Hat Sanatkârımız Sami Efendi', *Hayat Tarih Mecmuası* 5/1/5 (1969) 4-10.

51. — 'Hattat Sami Efendi'nin Dış Kirası', *Hayat Tarih Mecmuası* 4/2 (1969) 20-22.

52. — 'Yazı Nasıl Yazılır', *İslam Düşüncesi* 2/8 (1969) 505-12.

53. — 'Hat', *Türk Ansiklopedisi* 19 (Ankara, 1970), 49-60.

54. — 'Kadıasker Mustafa İzzet Efendi ve yazdığı Hilye-i Saadet', *Hayat* 47 (1970).

55. — 'Kanuni Devrinde Yazı San'atımız', *Kanuni Armağan.* (Ankara, 1970) (See : 269-89).

56. — 'Reis-ül-Hattâtin Kâmil Akdik', *Hayat Tarih Mecmuası* 7/2/7 (1971) 35-41.

57. — 'Tuğrakeş İsmail Hakkı Altunbezer', *Hayat Tarih Mecmuası* 7/2/6 (1971) 43-51.

58. — 'Hat Sanatında Resim-Yazılar', *Kubbealtı Akademi Mecmuası* 1/3 (1972) 65-72.

59. — 'Yazı San'atımızda Tababet', *Image* (Resimli Tıbbi Dergi, Roche) 11 (1972) 27-32.

60. — 'İranlı Ta'lik Ustadı Mir İmâd ül-Haseni', *Güneş* 18 (1973) 16-18.

61. — 'Türk yazı san'atında icazetnâmeler ve taklid yazılar', *VII. Türk Tarih Kongresi (Kongreye Sunulan Bildiriler II.* (Ankara, 1973) (716-27).

62. — 'Yazı tarihimizde hattat imza ve şecereleri', *VII. Türk Tarih Kongressi (Kongreye Sunulan Bildiriler II.)* (Ankara, 1973) (See: 728-32).

63. — 'Benzeri olmayan bir sanat albümü: Gazneli Mahmud Mecmuası', *Türkiyemiz* 5/14 (1974) 17-21.

64. — 'Mezar Kitâbelerinde Yazı San'atımız', *Türkiye Turing ve Otomobil Kurumu Belleteni* 49/328 (1975) 36-47.

65. — *Türk Sanatında Ebrû* (İstanbul, 1977).

66. Dürüst, K., 'Ebru Sanatı', *Türkiye Turing ve Otomobil Kurumu Belleteni* 50/329 (1975) 2-4 & 21-2 (English Summary).

67. Ersoy, O., *XVIII. ve XIX. yüzyıllarda Türkiye'de kağıt* (Ankara, 1973).

68. Habib Efendi (Ecümeni Maarif Âzasından). *Hat-ü-Hattâtin* (edited by Ebuzziya Tevfik), İstanbul, AH 1305/1887 AD.

69. İnal, İ. M. K., 'Hat ve Hattatlar', *Çınaraltı Mecmuası* 7 (İstanbul, 1941).

70. — *Son Hattatlar* (İstanbul, 1955).

71. İsfendiyaroğlu, F., *Galatasaray Tarihi* (İstanbul 1952) (See: 468-84).

72. İsmail Baykal, 'Hat Sanatı', *Güzel Sanatlar* 2 (1940) 33-48.

73. İsmail Hakkı (Baltacıoğlu), 'Türk Yazılarının Tetkikine Medhal', *Darülfunun İlâhiyat Fakültesi Mecmuası* 2/5 & 6 (1926) 111-36.

74. Kâğıtçı, M. A., *Historical Study of Paper Industry in Turkey/Historique de l'industrie Papetière en Turquie* (İstanbul, 1976).

75. Konyalı, İ. H., 'Abdülkadir Sayanç', *Tarih Hazinesi* 2 (İstanbul, 1951) 654-9.

76. Kumbaracilar, S., 'Ayasofya'nin Levhaları', *Hayat Tarih Mecmuası* 1 (1970).

77. Mehmet Sait., 'Kadın Hattatlar', *Sevimli Ay Mecmuası* 3/9 (İstanbul, 1926) 8-9.

78. Meriç, R. M., *Türk Tezyini San'atları* (İstanbul, 1937).

79. — *Türk Cild San'atı Tarihi Araştırmaları (I. Vesikalar)* (Ankara, 1954).

80. — 'Hicri 1131 tarihinde Enderunlu Şairler, Hattatlar, ve Musiki Sanatkârları Tezkiresi', *İstanbul Enstitüsü Dergisi* 2 (İstanbul, 1956) 139-68.

81. Muhammed, B., Abd Al-Halik Al-Mayhani, *Destûr-i Debîrî* (edited by Adnan Erzi) (Ankara, 1962).

82. Mustafa 'Ali. *Menakıb-ı Hünerveran* (edited by İbnülemin Mahmud Kemal) (İstanbul, 1928).

83. Mustakimzâde Süleyman Sadeddin Efendi, *Tuhfe-i Hattatin* (ed. İbnülemin Mahmud Kemal) (İstanbul, 1926).

84. Nefeszâde İbrahim. *Gülzari Savab.* (edited by Kilisli Muallim Rifat) (İstanbul, 1939).

85. Orgun, Z., 'Tuğra', *Türk Tarih, Arkeologya ve Etnografya Dergisi* 5 (1949) 203-20.

86. Öz, T., 'Hattatlarımız', *Aylık Ansıklopedi.* 2/5 (İstanbul, 1945) 67-70.

87. Özel, S., *Hat Örnekleri* (İstanbul, 1969).

88. Ramazanoğlu, G., 'Calligraphy: One of the most Decorative Turkish Arts', *Istanbul Hilton Magazine* (Winter 1975-6) 18-23.

89. Rüştü Bey. *Nuhbet-ül-etfal* (İstanbul, AH 1274/1857 AD).

90. Sertoğlu, M., *Osmanlı Türklerinde Tuğra* (İstanbul, 1975).

91. Suyolcuzâde Mehmed Necib. *Devhatül-Küttab* (ed. Kilisli Muallim Rifat) (İstanbul, 1942).

92. Şahinoğlu, M., *Anadolu Selçuklu Mimarisinde Yazının Dekoratif Eleman Olarak Kullanılışı* (İstanbul, 1977).

93. Şehsüvaroğlu, *Asırlar Boyunca İstanbul*. İstanbul (Cumhuriyet Gazetesi), 1953 (See: 12, 24, 115, 148, 204 & 84, 73, 184 & 198).

94. Tilgen, N., *Eyüplü Hattatlar* (1650-1950) (İstanbul, 1950).

95. Umur, S., *Osmanli Padişah Tuğraları* (İstanbul, 1980).

96. Unver, A. S., 'Siyakat Yazısı ve Kuyud-i Atika', *İstanbul Belediye Mecmuası* 8/87/15 (1931) 88-95.

97. — 'Türk Kalemtraşçıları', *Yücel* 6/34 (İstanbul, 1937) 1-7.

98. — *Karaman Sultanı Mehmet Beyin Hususi Kütübhanesine Ait Bir Kitapta Temellük Kitâbesi* (İstanbul, 1946).

99. — *Hattat Ahmed Karahisari (A Well-Known Turkish Calligrapher Karahisari Ahmed Efendi, 1469-1556).* (İstanbul, 1948).

100. — 'Hattat Mustafa Râkım Efendi: 1757-1826', *Tarih Dünyası* 1/7 (1950) 271-275.

101. — *Hekimbaşı ve Hattat Kâtipzade Mehmed Refi* (İstanbul, 1950).

102. — 'Kalemtıraşçılık Tarihimiz', *Tarih Dünyası* 2/13 (1950) 545-49.

103. — *Amasyalı Hamdullâh Efendi ve Tıp Tarihimizdeki Yeri* (İstanbul, 1953).

104. — *Eski Fatih Camii Bir Çini Pano* (İstanbul, 1953) (50 Sanat Sever Serisi: No. 10).

105. — *Hattât İsmail Zühdü Efendi* (İstanbul, 1953) (50 Sanat Sever Serisi: No. 1).

106. — *Hattat Karahisârî Ahmed Efendi ve Altunlu Besmelesi.* (İstanbul, 1953) (50 Sanat Sever Serisi: No. 11).

107. — *Hattat Kazasker Mustafa İzzet: Hayatı ve Eserleri* (İstanbul, 1953) (50 Sanat Sever Serisi: 9).

108. — *Hattat Mahmud Celâleddin Efendi ve İstanbul Fethini Müjdeliyen Hâdis* (İstanbul, 1953) (50 Sanat Sever Serisi: No. 4).

109. — *Hattat Mustafa Râkim Efendi* (İstanbul, 1953). (50 Sanat Sever Serisi: No. 3).

110. — *Hilyei Saadet Hattat-ı Mehmed Sevki* (İstanbul, 1953) (50 Sanat Sever Serisi: No. 6).

111. — *Tezyini Çifte Besmele* (İstanbul, 1953) (50 Sanat Sever Serisi: No. 2).

112. — *Türk Yazı Çeşitleri ve Faideli Ba'zı Bilgiler.* (İstanbul, 1953).

113. — 'Baba Nakkaş', *Fatih ve İstanbul Dergisi* 7-12 (1954) 169-79.

114. — *Reisül Hattatin Hacı Kâmil Akdik: Hayatı ve Eserleri* (İstanbul, 1954) (50 Sanat Sever Serisi: No. 12).

115. — *Hattat ve Tuğrakeş İsmail Hakkı Altunbezer (1869-1946) Hayatı ve Eserleri* (İstanbul, 1955) (50 Sanat Sever Serisi: No. 13).

116. — *Mehmed Esad Yesarî: Hayatı ve Eserleri* (İstanbul, 1955) (50 Sanat Sever Serisi: No. 14).

117. — *Hattat Sefik Bey (1819-1880) Hayatı ve Esenleri* (İstanbul, 1956) (50 Sanat Sever Serisi: 15).

118. — *Hattat Ali bin Hilâl: Hayatı ve Yazıları* (İstanbul, 1958).

119. — *Hattat Mehmed Hulûsi (1869-1940)* (İstanbul, 1958) (50 Sanat Sever Serisi: No. 16).

120. — *Leylek Dede 'Dede Stork'* (İstanbul, 1958).

121. — 'XV. yüzyılda Türkiye'de kullanılan kağıdlar ve su damgaları', *T.T.K. Belleten* 26/104 (1962) 739-62.

122. — *Türk İnce El San'atları Tarihi* (İstanbul, 1964).

123. — 'Hattat Hafız Osman ve Yazdığı Kuran i Kerimler', *Türk Yurdu* (September, 1967) 3-7.

124. — 'Yazdığı Kur'anı Kerimlerle Meşhur Hattat Hafız Osman Efendi', (Introduction to a photoreproduction of a Kuran written by Hafiz Osman) (İstanbul, 1968).

125. Uyar, V. S., 'Hattatlar Armağan', *Konya Halkevi Dergisi* (1946) 93-4 & (1950) 135-6.

126. Uzluk, F. N., 'Hattat olarak Sabuncuoğlu Şerafeddin', *Dirim Mecmuası* 9/10 (İstanbul, 1951).

127. Uzluk, S., *Mevlevilikte Resim, Resimde Mevleviler* (Ankara, 1957).

128. Yazir, M., *Eski Yazıları Okuma Anahtarı* (İstanbul, 1942).

129. — *Medeniyet Aleminde Yazı ve İslâm Medeniyetinde Kalem Güzeli (I.)* (edited, revised and expanded by Uğur Derman) (Ankara, 1972).

130. — *Medeniyet Aleminde Yazı ve İslâm Medeniyetinde Kalem Güzeli (II.)* (edited, revised and expanded by Uğur Derman) (Ankara, 1974).

131. — *Siyakat Yazısı* (İstanbul, 1941).

132. Züber, H., *Türk Süsleme Sanatı* (Ankara, 1972).

PAINTING

1. Aslanapa, O., *Turkish Art and Architecture* (London, 1971).

2. Atil, E., 'Ottoman miniature painting under Sultan Mehmed II,', *Ars Orientalis* IX (1973), pp. 103-121.

3. — 'The Art of the Book', *Turkish Art* edited by E. Atil (Smithsonian Institution, Washington D.C., 1980) pp. 137-238.

4. Atasoy, N., *Türk Minyatür Sanatı bibliografyası* (İstanbul, 1972).

5. Atasoy, N., Çağman, F., *Turkish Miniature Painting* (İstanbul, 1974).

6. Atasoy, N., Çağman, F., Grube, E. J., 'Topkapı Sarayı Collection', *Islamic painting* (Tokyo, 1978).

7. Binney, E., *Turkish treasures from the collection of Edwin Binney 3rd* (Portland, 1979).

8. — *Turkish miniature paintings & manuscripts from the collection of E. Binney 3rd* (New York, 1973).

9. Çağman, F., 'Turkish miniature painting', *The Art and Architecture of Turkey*, edited by E. Akurgal (New York, 1980, pp. 222-248).

10. Çağman, F., Tanindi, Z., *Islamic miniature painting* (İstanbul, 1979).

11. Gray, B., 'Two portraits of Mehmet II', *Burlington magazine*, 61, 1932, pp. 4-6.

12. Grube, E. J., 'Miniatures in the albums H.2147, 2153, 2162 in the Topkapı Sarayı collection and some related material', *Pantheon*, XX, 1962 pp. 213-26, 306-13.

13. — 'Notes on Ottoman painting in the 15th century', *Festschrift fur Katarina Otto-Dorn*, Malibu, California. Forthcoming.

14. Meredith-Owens, G. M., 'Ottoman Turkish painting', *Islamic painting and the Arts of the book*, The Keir collection IV (London, 1976), pp. 223-30.

15. Minorsky, V., *The Chester Beatty Library, A catalogue of the Turkish manuscripts and miniatures* (Dublin, 1958).

16. Stchoukine, I., *La peinture Turque*, Vol. I, Paris, 1966; Vol. II, Paris, 1971.

17. Sakisian, A., 'La miniature Turc à l'exposition d'art Persan de Burlington House', *Syria* XII, 1931 pp. 163-72.

18. UNESCO, *Turkey Ancient miniatures* (Paris, 1961).

19. Yetkin, S. K., *L'ancienne peinture Turque du XIIe au XVIIIe siècle*, n.p., 1970.

Index

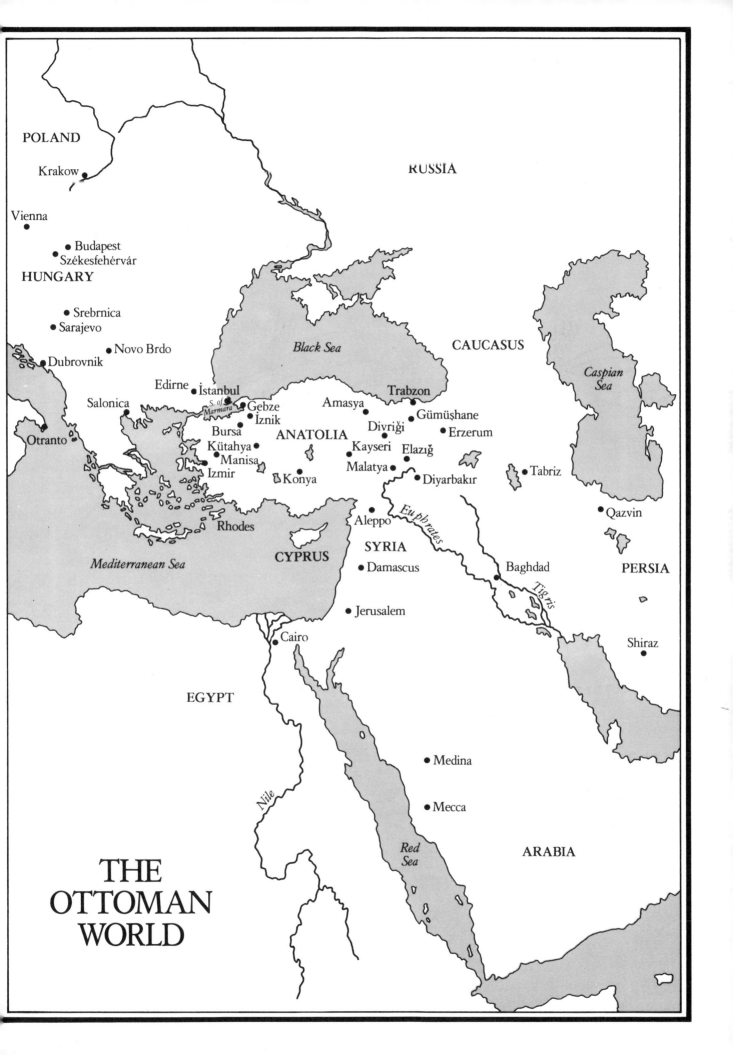

POLAND

Krakow

Vienna

Budapest
Székesfehérvár
HUNGARY

Srebrnica
Sarajevo
Novo Brdo
Dubrovnik

RUSSIA

Black Sea

CAUCASUS

Caspian
Sea

Edirne · İstanbul
Salonica
S. of
Marmara
Gebze
İznik
Bursa
Kütahya
Manisa
Izmir
ANATOLIA
Konya

Trabzon
Amasya
Gümüşhane
Divriği
Erzerum
Kayseri
Elazığ
Malatya
Diyarbakır

Tabriz

Otranto

Rhodes

Mediterranean Sea

CYPRUS

SYRIA

Aleppo

Euphrates

Damascus

Jerusalem

Cairo

Tigris

Baghdad

Qazvin

PERSIA

Shiraz

EGYPT

Nile

Medina

Mecca

Red
Sea

ARABIA

THE
OTTOMAN
WORLD

Orhan 1281-1324

Murad I 1360-1389

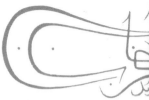

Bayezid I 'The Thunderbolt' 1389

Mehmed II 'The Conqueror' 1444-1446,1451-1481

Bayezid II 1481-1512

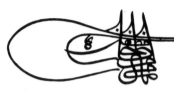

Murad III 1574-1595

Mehmed III 1595-1603

Ahmed

Murad IV 1623-1640

İbrahim 1640-1648

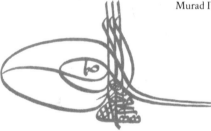

Mustafa II 1695-1703

Ahmed III 1703-1730

Mahm

Abdülhamid I 1774-1789

Selim III 1789-1807

Mustafa IV 1807-1808

Murad V 1876

Abdülhamid II 1876-1909